TOO MANY CHILDREN LEFT BEHIND

TOO MANY CHILDREN LEFT BEHIND

The U.S. Achievement Gap in Comparative Perspective

Bruce Bradbury,
Miles Corak,
Jane Waldfogel,
and Elizabeth Washbrook

Russell Sage Foundation
New York

The Russell Sage Foundation

The Russell Sage Foundation, one of the oldest of America's general purpose foundations, was established in 1907 by Mrs. Margaret Olivia Sage for "the improvement of social and living conditions in the United States." The foundation seeks to fulfill this mandate by fostering the development and dissemination of knowledge about the country's political, social, and economic problems. While the foundation endeavors to assure the accuracy and objectivity of each book it publishes, the conclusions and interpretations in Russell Sage Foundation publications are those of the authors and not of the foundation, its trustees, or its staff. Publication by Russell Sage, therefore, does not imply foundation endorsement.

Library of Congress Cataloging-in-Publication Data

Bradbury, Bruce.
  Too many children left behind : the U.S. achievement gap in comparative perspective / Bruce Bradbury, Miles Corak, Jane Waldfogel, & Elizabeth Washbrook.
      pages cm
  Includes bibliographical references and index.
  ISBN 978-0-87154-024-9 (pbk. : alk. paper) — ISBN 978-1-61044-848-2 (ebook)
    1. Children—Social conditions.   2. Poor children—United States.
    3. Education—United States.   I. Corak, Miles.   II. Title.
  HQ792.U5B7243 2015
  305.230973—dc23   2015005102

The paper used in this publication meets the minimum requirements of American National Standard for Information Sciences—Permanence of Paper for Printed Library Materials. ANSI Z39.48-1992.

Text design by Suzanne Nichols

RUSSELL SAGE FOUNDATION
112 East 64th Street, New York, New York 10065
10 9 8 7 6 5 4 3 2 1

Contents

Technical Appendix is available at: https://www.russellsage.org/sites/all/files
/Technical%20Appendix%20to%20Bradbury%20et%20al%202015.pdf

List of Illustrations

About the Authors |

BRUCE BRADBURY is associate professor at the Social Policy Research Centre at the University of New South Wales, Australia.

MILES CORAK is professor of economics at the Graduate School of Public and International Affairs at the University of Ottawa.

JANE WALDFOGEL is professor of social work and public affairs at the Columbia University School of Social Work and visiting professor at the Centre for Analysis of Social Exclusion at the London School of Economics and Political Science.

ELIZABETH WASHBROOK is lecturer in Quantitative Methods for Education at the Graduate School of Education and a member of the Centre for Multilevel Modelling at the University of Bristol, United Kingdom.

Acknowledgments

WE HAD THE great pleasure of being visiting scholars at the Russell Sage Foundation (RSF) in 2013–2014. Our year together at RSF provided us with the ideal platform from which to research and write this book. We are deeply grateful to former RSF president Eric Wanner and current president Sheldon Danziger for their support and inspiration. We are also grateful to Jim Wilson, who coordinated the CRITA (Cross-national Research on the Intergenerational Transmission of Advantage) project at RSF; our partnership on that project laid the groundwork for this one. And we are grateful to the other visiting scholars and all the other members of the RSF family who made our year there so productive—and so enjoyable. We offer a particular thanks to Suzanne Nichols for her help publishing this book, and to David Haproff for his help getting its message out. Our work on this project has also been supported by a grant from the Australian Research Council (grant number DP130103440) and by infrastructure support from the Eunice Kennedy Shriver National Institute of Child Health and Human Development (NICHD) (grant number P2CHD058486 awarded to the Columbia Population Research Center). The content is solely the responsibility of the authors and does not necessarily represent the official views of the NICHD or the National Institutes of Health (NIH). We also benefited from earlier support from the Sutton Trust, as part of their research on social mobility led by Lee Elliott Major.

A large team of research assistants worked with us on the analyses for this book: Melissa Wong and Anna Zhu in Australia; Ashton Brown and Seda Gunduz in Canada; and Karen Chatfield and RaeHyuck Lee in the United States. We could not have done it without them.

We are also grateful to the individuals and agencies that collected and managed the data we used and made it possible for us to access them. We are especially indebted to the families who voluntarily provided their information to the studies upon which we drew. The Australian results are based on unit record data from Growing Up in Australia: The Longitudinal Study of Australian Children. This study is jointly conducted by the Australian Government Department of Social Services (DSS), the Australian Institute of Family Studies (AIFS), and the Australian Bureau of Statistics (ABS). The findings and views reported in this book are those of the authors and should not be attributed to DSS, AIFS, or the ABS. The analysis of the data from Canada presented in this book was conducted at the Carleton, Ottawa, Outaouais Research Data Centre (COOL-RDC), which is part of the Canadian Research Data Centre Network (CRDCN). The services and activities provided by the COOL-RDC are made possible by the financial or in-kind support of the Social Sciences and Humanities Research Council of Canada (SSHRC), the Canadian Institutes of Health Research (CIHR), the Canadian Foundation for Innovation (CFI), Statistics Canada, Carleton University, the University of Ottawa, and the Université du Québec en Outaouais. The views expressed in this book do not necessarily represent those of the CRDCN or its partners. In the United Kingdom, we are grateful for the support of the Centre for Longitudinal Studies at the Institute of Education, University of London, for the use of these data and to the U.K. Data Archive and Economic and Social Data Service (ESDS) for making them available (University of London, Institute of Education, Centre for Longitudinal Studies 2012a, 2012b, 2012c, 2012d, 2014). We also acknowledge the funding of the data collection by the Economic and Social Research Council (ESRC) and the consortium of U.K. government departments led by the Office for National Statistics (ONS). However, none of these organizations or individuals bears any responsibility for the analysis or interpretation of these data. The U.S. results are based on restricted-use data from the Early Childhood Longitudinal Study: Kindergarten Class of 1998–99 (ECLS-K). This study is sponsored by the National Center for Education Statistics (NCES) at the U.S. Department of Education and conducted by Westat with assistance from the Survey Research Center (SRC) and the School of Education at the University of Michigan and from Educational Testing Services (ETS). The findings reported in this book are solely the responsibility of the authors and do not necessarily represent the official views of NCES or other agencies.

Finally, our intellectual debts are many. We are particularly grateful to a group of scholars who came to Russell Sage for a workshop in the fall of 2013 to help us think through issues related to inequality of achievement and what schools can do: Tom DiPrete, Adam Gamoran, Anna Haskins, Larry Hedges, Miyako Ikeda, Christopher "Sandy" Jencks, Ben Jensen, Jim Liebman, Lee Elliott Major, Philip Merrigan, Richard Murnane, Sean Reardon, and Randall Reback.

We also had helpful conversations with Jeanne Brooks-Gunn, Andrea Elliott, John Ermisch, John Roemer, and Tim Smeeding. Finally, we are deeply grateful to Dick Murnane and Sean Reardon, who read the book closely and provided us with many helpful suggestions for improving it.

Chapter 1 | Introduction

THE AMERICAN DREAM—the idea that all children should be able to succeed regardless of the economic circumstances into which they were born—is widely shared by parents in the United States, as well as in many other countries. Parents want the best for their children, and society as a whole has an interest in seeing all children reach their fullest potential without being held back by the circumstances of their birth.

But is the American Dream a reality? Is it a reality for just some and not others? If the American Dream is not widely attainable, what can the United States do—if anything—to make opportunity a reality for all Americans? And what can this country learn from other countries in meeting this challenge?

We are writing this book to shed light on these crucial issues by tackling three central questions that motivate our story:

1. How large is the achievement gap between children from low-socioeconomic status families and those from high-socioeconomic status families?

2. When does this gap emerge? How much inequality is already present at school entry, and what happens to the gap as children move through school?

3. What can the United States learn from other countries to make success more common regardless of family background? More broadly put, does it have to be this way?

We answer these questions by focusing on the development and progress of children during the primary school years and in some cases beyond. We look at their starting point on the cusp of formal schooling at age four or five, describe their accomplishments in their early teen years, and chart the ups and downs of their development in between. Another

1

way we answer these questions is by making two types of comparisons: between children raised by families at different rungs on the ladder of socioeconomic success, and between children in the United States and children in three similar countries—Australia, Canada, and the United Kingdom. We very intentionally chose these three countries for this comparative analysis because culturally, historically, and institutionally they have a good deal in common, and also because there has long been a good deal of communication and borrowing of policy ideas between their governments. Is there as much inequality in the development of more- and less-advantaged children in these peer countries as there is in the United States? Or do the experiences of Australia, Canada, and the United Kingdom suggest that the United States could do better?

THE AMERICAN DREAM, LUCK, AND OPPORTUNITY

"Equality of opportunity" and "opportunity for all" are central themes of a compelling story that Americans tell themselves—a story about their children's futures, but also a story about the country.

It is a story about hope—the hope that with hard work and perseverance, children will become all that they can be. But it is also a story about fairness—the rules of a game in which success is sometimes determined by circumstances beyond one's control.

Sometimes luck, good or bad, sets people on a path in life that they did not anticipate and may certainly not have chosen. Opportunity is a matter of chance, and "down on your luck" is a phrase that, in many different ways, has real meaning. But at the same time, "good luck comes to those who work hard" is not just a hollow mantra: it can be a powerful explanation for one's station in life.[1]

Americans do not believe that luck is the central ingredient of success. In a public opinion poll designed to explore attitudes toward the American Dream and how people can move up the income ladder, only about one-fifth of respondents said that luck is essential or very important, but about 90 percent said that hard work and ambition are important.[2] The same poll asked what the American Dream means and found that Americans feel that financial security is certainly a part of the definition, but not the most important part. For many, the American Dream is linked to equality of opportunity and means "being able to succeed regardless of the economic circumstances in which you were born" and, relatedly, "being free to accomplish anything you want with hard work."

Whatever the case in reality, Americans believe that the pathway to success is not about good luck, but about hard work and ambition. Nevertheless, overwhelming proportions of Americans also feel that having a good education, and having access to quality schooling from kindergarten through high school, is essential, or at least very important, to getting ahead in life. In short, ambition, hard work, and the opportunity to get a good education are the ingredients of upward mobility and the chance to attain the American Dream.

Americans want their children to have these ingredients for success.

But hard work can't always overcome bad luck, and children in particular have no responsibility for the circumstances that ultimately determine their capacities and skills: the circumstances of their birth and the schools and communities in which they are raised. If Americans do not come to appreciate the details of how children develop the capacity to become all that they can be, the compelling story they tell themselves about equality of opportunity and the future of America's children will remain more of a dream than a reality.

A TALE OF TWO CHILDREN

Three-year-old Johnny, the compelling subject of a story in the *New York Times* by Nicholas Kristof, learned to speak later than most children—because he had a hearing problem that was not diagnosed until he was eighteen months old. He was in the midst of an important transition, one that would play a big role in determining his station in life while revealing the shortcomings of today's American Dream. As Kristof reported, Johnny eventually received "medical treatment that restored most of his hearing, but after such a long period of deafness in infancy, it's unclear if he will fully recover his ability to communicate."[3]

Johnny had the misfortune of encountering bad luck in early childhood. The years from infancy to preschool age are a crucial period in a child's life, offering preparation for the wider world, which most importantly includes formal schooling. Competencies associated with what developmental psychologists call "readiness to learn" require a stimulating and caring environment if they are to develop to their fullest extent. The development of these skills also requires attention and resources to address and compensate for unforeseen setbacks and unfortunate events. Bad luck at this stage in life can limit a child's sensory, cognitive, or behavioral development in ways that limit future possibilities. Language and behavioral skills are central ingredients for successfully starting primary schooling, and they shape a child's future success, reverberating all the way to high school graduation and college attendance and completion.

The human brain has a certain "plasticity," particularly during the early years.[4] Neural development is extremely dynamic during the first weeks, months, and years of life and proceeds through a series of stages that last at least until puberty, if not into the teen and early adult years. But the early years are very important. The scientific study of the human brain has found that people are born with many more neurons than they will ever need. Human development proceeds through stages as the brain responds to a stimulating environment, sculpting and pruning neural pathways to a fine level of efficiency. This permits the development of age-specific competencies, which in turn offer the capacity for even more interaction with an increasingly stimulating environment. These competencies are behavioral and include self-control, perseverance, and the social skills associated with empathy. These competencies are also cognitive, prime among them being language development. The University of Chicago economist and Nobel laureate James Heckman has emphasized that "skills beget skills," by which he means that development involves a series of sequential steps that build on each other, with earlier steps influencing the length of the strides that can be taken later in life. Investments in children and teens during the school years prove to be much more productive if prior investments during the early years developed their capacities to the greatest extent possible.

These investments certainly include sufficient financial resources. Poverty limits the capabilities of children for a whole host of reasons ranging from inadequacies in nutrition, limited access to the goods and services that foster the kind of stimulating environment that is important for behavioral and cognitive development, and a limited ability to deal with the fallout from unexpected events such as accidents and sickness. The growing income inequalities in the labor market since the late 1970s have increasingly become shadowed in the resources available for children. Professors Greg Duncan and Richard Murnane have documented a growing and significant gap in what they refer to as "enrichment expenditures" made by families at the top and the bottom of the income distribution.[5] These include spending on books, computers, high-quality child care, summer camps, private schooling, and other resources that offer a motivating and nurturing environment for children. A generation or more ago, during the early 1970s, a typical family in the top fifth of the income distribution spent about $3,850 per year on resources like these, four times as much as the typical family at the bottom of the income distribution, which spent about $925. This is certainly a large gap, but by 2005 it had grown tremendously, to $9,800 versus $1,400. And while there is some debate in the academic literature about how much money really matters in the lives of young children, convincing studies have shown that in many poor households more money eases stress, enables better parenting, and is an important resource for dealing with the unexpected.[6]

At the same time, money is not all that matters: good parenting and the quality of the time children spend with their parents, with significant others, and in the wider community are also important. Poverty of expectation, experience, and emotional support can negatively affect children regardless of how financially secure their families are.

The experiences of a child like Johnny have their roots in a family living in straitened circumstances, but the solutions seem more complicated than just giving such families more money, helpful as that might be. Johnny was still struggling with learning to speak because his deafness at birth had gone undiagnosed for so long. Although treatment had restored much of his hearing, the long period of deprivation might have permanently limited his speaking ability. This is how luck touched Johnny in a bad way—the bad luck of being born into a poor family. As Kristof chronicled, his mother was caring and loving but at the same time had many other worries and concerns, from bills to be paid to frozen pipes in their trailer home that needed fixing, to a broken car that limited access to work and other resources. If Johnny had been born into a better-off family to parents who were equally as loving but also had more time, more resources, and more connections to the wider community, his medical condition might have been addressed much sooner, or more effectively. Johnny had also had the bad luck of not having other social supports, like routine visits with a health practitioner who might have discovered the problem and started remedial treatment sooner. Johnny's mother had to reach out to a children's aid group for help in understanding and treating her son's affliction. If social programs had been easier to access and more of a help to his mother, perhaps Johnny's challenges would not have become so great. Kristof used his story in the *New York Times* as a call for more effective and active public policies, asking for a broadening of "the conversation about opportunity, to build not just safety nets for those who stumble but also to help all American kids achieve lift-off."[7]

Obviously, we have no way of knowing how Johnny's story will unfold, how lucky he will be, how much the early challenges he faced will matter. But we might quite reasonably imagine that his starting point in life could have been very different, and that the compelling narrative of equality of opportunity might not have taken such an unexpected and sharp turn for him had he been born into another family or into a different social and public policy environment.

A glimpse into what might have been for Johnny comes from the story of a second child, Alex, who was also born with a hearing problem and who also did not receive a diagnosis until he was a toddler. But unlike Johnny, he was born into a family with resources with which to tackle his problem. As *New York Times* writer Katherine Bouton details in her story (which appeared just a few months after the story about Johnny), Alex's mother (a science writer) and father were able to ensure that he received excellent medical treatment and also were able to provide Alex with a "language-rich environment," which is a key factor predicting early vocabulary development and later success in school. Bouton describes how well Alex was doing as an early adolescent, at age eleven. He attended the same local private school as his two older siblings, enjoyed playing lots of sports, and—most impressively—scored 100 percent on a speech recognition test. As his mother commented, "Whatever Alex missed by the delay, he's made it up." She also noted: "It's partly that he's lucky."[8]

It might seem ironic that Alex's mother sees him as lucky. After all, he was born with a serious hearing problem. But she is right—he was lucky to have parents who could arrange first-rate medical treatment for him and also provide him with lots of language stimulation so that he could benefit to the fullest from that treatment. So, in this respect, he was indeed lucky.

OPPORTUNITY FOR ALL?

The diverging paths and life chances of these two children—and many others like them—provided the motivation for our book. Probably every reader can bring to mind a similar case of contrasts—a story of a child from a family of lesser means who is held back by early challenges, in contrast with a child from a more-advantaged family who is given a helping hand to overcome adversity. We can also picture a talented child who never really reaches his or her full potential owing to lack of resources and opportunities, a story that contrasts with that of a similarly talented child who achieves great success because that talent was nurtured and given the chance to flourish. It's a story as old as Mark Twain's *The Prince and the Pauper,* or perhaps even older. It is also a story that runs counter to our understanding of, and aspirations for, the American Dream.

Taking a step back from these two children, and others who come to mind, do we see a similar story in the larger landscape of American children? Unfortunately, the answer seems to be yes. Children's success in school, and in life, is very much tied to their family background, and more so in the United States than in other countries.

We draw this conclusion from a range of U.S. and international evidence that has accumulated over the last decade or so as increasing attention has been focused on how countries fare with regard to not only their average school achievement but also inequality in achievement. In the United States, the No Child Left Behind (NCLB) Act of 2001, the landmark federal education reform enacted in 2001, set the goal that states should not only raise their average levels of student proficiency but also close achievement

Box 1.1   Overview of the Child Cohort Studies

	United States	United Kingdom	Australia	Canada
	Early Childhood Longitudinal Study: Kindergarten Class of 1998–99 (ECLS-K)	Millennium Cohort Study (MCS)	Longitudinal Study of Australian Children: Kindergarten Cohort (LSAC-K)	National Longitudinal Study of Children and Youth (NLSCY)
Cohort birth dates	1992–1993	2000–2002	1999–2000	1991–1994
Common ages when children are assessed	Five, nine, and eleven	Five, seven, and eleven	Five, nine, and eleven	Five, nine, and eleven

gaps—that is, gaps in test scores between less- and more-advantaged groups.[9] And across countries, international reports from comparative test series such as the Program for International Student Assessment (PISA) and the Trends in International Mathematics and Science Study (TIMSS) generate headlines not just about how countries rank on average but also about how their lowest- and highest-performing students fare.[10]

Results from international test score data indicate that the United States has a problem with inequality of student achievement, and more so than peer countries, including the three we focus on here (Australia, Canada, and the United Kingdom).[11] But because these results draw on tests administered to fifteen-year-olds (or adults), they cannot tell us about inequality in the all-important early childhood period, nor about how inequality develops between early childhood and adolescence. Do children from different backgrounds start school on relatively equal footing but then see their paths diverge as they move through school? Or are children starting school already unequal? If so, what happens to that inequality over time? And as children move through the school years, is inequality growing for children of all initial ability levels, or is it particularly the children who started out with the greatest challenges, or those who had the most potential, who feel the lack of socioeconomic resources most keenly?

To address these questions, we make use of large-scale and very detailed surveys that follow cohorts of children over time in each of our four countries (see box 1.1). In particular, we make use of assessments of the children when they are age four or five, at around the time of school entry, and then repeated assessments at later ages as they move through school. We can follow all our children to at least the age of eleven, at the time they are finishing up primary school, and we can follow our U.S. children even further, to age fourteen, when they are about to enter secondary school.

Our focus is on the gaps in achievement between children of different family backgrounds, and how those gaps in the United States compare to those in our three other countries. We do not argue that societies should try to compensate for all the different sources of unequal opportunity. For many characteristics, this is neither politically nor even scientifically possible. But we do wish to explore the impact of some important and potentially modifiable social and economic resources. Cross-national comparisons provide a powerful tool for exploring the economic and social policies that are feasible in modern societies. Our four countries share a common culture and economic system, and a similarly wide distribution of parental and family personal capabilities. As we shall see, however, the gaps in outcomes between children from different socioeconomic backgrounds do vary significantly across these countries. Although it might not be possible to eliminate all of the inequality of opportunity associated with genes and families, our comparative cases illustrate that there are other countries similar in many respects to the United States where gaps between families of different socioeconomic backgrounds are significantly smaller.

AN OUTLINE OF THE BOOK

Our analysis begins in the next chapter by discussing the meaning of equality of opportunity. We look at how philosophers and economists have distinguished between circumstances beyond an individual's control, circumstances for which individuals should in some sense be compensated, and choices for which individuals should be held responsible. We also discuss the concept of bottlenecks, which impede opportunity and stunt children's life chances. We clarify how this conceptual framework can be used to concretely measure inequalities and bottlenecks in the development of young children, and we elaborate on what it offers as a plot line for telling a story based on the lives of thousands upon thousands of American children, as well as children from the other three countries we study.

Our book is motivated and structured around three important themes that Johnny's and Alex's stories led us to ponder. The first theme concerns the resources available to families with children. Poverty and wealth, in all their dimensions, are important drivers in forming children's capabilities and opportunities, for reversing bad luck, and for creating good luck. The second theme has to do with what is missing from the tale of these two children: What happens to children between early childhood and early adolescence? Just how does a child like Alex manage to do so well in spite of his early challenges? Will a child like Johnny overcome his early setback, and will his years in primary school give him the liftoff he needs to succeed in high school and beyond? The third theme arises from wondering about how things could be different. What can families, schools, and other aspects of society do to lock in the advantages of capable four- and five-year-olds? What can they do to boost the chances of progress for those children whose starting line is way behind the starting line of other children so that we truly have opportunity for all, regardless of a child's family background?

Chapter 3 addresses the first theme, the issue of the resources available to children. Poverty and wealth, both monetary and nonmonetary, are important undercurrents of a child's experience. In this book, we see children as being supported, monetarily and nonmonetarily, by their families, by the jobs and wages available to their parents in the world of work, and by the public and other community supports designed to serve them. These three interacting webs of support—family, work, and the public sector—are for some children so threadbare as to offer only the most basic safety net, but at the same time so interwoven for other children as to offer a resilient springboard that allows them to bounce back lightly in times of bad luck and to reach even higher heights in times of good luck.

The education level of the most-educated parent is our marker of socioeconomic status, signaling differences in resources. For us, more education indicates—perhaps imperfectly—that parents have on average more money, but also more of the other resources that matter for their children, like the language-rich environment that was so crucial for Alex. In chapter 3, we document the differences in the family backgrounds and environments, financial resources, and time and care for children who are raised by parents from low-, medium-, and high-socioeconomic status (SES) groups, as defined by their parents' education levels.[12]

We are interested in learning whether the disparities in resources between children from more- and less-advantaged families in the United States are distinctive, or whether similar disparities are evident in the other countries we examine. Our analysis reveals three striking findings. First, we find that Canada stands out from the United States and the other two countries in having more family resources, on average, available to children. In particular, the typical Canadian parent has more education, a key marker of socioeconomic status and a key input into child development. Second, although family resources are skewed by socioeconomic status in all four countries, this inequality is starkest in the United States. U.S. children born to less-educated parents have parents who not only have less formal education but also, on average, are younger, are more likely to be single at the time of the child's birth, and are less likely to be in a stable couple during their child's early years. Less-educated parents in the United States are also more likely to be foreign-born and to have health problems. And importantly, families with low levels of education also have lower incomes. But third, and ironically, we find that the U.S. social safety net and supports for working families do the least among the four countries to combat inequality. The meager public policy response in the United States leaves children from low-SES families doubly disadvantaged relative to their peers in the other three countries.

Chapters 4, 5, and 6 form the heart of our story. Chapter 4 builds on these descriptions of resource disparities to show that socioeconomic status is already reflected in the starting line of skill levels for young children at the age of school entry, and that this pattern differs across countries with different economic, social, and policy contexts. The next two chapters then address our second theme: How do the gaps between children from different backgrounds grow or shrink during the school years? Just what happens between the starting line and the finish line—between the early years and the cusp of high school? We need to know more about the past of a child like Alex—about what got him to where he is—to know what can be done to improve the future of a child like Johnny.

In these chapters, we summarize the major lessons from a detailed study of more than eight thousand American children in order to trace out the experiences of children during a period in their lives when they interact with broader social influences, and particularly the education system. These children are chosen to be representative of the entire population of four- and five-year-olds during the late 1990s, and we follow each and every one of them through the course of their primary school years up to the eighth grade, when they are on the cusp of high school.

We use similar information on Australian, British, and Canadian children. Making comparisons between children high on the socioeconomic ladder and those lower on the ladder is one way to address our third theme: How could things be different? In other words, what are the potential policy options? Another complementary way to address this theme is to compare the SES gaps between children across these countries. Ultimately, we would like to know more about why patterns and inequalities in child development are different across these countries, and what impact it would have on American schools and children to borrow the design of particular aspects of education or other policies in other countries. But before we can even think about these questions, we need to know if in fact there are differences across the countries. That is the challenge addressed by our comparative analysis.

Looking at children at the start of school, in chapter 4 we find that inequalities in children's cognitive skills at school entry are significantly larger in the United States than they are in the other three countries. The poor showing of the United States reflects not just a relatively large gap in skills between low- and middle-SES children but also a large skills gap between middle- and high-SES children. These skills gaps parallel the family resource gaps documented in chapter 3, which are also more pronounced in the United States than in the other three countries. At the same time, we find that enrollment in preschool, which could offset some of these inequalities, remains highly skewed by socioeconomic status in the United States and thus plays a less equalizing role than it otherwise might play.

What happens to the gaps as children move through school? In chapter 5, making use of the repeated assessments of children in our four countries to describe inequalities in their achievement by family socioeconomic status at three common time points from ages five to eleven, we find that children in the United States not only start primary school more unequal but also finish primary school more unequal than children in the other countries. As we discuss throughout the book, social scientists have long debated the sources of inequality in school achievement and how much might be due to schools themselves versus factors outside of schools. We find evidence that both out-of-school and school factors are likely to play a role in the greater inequality in the United States. Inequalities in family backgrounds and resources for school-age children—as indicated by measures such as access to a computer or books and participation in extracurricular and summer activities—are substantial, particularly in the United States. These disparities in out-of-school resources coexist with considerable inequalities in schools as measured by factors such as private school enrollment, exposure to high-SES peers, teacher experience, and ability grouping—again, particularly in the United States. So the fact that in the United States gaps are high—and do not narrow—during the school years is likely due to both out-of-school and school factors.

In chapter 6, we continue our analysis of children during the school years, taking advantage of the very detailed data we have for the United States, which uniquely measure outcomes in a comparable metric for a large sample of children on six occasions between kindergarten and eighth grade. Using these detailed data on individual children's trajectories, we find that the majority—60 to 70 percent—of the SES gap in achievement at age fourteen in the United States can be attributed to differences already present at school entry. However, a substantial portion—30 to 40 percent—emerges during the school years. So there is a role for policy interventions in both periods.

In the final chapter, we relate our findings to a very well-developed academic literature on what families, schools, and other sectors of society can do to improve the skills and competencies of children and narrow the gap between the achievements of children from the highest and lowest rungs on the socioeconomic ladder. What reforms would promote equality of opportunity? Researchers who adopt methods allowing for cause and effect to be clearly delineated are much better placed to make specific suggestions. Some of this research is based on experimental methods comparing control and treatment groups, much in the way that pharmaceutical companies demonstrate the effectiveness of a new drug through randomized controlled trials.[13] We hope that our portrait of the progress of American children during their school years, highlighted by and contrasted with the experiences of children in other countries, can add to this discussion.

In their powerful recent book, *Restoring Opportunity*, professors Greg Duncan and Richard Murnane describe a whole host of school policies that formal evaluations have shown to be effective in improving achievement for disadvantaged children.[14] Part of their agenda for the reform of American schooling is based on particular cases and examples, be they particular preschools in the Boston public school system or elementary schools like those in the University of Chicago Charter School Network. The value of the international comparisons we make might lie in helping us appreciate the extent to which the effective qualities of these schools can—or for that matter, cannot—be scaled up to a national level. It is one thing to demonstrate the effectiveness of model school reforms that may require more resources or significant institutional and managerial changes, but it is another to demonstrate that they can be brought to scale and implemented across an entire country. The case for such school reforms is stronger if they are already part of the national system in other countries.

OUR MAJOR QUESTIONS

It is our intention in this book to answer three sets of questions about the U.S. achievement gap.

1. How large is the achievement gap between children from low-SES families and those from high-SES families?

We estimate that the degree of inequality of opportunity is significant in the United States. Family background is significantly related to the competencies of young children, both at school entry and in eighth grade. Children from low-SES families lag behind their counterparts from high-SES families, in both reading and math, by a full standard deviation at school entry (see figure 1.1). Elsewhere, the situation is different. Succeeding regardless of the economic circumstances into which one is born is

Figure 1.1   Inequality in language/reading skills at ages four and five is greater in the United States than in other comparable countries.

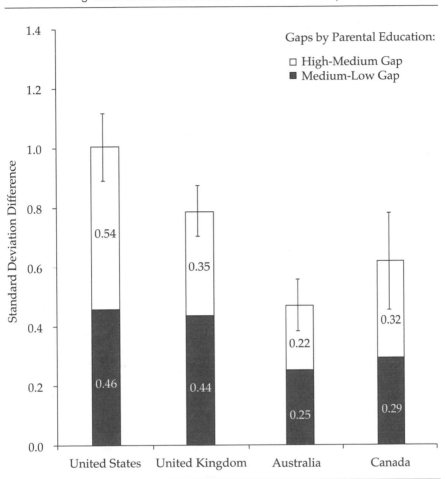

Source: Authors' calculations using data from the ECLS-K, MCS, LSAC-K, and NLSCY.
Notes: The figure shows the gaps in average language and reading test scores between children from families with different levels of parental education. The "high-medium gap" is the difference between children with a college-educated parent and those whose parents have only some college. The "medium-low gap" is the difference between children with a parent with some college and children whose parents have no more than a high school degree. The total length of each bar is the "high-low gap"—the difference between children with a college-educated parent and those whose parents have no more than a high school degree. Test scores are standardized in all countries to have mean zero and unit variance. Black lines are 95 percent confidence intervals for the high-low gap (the total length of the bar). See chapter 4 for further details.

more likely in Australia and, particularly, Canada than in the United States or the United Kingdom.

In some of these countries, inequality is a more serious problem for boys than for girls. This is not the case in the United States or Australia, but does hold with regard to some outcomes we examine in the United Kingdom and Canada.

2. When does this gap emerge? How much inequality is already present at school entry? What happens to the gap as children move through school?

The gap between the achievement of the average child from a family in which one parent has a college degree or more and that of the average child from a family with at most a high school diploma is already significant before these children start kindergarten. During the school years the gap between them never narrows, but on average it also does not widen by very much (see figure 1.2).

These average patterns, however, conceal another fact: the children of families lower on the socioeconomic ladder actually do not make as much progress as those who start out with the same ability at school entry but whose parents are more educated (see figure 1.3). The potential displayed by high-achieving low-SES children in kindergarten tends to wither away over time, while high-SES children who started off below average seem able to make up ground on other children during the school years.

Children's positions in the achievement distribution actually move around a lot during the school years, with many either surging ahead or dropping behind for short periods. We would expect this fluidity to weaken the association between family background and children's achievement over time. The fact that it does not—that the gaps do not narrow—implies a cumulative effect of socioeconomic status that continues well beyond the preschool period into adolescence. We estimate that some 30 to 40 percent of the gaps we observe at the start of high school can be attributed to factors that only come into play *after* children enter school.

It is important to note that the factors driving the gaps during the school years might have to do with schools, they might reflect the influence of factors outside of schools, or they might stem from a combination of the two. So the fact that gaps do not narrow during the school years does not mean that schools are not playing an equalizing role. It might be that gaps would grow even wider in the absence of schooling, and in fact there is evidence to support this interpretation in the phenomenon of "summer learning loss": low-SES children often lose ground relative to their more-advantaged peers during the summer, when they are not in

Figure 1.2   Average reading scores of U.S. children from different SES groups—and the gaps between them—change relatively little between kindergarten and eighth grade.

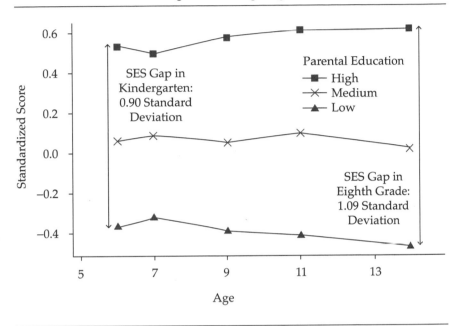

Source: Authors' calculations using the ECLS-K.
Notes: The chart plots the average standardized reading scores of children from the three SES groups, defined by their parents' level of education, at spring kindergarten (age six), first grade (age seven), third grade (age nine), fifth grade (age eleven), and eighth grade (age fourteen). The "SES gap" is the difference in average scores of children in the low-SES group (parents have only a high school degree or less) and the high-SES group (at least one parent has a college degree). See chapter 6 for further details.

school. Gaps during the school years might also reflect the increasing importance of early differences in vocabulary and background knowledge to children's test scores in the later elementary school years and beyond as they make the transition from learning to read to reading to learn.

3. What can the United States learn from other countries about making children more successful regardless of family background? More broadly put, does it have to be this way?

Our three country examples provide interesting points of comparison. Although we cannot say precisely which factors account for their greater

Figure 1.3   Over time, achievement gaps emerge between low- and high-SES children who start school with the same level of reading ability—high-SES children always develop an advantage, whether they start with high, average, or low ability in kindergarten.

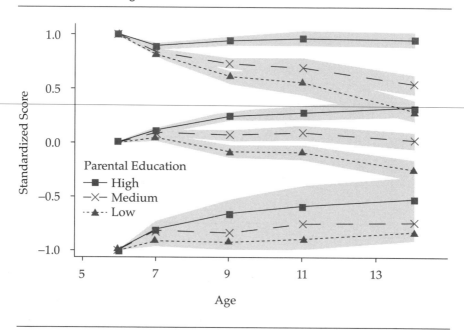

Source: Authors' calculations using the ECLS-K.
Notes: The lines depict the predicted scores in grades 1 through 8 (at ages seven through fourteen) of children with three specific reading test scores in kindergarten (+1, 0, and –1 standard deviations above the mean). We allowed the predicted scores associated with a given initial score to differ with SES. We calculated a quadratic relationship between spring kindergarten score and later test score separately for each group (with fall kindergarten scores used as instruments to correct for measurement error) and generated predictions from these models. Shaded areas are 95 percent confidence intervals that indicate the precision with which we can predict later outcomes. See chapter 6 for details.

equality of opportunity, Australia, Canada, and the United Kingdom do provide proof that the outcomes of children from different backgrounds can be more equal than they are in the United States today.

Canada and, to a lesser extent, Australia have more equality among children than the United States does. Their smaller SES gaps are present already in early childhood and persist through the school years. Compared to the United States, low-SES families in Canada and Australia have more resources for children—the parents are older, are more likely to be married or residing together, and have higher incomes. In Canada, parents are also more likely to read to the children. Low-SES children in both Canada and Australia also receive more supports from the public sector. Both countries provide universal health insurance as well as child benefit programs that provide income support to families with children. Both now provide substantial paid parental leave to allow new parents to stay home with their infants. Australia provides free universal preschool; Canada does as well in some provinces.

The U.K. example is also informative. Like the United States, the United Kingdom has a lot of inequality between families, and this is reflected in a fairly large SES gap in achievement before school entry. The fact that the SES gap in children's achievement in the United Kingdom is not as large as it is in the United States may be due to more universal supports for low-SES families, such as universal health insurance, universal preschool, child benefits, and so on. The United Kingdom also appears to be a country where the SES gap may narrow during the primary school years, unlike the situation in the United States. This may be due to the United Kingdom's more uniform national curriculum as well as recent school reforms that emphasize raising the achievement of low-SES children and provide extra funds to schools to help them accomplish this goal.

One common—and surprising—finding across countries is that the majority of the SES achievement gap is already present at school entry. When we set out to write this book, we expected to find that at least half the gap in achievement would emerge during the school years. But to our surprise, most of the gap in skills between low- and high-SES children, and most of the difference in the magnitude of that gap across countries, was already present at school entry. This has important implications for the timing and nature of policy remedies.

Because the majority of the achievement gap between low- and high-SES children has its origins prior to school entry, addressing the gap clearly will require interventions in early childhood. In particular, there is an important role for evidence-based parenting programs and preschool programs, as well as income support programs to reduce poverty and financial strain among families with preschool-age children. Such programs would go a long way toward evening out the disparities in resources available to young children in the United States and, in turn, the disparities in their early development. And reducing those early gaps would make it easier to combat inequality during the school years, since children would come to school on a more even footing and with a greater likelihood of being among peers who, like them, are better prepared.

But there is also a role for policies to address inequality during the school years. Both within and beyond our four countries, what is now a considerable body of evidence on school policies that help promote equity suggests that the following school reform policies would be most effective in helping to reduce SES achievement gaps: recruiting, supporting, and adequately compensating more effective teachers; implementing more rigorous curricula; and raising expectations and providing more support for low-achieving children. There may also be a role for extending the school day or school year.

Inequality during the school years may also reflect the influence of out-of-school factors. The family, community, and public-sector factors that are important in early achievement are also likely to play a role in achievement during the school years. So there is also a role for policies that provide support for student learning outside of school, from after-school and summer programs to help address out-of-school learning differentials to income support programs to help ease financial pressures and stresses on families.

CONCLUSION

Children from low-SES families face considerable challenges, and more so in the United States than in other countries. Their parents not only lack education but also tend to be younger, to live in less stable families, and to have lower incomes. These initial inequalities are augmented by a less active social safety net than is provided by peer countries. Unlike their counterparts in other countries, less-advantaged families in the United States do not have paid parental leave, universal preschool, reliable income supports, or (until recently) access to universal health insurance. It is little wonder that their children come to school less ready than higher-SES children, and further behind than their peers in Canada, Australia, and the United Kingdom. Once they are in school, children from low-SES families face school systems that struggle with widely disparate readiness among their students and with many other children with similar family backgrounds. Low-SES children also attend schools that, reflecting residential segregation, are segregated by income and have fewer school resources, including important inputs like teacher quality. So again, it is little wonder that gaps across social groupings are not closing during the school years and, if anything, are widening instead.

But the challenge to equal opportunity in the United States is not just driven by the situation of low-SES families. Something is going on at the middle and the top as well.

For children from high-SES families, it is in many ways the best of times. Not only are their parents highly educated, they also are more likely than parents in other families to be married, and they have much higher incomes than such families had in the past or than such families have in other countries. Sociologist Sara McLanahan calls this a pattern of "diverging destinies": family and other resources have been increasingly concentrated in the high-SES families, while the low-SES families have become increasingly disadvantaged. In addition to having more resources, high-SES families are also investing a larger share of their resources in their children in a phenomenon that we have likened to an arms race. The result is high-SES children pulling away from others—pulling away not just from the low-SES children but also from those in the middle.

Meanwhile, the families in the middle are experiencing what we call a "middle-class squeeze." Parents are working long hours but not seeing income gains. Nor do they receive much support from government policies relative to their counterparts in other countries. They do not receive universal paid parental leave or universal preschool, and until recently they did not have access to universal health insurance. They fear that the schools their children attend are just mediocre, but they do not have the resources available to the more affluent to supplement school with out-of-school enrichment activities and summer programs or move their children to private school. Parents in the middle worry about whether their children will do well enough to get into a good college, and they worry about how they will manage to pay for it. Thus, to close the unacceptably large achievement gap in the United States will require doing something about achievement not only for children from low-SES families but also those from middle-SES families. Both groups are struggling, and not doing as well as their peers in other countries. That is why we favor policies that will help a broad range of families rather than ones narrowly targeted at the most disadvantaged. To this end, we emphasize three key policy directions for the United States:

1.   Provide more support for early learning through more widespread availability of evidence-based parenting programs for families with infants and toddlers and through universal preschool for three- and four-year-olds

2.   Raise family incomes for the poor and near-poor through measures such as increasing the minimum wage and expanding the Child Tax Credit and Earned Income Tax Credit

3.   Improve the quality of teaching and learning in schools by recruiting, supporting, and adequately compensating more effective teachers, implementing more rigorous curricula, and setting higher expectations and providing more support for low-achieving students

The challenge involved in achieving the American Dream of equal opportunity—for children like Johnny as well as children like Alex—is not a simple one. The SES gap in achievement is large, and it has many causes. But it is not intractable. The evidence from our peer countries indicates clearly that the United States can do better, and that we need not leave so many children behind. We hope this book will help in making that dream a reality.

Chapter 2 | The Meaning and Measurement of Equal Opportunity

IF WE ARE to determine whether the United States is living up to its dream of opportunity for all, we must first define what we mean by "equal opportunity" and how it might be measured. We do so in this chapter, drawing on the work of the political economist John Roemer, on gaps in outcomes and equality of opportunity, and the work of the philosopher and legal scholar Joseph Fishkin, on the process through which gaps evolve over time, potentially resulting in "bottlenecks" at certain stages of development.

We also provide a first look from our data at the distribution of test scores of American children from different socioeconomic status groups just before high school. Our data confirm the pattern seen in international test score data for high school students—there is a great deal of inequality in test scores for children in the United States. We then go on to provide what international test score data cannot—the comparable distributions of test scores for the same children at school entry. Our results add to that picture by showing that substantial inequality is for the most part already present when children start school.

CHILDREN'S OUTCOMES AND BACKGROUNDS

In focusing on the nature of equal opportunity and children's outcomes, we make use of tests administered to children in the United States, the United Kingdom, Australia, and Canada. These tests are given to only a small fraction of young people in each of these countries, but that fraction is carefully chosen to be representative of the country's young people.

In this chapter, we focus on the United States and use information on roughly 9,000 children who were chosen to be representative of the almost 4 million children born in 1993. These children started kindergarten in 1998, when they were about five years old, and were followed to 2007, when they were about fourteen years old.[1] Their test scores are meant to offer a picture of how the country's children are doing.

Figures 2.1 and 2.2 show some basic results from a series of questions meant to assess the mathematics and reading skills of these children when they were fourteen years old during the spring of their eighth-grade year, when they were about to make the transition to high school. Whatever the lives of fourteen-year-olds have to offer, and however they choose to define their own life goals, they will find it easier to seize opportunities if they know how to read critically and are proficient in math skills. And certainly the more refined these skills, the greater their chances of passing through one important gateway in life—successfully completing and graduating from high school.

These figures show two things. First, we might be surprised at the low average level of proficiency. Fewer than four in ten fourteen-year-olds are able to manipulate fractions or critically evaluate a written text. A good deal has been made of these sorts of facts. The Organization for Economic Cooperation and Development (OECD), a think tank for the United States and other rich countries, has produced numerous reports on children's scores on mathematics, literacy, and science tests; designed in a way to measure important life skills, these tests have documented the relatively poor performance of American teens.[2]

The second striking revelation from these figures is the strong relationship between skills and family background, particularly the fading away of achievement for children from less-advantaged backgrounds. This pattern is clear for all but the most basic mathematics and reading skills. Children raised in households in which at least one parent has a college degree perform noticeably better than those whose parents have some education beyond high school but no college degree, although they, in turn, do better than those with parents who did not continue their schooling beyond high school or did not complete high school.

The gap between the children from the highest-status families and those from the lowest is clearly noticeable for all but the most basic skills, and it becomes wider and wider for the successively more sophisticated skills. For example, 58 percent of eighth-graders in the high-parental-education group are proficient in the use of fractions, compared to 18 percent of the children whose parents are in the low-educated group.

This gap across these groups is our main concern. As we detail in later chapters, we measure socioeconomic status primarily using the level of

Figure 2.1   Proficiency in mathematics fades as family background becomes less advantageous: children from the highest-status families are much more likely to master mathematics skills than those from the lowest-status families.

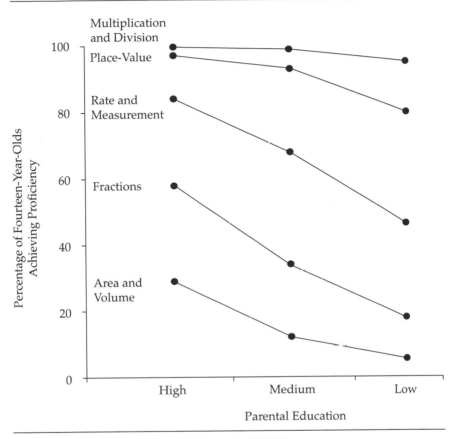

Source: Authors' calculations using data from the ECLS-K.
Notes: The average proportion of all fourteen-year-olds attaining maximum proficiency in each skill is: 97.6 percent for multiplication and division, 89.5 percent for place value, 65.2 percent for rate and measurement, 35.4 percent for fractions, and 15.1 percent for area and volume. Parental education refers to the schooling attainment of the most-educated parent. This figure uses data on 7,340 children, of whom 36 percent were in the high education group, 31 percent in the low education group, and the remainder in the medium education group (when this sample is appropriately weighted). The ECLS-K sample was selected in 1998 to be representative of the 3.9 million American children who started kindergarten in that year and who were generally fourteen years old in 2007. See the technical appendix for further details of the samples and weights used in our analyses.

Figure 2.2   Proficiency in reading skills also fades as family background
becomes less advantageous: children from the highest-status
families are much more likely to master reading skills than those
from the lowest-status families.

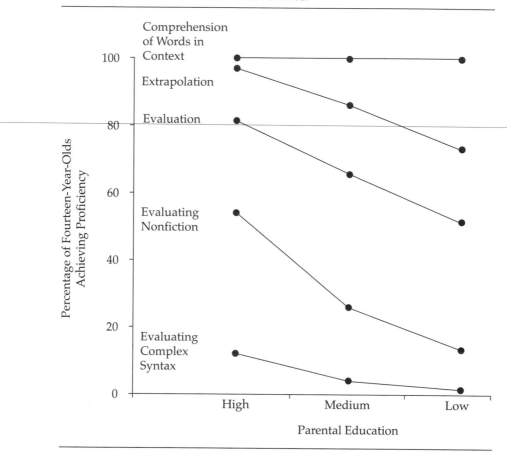

Source: Authors' calculations using data from the ECLS-K.
Notes: The average proportion of all fourteen-year-olds attaining maximum proficiency in
each skill is: 99.7 percent for comprehension of words, 84.9 percent for extrapolation, 65.7
percent for evaluation, 30.3 percent for evaluating nonfiction, and 5.8 percent for evaluating
complex syntax. Parental education refers to the schooling attainment of the most-educated
parent. This figure uses data on 7,500 children, of whom 35 percent were in the high education group, 32 percent in the low education group, and the remainder in the medium education group (when this sample is appropriately weighted). The ECLS-K sample was selected
in 1998 to be representative of the 3.9 million American children who started kindergarten
in that year and who were generally fourteen years old in 2007. See the technical appendix
for further details of the samples and weights used in our analyses.

education of the most-educated parent. Social scientists have used a number of different indicators of socioeconomic status according to different perspectives and purposes for their analyses and according to the information available to them. Our decision to use parental education as our primary indicator of socioeconomic status is based on both theoretical and statistical considerations. The theoretical justification is that parental education is an excellent marker for family resources and environment, as well as family values and beliefs. We also recognize that parental education may reflect innate characteristics that are passed on between parent and child, a more subtle and enriched environment, and the interactions between the two. Statistically, education may suffer less from measurement error than income, the other commonly used indicator of socioeconomic status. Education is a good measure of a person's likely lifetime earnings and, as a result, should give a more accurate picture of permanent material resources. In addition, empirical research shows that parental education is strongly associated with child outcomes. We have also looked at differences across parental income groups, and when appropriate we draw attention to any results for which the cross-national pattern according to income is different than that based on parental education.

Although we focus primarily on the mathematics and reading skills that young children develop—as measured in the battery of questions administered in the surveys we use—these surveys ask many questions on other aspects of cognitive and behavioral skills, as well as child health, and we also make use of these indicators.

What should we make of the test results presented in figures 2.1 and 2.2? The gaps evident in both figures are certainly important in understanding why overall average levels of attainment might be considered too low in the United States. Raising the skills of children from the least-advantaged families seems like the surest way to have a big impact on the overall average. But we also contend that the gaps are important in understanding inequalities of opportunity in American society. Are these test results showing us a tilted playing field—a field in which a child's life chances are significantly influenced by family origins? And is it fair that children born to different groups of parents enter high school with such different levels of skills?

EQUALITY OF OPPORTUNITY

Professor John Roemer is an expert in the meaning and measurement of "equality of opportunity." To appreciate and understand his research, we need to begin by recognizing that not all of the inequalities we see around us are objectionable from an ethical point of view. Roemer's theory of equality of opportunity is based on the idea that some inequalities are morally acceptable, while others are not. To make this distinction we need to know to what degree individuals are responsible for their outcomes in life: to what extent, in other words, are these outcomes the result of circumstances beyond an individual's control, and to what extent do they reflect an individual's effort?[3]

Effort follows from the choices that individuals make, and Roemer argues that people should be held responsible for their choices. If inequality is the result of choice, then we should not think of it as a problem, at least from a moral standpoint. But Roemer also recognizes that some part of inequality in the outcomes we care about is the result of circumstances beyond an individual's control, circumstances for which he or she should not be held responsible. Inequality due to circumstance is not morally acceptable.

Much of Roemer's research on this topic deals with adult outcomes, like incomes and health, and in these cases it is particularly important to draw the distinction between effort and circumstance. He suggests that we draw this line by ranking individuals within the groupings that distinguish them by their circumstances. As an example, when he considers adult incomes, he ranks individuals from bottom to top within each of the categories that define the circumstances beyond their control—say, their family origins as indicated by their parents' education. All individuals from high-educated families are ranked from lowest to highest incomes, and all individuals from low-educated families are ranked from lowest to highest. Equality of opportunity occurs not when incomes are equal for everyone, but rather when the distribution of incomes across the different types of individuals is the same. Roemer asks that we compare the incomes of individuals who have the same rank across the different categories of family background. If the income of someone from a well-to-do family is higher than it is for someone from a relatively less well off family who is at the same rank in the distribution, then this indicates inequality of opportunity. In this scenario, a glass floor supports those people from advantaged families, while a glass ceiling may limit opportunity for those from less-advantaged ones.

But it is important to note—as Roemer clearly acknowledges—that a good deal hinges on how we define these categories. All the differences in outcomes that are not accounted for by the groupings are assumed to reflect effort. There are many factors that we may feel are beyond an individual's control and should also be accounted for when drawing the line between effort and circumstance, between personal responsibility and bad or good luck. And it is quite reasonable to also suggest that drawing this line reflects value judgments over which reasonable people, or citizens of different countries, may well disagree.

It is also important to note, perhaps counterintuitively, that controlling for only one circumstance, like family background in the above example, and leaving everything else aside—including, in the extreme, genetic endowments—is likely to *understate* the amount of inequality of opportunity. That is, if we were able to take a factor like genetic endowment into account, our estimate of inequality of opportunity would be larger, because children who have had the bad luck to be born without the genes that lead to success will find it extremely difficult to do as well in the things that matter to them as those who are more fortunate. Children with "bad genes" will have less opportunity.[4]

Indeed, "where children are concerned," Professor Roemer and his co-author Alain Trannoy write, "all inequality should be counted as due to circumstances, and none to effort. . . . Children should only become responsible for their actions after an 'age of consent' is reached, which may vary across societies. Both nature and nurture fall within the ambit of circumstances for the child."[5]

Roemer also points out that parents influence their children, and the opportunities available to them, in a number of ways. Societies may quite reasonably differ in the extent to which children should in some sense be compensated for the resulting inequalities in their life outcomes. For example, parents may use their social connections for the benefit of their children, and these resources may vary across socioeconomic groups. Some parents may use their network to get their children better playmates, teachers, schools, or even jobs. Overt nepotism is an extreme example. But there are other influences that are subtler, or even outside of full parental control. Children are influenced by the climate or culture of their families, which can also influence not just their skills, both social and cognitive, but also their beliefs and outlook on life. Certainly children resemble their parents for a whole host of reasons, but they also resemble them because of the genetic transmission of traits. These are all influences that Roemer argues should be compensated for by equal opportunity policies.

Parents also play an important role in forming the preferences and aspirations of their children; indeed, for many people that is the very point, and the deepest goal, of raising a family. This is a subtle but important influence on children. Although we might agree that some children should not fall behind others in the development of important life skills because their parents lack the "connections" or "power" to make important resources available to them, at the same time we might be ambivalent about how much of the influence of family background is not defensible and should be leveled in some way by compensating those in less-advantaged circumstances. "If one does not admit this," cautions Professor Roemer in the paper written with Alain Trannoy, "then it is difficult to justify why we do not advocate raising children collectively."[6] Equality of opportunity comes down to understanding the sources of differences between outcomes across socioeconomic groups, and then making a value judgment on their acceptability in the context of broader social goals associated with the autonomy of individuals and families.

This has led at least one philosopher to argue that societies can never completely close socioeconomic gaps because of the "problem of the family."[7] Sociologists like Christopher Jencks and Gøsta Esping-Andersen have also made this point.[8]

We focus our attention on differences in opportunity related to family background. Our approach is not to argue that we should try to compensate for all the different sources of unequal opportunity. For many characteristics, this is neither politically nor scientifically possible. But we do wish to explore the impact of some important and potentially modifiable social and economic resources. Cross-national comparisons provide a powerful tool for exploring the range of economic and social policies that are feasible in modern societies. Our four countries share a common culture, a common economic system, and a similarly wide distribution of parental and family personal capabilities. As we shall see, however, the gaps in outcomes between children from different socioeconomic backgrounds vary significantly across these countries. Although it might not be possible to eliminate all of the inequality of opportunity associated with genes and families, the fact is that gaps between families of different socioeconomic backgrounds are significantly smaller in other countries that, in many respects, are similar to the United States.

UNEQUAL OUTCOMES

Roemer's way of thinking about inequality of opportunity can be illustrated in concrete form by examining the reading and math test scores of the fourteen-year-old American children of interest to us. We can group children according to socioeconomic status, rank them within each group on the basis of their test scores, and then compare the achievement levels of children who have the same rank (and thus, by implication, have exerted the same amount of "effort") but happened to be born to parents with different levels of education.

We are able to measure math and reading skills with a much wider battery of questions and tests than the small number used to create the basic competencies depicted in figures 2.1 and 2.2. This more comprehensive assessment is directly related to these specific competencies, but it has the advantage of allowing a finer and continuous measurement of underlying skills. Unlike height or weight, there is no natural unit of measurement for reading or math skills. The scale on a test is completely arbitrary: a ten-point gap on one test can mean the same thing as a fifty-point gap on another test. We tackle this problem by expressing all outcomes in standard deviation units and adjusting the measures so that the average child is assigned a score of zero on every test. This method has several advantages, and is commonly used by education researchers. If the distribution of test scores follows the bell-shaped normal curve (and many tests are designed to give just this distribution), then each score corresponds to a known percentile rank. Two-thirds of individuals will have scores lying between −1 and +1. About 2.5 percent of individuals will have a score less than −2, and 2.5 percent will have a score beyond 2. Hence, three standard deviation units will span the scores attained by the vast majority of the population, regardless of which test was administered. This property allows us to compare inequalities in outcomes measured in a host of different ways, such as for different domains of development, at different child ages, and in different countries.

The horizontal axes of figures 2.3 and 2.4 mark out all possible scores on a test in standard deviation units, first for mathematics and then for reading. Moving vertically from bottom to top indicates the proportion of students reaching no more than each particular test score. This proportion is calculated for students within each of our three different socioeconomic status groups. These figures can be read in two ways. First, we can pick a test score from the horizontal axis—for example, the average test score of zero—and draw from there a vertical line upward, noting where it intersects the three curves. This tells us that only about 25 percent of children from high-SES families score less than the average for all children in mathematics in eighth grade; the corresponding number is about 50 percent for the medium-SES group, and it reaches almost 70 percent for children in the low-SES group. Differences in these percentages are one type of socioeconomic status gap.

Roemer's analysis of equal opportunity, however, encourages us to measure these gaps in a different way. A test of whether equal opportunity holds is whether the three lines for the different groups lie on top of another. Horizontal gaps between the lines indicate that children with the same rank position within a group have different outcomes, and the size of that gap gives a measure of the degree of inequality of opportunity.[9]

An important implication of Roemer's theory is that a complete analysis of inequality of opportunity requires us to consider the full distribu-

Figure 2.3 Inequality of opportunity in mathematics skills at age fourteen is indicated by the gap in test scores for equally ranked individuals across socioeconomic groups.

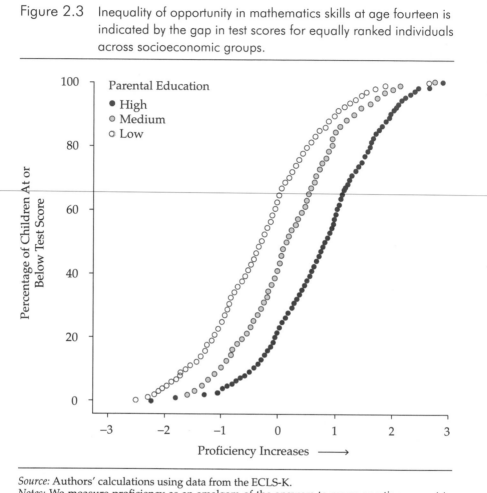

Source: Authors' calculations using data from the ECLS-K.

Notes: We measure proficiency as an amalgam of the answers to many questions meant to evaluate mathematics skills as a whole, accounting for biases in the test-taking process. These "theta scores" increase with increased proficiency, and as they increase they are related to higher competencies in mathematics skills. Here they are expressed as standardized scores. The average score on the test is normalized to zero, and the units (marked along the horizontal axis) correspond to standard deviations of the underlying theta scores. The series of dots sketches out the cumulative distribution functions within each of three groups according to parental education, which refers to the schooling attainment of the most-educated parent. As discussed in the note to figure 2.1, children are not equally divided between these three groups. This figure uses data on about 9,280 children from the ECLS-K sample, which was selected in 1998 to be representative of the 3.9 million American children who started kindergarten in that year and who were generally fourteen years old in 2007. Sample size is rounded to the nearest 10, in accordance with NCES reporting rules. See the technical appendix for further details of the samples and weights used in our analyses.

Figure 2.4   Inequality of opportunity in reading skills at age fourteen is indicated by the gap in test scores for equally ranked individuals across socioeconomic groups.

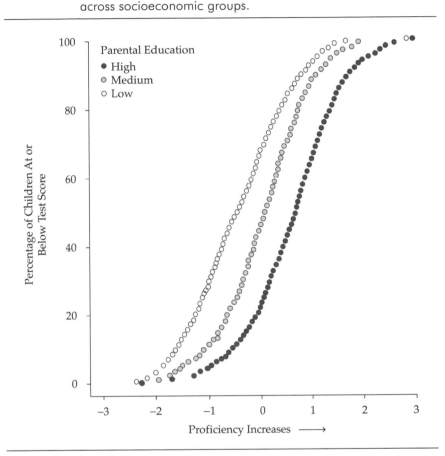

Source: Authors' calculations using data from the ECLS-K.

Notes: We measure proficiency as an amalgam of the answers to many questions meant to evaluate reading skills as a whole, accounting for biases in the test-taking process. These "theta scores" increase with increased proficiency, and as they increase they are related to higher competencies in reading skills. Here they are expressed as standardized scores. The average score on the test is normalized to zero, and the units (marked along the horizontal axis) correspond to standard deviations of the underlying theta score. The series of dots sketches out the cumulative distribution functions within each of three groups according to parental education, which refers to the schooling attainment of the most-educated parent. As discussed in the note to figure 2.2, children are not equally divided between these three groups. This figure uses data on about 9,220 children from the ECLS-K sample, which was selected in 1998 to be representative of the 3.9 million American children who started kindergarten in that year and who were generally fourteen years old in 2007. Sample size is rounded to the nearest 10, in accordance with NCES reporting rules. See the technical appendix for further details of the samples and weights used in our analyses.

tion of outcomes both within groups and across groups. Such a level of detail is infeasible, however, if we wish to compare inequalities across a large number of outcomes from different domains of development, ages, and countries. This is our intention. Some kind of summary statistic is needed that captures the overall horizontal difference between each pair of lines in a parsimonious way. We use the difference in the average test score of children in each status group, which is equivalent to the average of all the horizontal gaps in the figures if we were to calculate them for every possible percentage share. This is the area between pairs of curves in these figures. For the math scores in figure 2.3, the average scores of the low, medium, and high-SES groups are –0.47, 0.01, and 0.58, respectively, giving an overall high-low gap of 1.05 standard deviation units, which is very close to the horizontal gap at the fiftieth percentile. For reading, the average scores are 0.50, 0.01, and 0.61, giving a gap of 1.11 units. Hence, inequality of opportunity is slightly higher for reading than for math.

"BOTTLENECKS" AND OPPORTUNITY

Professor Joseph Fishkin is also an expert in the meaning and measurement of equality of opportunity. In thinking about how to measure equality of opportunity, we are encouraged by Professor Roemer's views to examine gaps in attainment across socioeconomic groups. Professor Fishkin's perspective adds to this by encouraging us to wonder about the process, and the changes in these gaps, as children grow older and make a host of transitions on their way to adulthood.

In other words, Fishkin's way of thinking about equality of opportunity asks us to consider the process of moving across the different stages in the life course. From this view, the kinds of movements that we see—or for that matter do not see—in these test score patterns need to be interpreted carefully. These tests are never perfect indicators of the underlying abilities they are attempting to measure, and to a certain degree the results for any particular child on any particular test day may reflect distractions when the test was administered that pulled up or pushed down his or her score. This sort of "noise" needs to be netted out before we can get a clear picture of change over time; a good part of our analysis in the following chapters adopts appropriate statistical techniques to account for this sort of randomness. Also, we must account for the statistical variation that is an inherent part of the survey-taking process and that introduces uncertainty in the attempt to make inferences about the entire population of children from a much smaller, though representative, sample.

But these statistical matters aside, Professor Fishkin is asking us to pay attention to the series of steps that children must take in becoming all that they can be, as well as to look at how different societies structure this process. He is conscious of the fact that we all must pass through certain gateways, or what he calls "bottlenecks," which he defines as: "narrow places through which people must pass if they hope to reach a wide range of opportunities that fan out on the other side. College education; developmental opportunities in early childhood; enough money to navigate a society where almost everything requires money—all these are examples of potential bottlenecks."[10]

Fishkin acknowledges that perfect equality of opportunity is not possible, somewhat in the same way that Roemer states that societies should not be seeking to completely eliminate the tie between parent and child outcomes. In particular, since parents have the freedom to decide how to raise their children, and since families are different in the resources available to them and in their approaches to parenting, opportunities for children are going to be different from the very start of their lives. Fishkin does argue, however, that we should be aware of and identify the crucial bottlenecks in our societies, and that we should either help move people through these bottlenecks or devise strategies for people to go around them so that they will be less important in determining life chances.

In thinking about how to measure equality of opportunity from this perspective, then, it is natural to focus on process and on change through time in the gaps between children in the basic skills that will be important to them regardless of their ultimate goal. It is also important to do this in a way that looks at the society as a whole and at the ways in which the particular crossroads that define the structure of opportunity add up to determine destination and outcome.

Figures 2.5 and 2.6 offer exactly the same information as the previous two pictures, but add the scores that the same children obtained on tests conducted at the start of kindergarten, when they were five years old. These tests are age-appropriate indicators of early numeracy and language skills; the latter, for example, involves showing children a series of pictures and verbally confirming that they know the word for the image, be it a bus or an umbrella. Recall that we are using "standardized" scores, expressed in standard deviation units, for every outcome measure at every age. These scores facilitate the comparison of inequality across outcome measures but, as a result, are not informative about differences in the absolute level of underlying skills. The math skills of all children, of course, improve massively between kindergarten and eighth grade, while the average score on a standardized test remains zero at both time points by definition. The test of whether inequality has widened (or narrowed) between kindergarten and eighth grade, therefore, is whether the three

Figure 2.5   Inequality of opportunity in mathematics skills at ages five and fourteen is indicated by the gap in test scores for equally ranked individuals across socioeconomic groups.

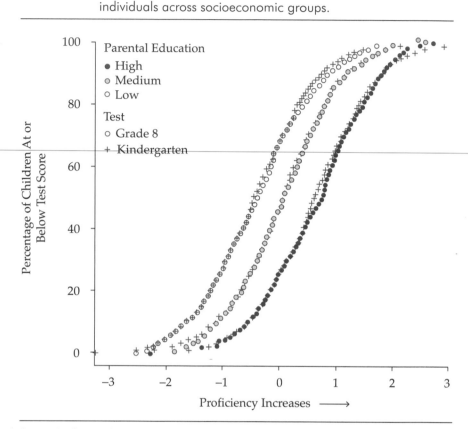

Source: Authors' calculations using data from the ECLS-K.
Notes: We measure proficiency as an amalgam of the answers to many questions meant to evaluate math skills as a whole, accounting for biases in the test-taking process. These "theta scores" increase with increased proficiency, and as they increase they are related to higher competencies in the mathematics skills depicted in figure 2.1. Here they are expressed as standardized scores. The average score on the test is normalized to zero, and the units (marked along the horizontal axis) correspond to standard deviations of the underlying theta score. The series of dots sketches out the cumulative distribution functions of standardized scores at age fourteen (as shown in figure 2.3), and the series of crosses sketches the same functions for about 18,630 children assessed in the fall of their kindergarten year. The functions are plotted separately for each of three groups according to parental education, which refers to the schooling attainment of the most-educated parent in the child's kindergarten year. The ECLS-K sample was selected in 1998 to be representative of the 3.9 million American children who started kindergarten in that year and who were generally fourteen years old in 2007. Sample size is rounded to the nearest 10, in accordance with NCES reporting rules. See the technical appendix for further details of the samples and weights used in our analyses.

Figure 2.6   Inequality of opportunity in reading skills at ages five and
fourteen is indicated by the gap in test scores for equally ranked
individuals across socioeconomic groups.

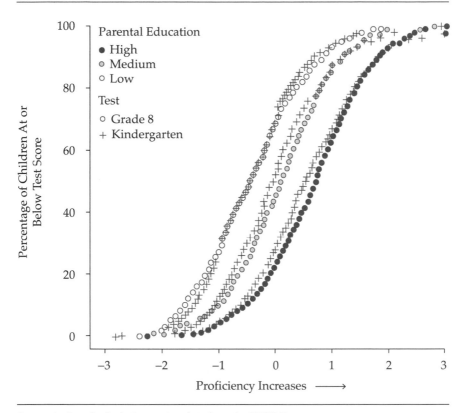

Source: Authors' calculations using data from the ECLS-K.

Notes: We measure proficiency as an amalgam of the answers to many questions meant to evaluate reading skills as a whole, accounting for biases in the test-taking process. These "theta scores" increase with increased proficiency, and as they increase they are related to higher competencies in the reading skills depicted in figure 2.2. Here they are expressed as standardized scores. The average score on the test is normalized to zero, and the units (marked along the horizontal axis) correspond to standard deviations of the underlying theta score. The series of dots sketches out the cumulative distribution functions of standardized scores at age fourteen (as shown in figure 2.4), and the series of crosses sketches the same functions for about 18,770 children assessed in the fall of their kindergarten year. The functions are plotted separately for each of three groups according to parental education, which refers to the schooling attainment of the most-educated parent in the child's kindergarten year. The ECLS-K sample was selected in 1998 to be representative of the 3.9 million American children who started kindergarten in that year and who were generally fourteen years old in 2007. Sample size is rounded to the nearest 10, in accordance with NCES reporting rules. See the technical appendix for further details of the samples and weights used in our analyses.

SES group lines at eighth grade (depicted as circles in the figures) are farther apart (or closer together) in terms of horizontal distance than they are in kindergarten (depicted as crosses).

The most striking result is how similar the distributions are at the two ages across the three socioeconomic status groups. The gap between similarly ranked children being raised in low- and high-SES families is, broadly speaking, not all that different whether it is measured in kindergarten, at the onset of formal schooling, or at grade 8—the cusp of high school—and this is generally the case whether we look children with relatively low- or high-rank positions within their group.

The figures do reveal that the change in the gap over time is not identical for all children. For example, the chart for reading points to a particularly strong widening of the gap between the lowest-achieving children in each group, at around the twentieth percentile rank or below (figure 2.6). Here the eighth-grade circles have shifted to the left of the kindergarten crosses in the low-SES group, but are positioned to the right for children from both the medium- and high-SES groups. Hence, the gap between groups seems to have unambiguously widened. The opposite pattern can be discerned at the top of the chart, where the relative test scores of the low-SES children at the eightieth to ninetieth percentiles have improved slightly (shifted right) in the eight years following school entry. But overall this variation seems relatively minor compared to the similarity of the distributions over time.

What does our summary measure of the average gap say about changing inequality as children move through school? We reported earlier that the high-low gap in eighth grade math was 1.08 standard deviation units. The equivalent gap in kindergarten was 1.04 units, a difference that is not statistically significant. For reading, the eighth-grade gap of 1.11 units can be compared with a gap of 1.01 at kindergarten, indicating a slight increase in inequality over time, but again, this is a remarkably similar inequality statistic given that eight years have passed between measurements.

The stability of the gaps revealed by figures 2.5 and 2.6 appears consistent with Fishkin's contention that developmental opportunity in early childhood acts as a bottleneck on later achievement. Children from families with low-educated parents begin school with a massive disadvantage in terms of their basic academic capabilities, and they are not able to close even a portion of that gap by the start of high school. Disadvantage from the preschool period appears to persist unchallenged throughout the school years. It is tempting to conclude that the sources of socioeconomic inequality in achievement are rooted entirely in the early years, that "not much happens" during the school years either to exacerbate or to ameliorate the gaps, and perhaps even that policy to reduce inequality should focus solely on the preschool period.

Our empirical analyses probe this characterization of early development as a bottleneck. We explore whether the magnitude of the socioeconomic status gap, and its stability over time, is a feature unique to the United States or one common across comparable countries. Can we find evidence of routes to recovery for low-SES children who enter school with poor skills that appear lacking in the United States? And is a comparison of gaps at different ages the appropriate way to assess the long-term consequences of disparities among children at school entry? In fact, as we show in chapter 6, statistical analyses reveal a more nuanced picture than the simple attribution of all inequality to influences in early childhood. Although skills at school entry undoubtedly cast a long shadow on children's eventual achievement, there is considerable fluidity in the school years, and low-SES children continue to be systematically disadvantaged in learning experiences during this period.

HIGH-STAKES TESTS AND THE ARMS RACE

The United States was a world leader in the development of universal public education.[11] A key principle was the idea that schooling would help level the playing field and promote more equal opportunity than had existed in the countries from which most American families had emigrated.

Seen in this light, tests would play a role in building the meritocratic society that the United States aspired to be. As journalist and author Nicholas Lemann puts it in his book on the origins of the college admissions test, the SAT, and the role played by Harvard president James Bryant Conant and test developer Henry Chauncey:

> In the new, classless American society Conant hoped for, everyone should start on an equal footing, and the abler graduates would rise to high positions strictly because they deserved to. They should not, however, be able to confer special advantages upon their children; America could use "the powers of government to reorder the 'haves and have-nots' in every generation to give flux to our social order." And how would such a society be achieved and managed? Through public education. "Abilities must be assessed, talents must be developed, ambitions guided," Conant wrote. "This is the task for our public schools." And, he might have added, for Henry Chauncey and the SAT.[12]

In this view, tests are a sorting mechanism, one that helps society identify the most able so that they can pass through the gateways to various higher levels of education or employment. In principle, tests are an objective measure—more objective than selecting children for higher education or employment based on other attributes, such as their family's status or connections. But if tests are high-stakes, and if children's scores on tests are affected by other factors like family background, then those tests can instead become bottlenecks, holding children back from achieving their full potential.

Bottlenecks have another pernicious effect. Because they have a zero-sum element—you either get through them or you don't—they can lead to a race of special efforts and expenditures on the part of families. This race will be greater the more incentive parents have to invest in it and the more resources they have to do so. Several analysts have pointed out that this is now the case in the United States and, to a lesser extent, in the United Kingdom.[13] Parents see a lot of inequality in the labor market and worry about the position their children will occupy. High-SES parents also have higher incomes relative to other families than they had in the past. These two factors combined have led to increased competition to invest in children and ensure that they will succeed on the all-important tests that provide the gateway to college admission.

Australia and Canada differ. Canada does not rely on high-stakes tests for college admission. Instead, students are evaluated based on their grades in high school. So the system is more forgiving and there are more ways to achieve success, as Fishkin would recommend. A further point of difference is that in both Canada and Australia college admission itself is not as "make or break" as it is in the United States and the United Kingdom. Colleges are not as sharply differentiated by quality, and other forms of higher education and training (technical schools, apprenticeships, and so on) are available and accessible to lower-scoring students.[14] As a result, and because the college wage premium is also lower, there is less earnings inequality in Canada and Australia than in the United States and the United Kingdom.[15] When it comes to parents' incentives to invest in an arms race to boost their children's achievement, and their ability to do so, we would expect to see less of an arms race in Canada and Australia than we do in the United States and the United Kingdom.

Although we have emphasized the spillover effects of high-stakes tests on families' behavior, we should not neglect the effects on schools. If schools are preparing students for high-stakes tests, what are the consequences for equality of opportunity? Does the schooling system ensure that each child reaches his or her full potential, or does it serve to identify the most able children and ensure that they are well prepared to pass high-stakes tests? To return to the metaphor of a bottleneck, will early screening and testing be a bottleneck that allows only certain children to pass, or will early assessments be used to help all children learn and achieve as much as they can?

Again, there are feedback loops here between inequality in schooling systems and the overall level of inequality in society. The more unequal the distribution of incomes, and the more tied school enrollments are to parental income, the greater the likelihood that schools, rather than leveling the playing field, may end up contributing to higher inequality in the future. Breaking this cycle requires conscious efforts, such as compensatory funding and teaching methods that focus on all parts of the ability and socioeconomic distribution.

WHERE DO WE GO FROM HERE?

The differences in academic skills of American children across socioeconomic groups signal inequality of opportunity, an inequality that should be a concern. To understand these gaps we must learn more about the process through which they arise, in particular the bottlenecks that might be hindering the achievement of children with lower-educated parents.

Our first look at the data for children in the United States suggests substantial inequality of achievement. A significant gap across socioeconomic groups is already evident at school entry at age five and is still present when children are on the verge of entering high school at age fourteen. In the following chapters, we look more closely at the socioeconomic status gap, drawing on our detailed data for the United States and bringing in data from our three comparison countries. We begin in the next chapter by looking at the resources available to children in our four countries. Are family resources and investments more unequal in the United States, and if they are, what role do others (employers and the public sector) play in augmenting or alleviating this greater inequality?

Chapter 3 | Resources for Children

ALTHOUGH THEY USE different terms to describe them, psychologists, sociologists, and economists agree that a variety of resources are critical for child development. This chapter describes the role of resources in child development and then sketches the situation of children from different family backgrounds—in terms of the resources they receive in early childhood—in our four countries. We focus in particular on the role played by three main sources of support—families, employers, and the government—in providing resources for children. Just how is the balance between these sources struck, and what does it imply for the resources available to children of different family backgrounds in the United States compared with the United Kingdom, Australia, and Canada?

Addressing these questions highlights three striking findings. First, Canada stands out from the United States and the other two countries in the higher level of family resources available to children. The distinctive position of Canada is seen most clearly in parental education, a key marker of socioeconomic status and a key input into child development. Second, family resources are skewed by socioeconomic status in all four countries, but most sharply in the United States. Third, the U.S. social safety net and supports for working families do the least among the four countries to combat inequality, leaving children from low-SES families in the United States doubly disadvantaged relative to their peers in the other countries.

THE DETERMINANTS AND STAGES OF CHILD DEVELOPMENT

Philosophers and social scientists have for centuries debated the relative importance of nature versus nurture. The seventeenth-century British philosopher John Locke espoused a tabula rasa, or blank slate, view of development. Applying this point of view, the twentieth-century American psychologist John Watson famously claimed that if given a healthy child at birth, he could mold that child into "a doctor, lawyer, artist, merchant-chief and yes, even beggar-man and thief, regardless of his talents, penchants, tendencies, abilities, vocations, and race of his ancestors."[1] Others have argued the opposite, that heredity is destiny, and would agree with the assertion of the nineteenth-century English scholar Francis Galton that "there is no escape from the conclusion that nature prevails tremendously over nurture."[2]

The truth, of course, lies somewhere in the middle. There are strong genetic influences on development *and* strong environmental influences. Most importantly, we have come to recognize the crucial role played by gene-environment interactions. The role that genes play for any given child depends crucially on the environment that the child experiences.[3] Even how a gene functions in the body—how it is expressed—can be affected by the environment through what are referred to as "epigenetic processes."[4] Thus, environment can go a long way toward either increasing the role of slight genetic advantages or disadvantages or mitigating them. The implication for our analysis is that the tendency of low-SES children to score lower on average on cognitive tests than high-SES children is likely due to a combination of factors—some related to differences in genes, some related to differences in environment, and probably the largest portion related to gene-environment interactions.[5]

Psychologists view human development as unfolding through a series of developmental stages, each of which has unique challenges and milestones.[6] The role of the environment starts early, as children are influenced even prenatally by the stresses and toxins to which their parents are exposed, and environment continues to play an important role in development throughout childhood.

The infant and toddler stages, taking up roughly the first three years of life, are a period of tremendous growth but also tremendous vulnerability. Human infants are unique in their long period of dependence on an adult caregiver, and their needs for care go beyond the purely material. To grow and thrive, infants need sensitive and responsive caregiving that is warm, nurturing, and consistent. Toward the end of the first year, infants move into the toddler stage as they begin to walk and move around more independently. Key challenges in this stage include learning how to use language and developing other early cognitive skills related to thinking, memory, and relationships. There are also developmental tasks related to social and emotional development. It is important that infants develop secure attachments to the adults who care for them. These attachments provide the foundation for healthy social interactions as toddlers begin to engage with peers and others outside the home.

Children ages three to five move into the preschool stage. Often they are starting to spend more time outside the home, in settings such as day care centers and preschools. Cognitive development, and particularly thinking and language skills, proceed rapidly in this stage. Preschool-age children also develop a stronger number sense and skills related to reading. In the social and emotional domain, preschool-age children are developing skills related to forming friendships and getting along with peers. They are also learning to control their attention, emotions, and behavior, a set of skills referred to as "self-regulation" and "self-control."[7]

The next stage, middle childhood, encompasses ages six to ten. At one time, this stage was thought to be a latency period when not much was happening developmentally, but we now understand that this is in fact a period of tremendous growth and learning. Children are enrolled in school and are mastering important content, including, most importantly, learning to read (which most children accomplish by age seven) and then making the transition to reading to learn. Children are also augmenting and applying their social and emotional skills. In addition to developing greater capacities for self-regulation and self-control, children are also learning to persist in tasks and to be conscientious about completing tasks.

Early adolescence begins around age eleven. This is a challenging period, both academically and socially. Children this age are often making the transition out of their elementary or primary schools to larger middle or secondary schools, where academic standards are typically more rigorous and social dynamics more intense. Adolescents are also experiencing a host of changes associated with puberty and entering a period when their experience of rewards, and their enjoyment of peers, is heightened. At the same time, adolescents' brains are still developing. In particular, they do not yet have fully developed skills in self-regulation. They are thus very susceptible to engaging in risky behaviors (such as substance use, early sexual activity, and crime), prompted by their own emerging feelings as well as by the influence of peers. The psychologist Larry Steinberg likens adolescent behavior in this period to driving a car equipped with a gas pedal but without good brakes.[8]

Successful development in each of these given stages lays the groundwork for future stages. Although for the most part development is not deterministic—early difficulties do not doom a child to later problems, nor do early successes provide an inoculation against later challenges—how a child develops in the early stages does influence his or her development in later ones. The economist James Heckman describes the links between early and later stages of development in his model of "dynamic complementarity." In this model, early skills lay the groundwork that enables the child to benefit from later learning opportunities. So "skills beget skills" and "learning begets learning." The result would be early skills gaps fanning out as children grow older. This fanning out could be averted if disadvantaged children received remedial services. Or it could be even more pronounced if children with initial advantages also benefit from more resources as they grow older, while children with initial disadvantages have access to fewer resources. We have much more to say about this in chapter 6. Here, the bottom line is that a good start in life is important, but a good start must be complemented by a series of later investments.

THE INPUTS TO CHILD DEVELOPMENT AND WHO PROVIDES THEM

As the preceding discussion suggests, at each stage of development a host of factors influence child development. Psychologists helpfully distinguish between inputs and actors that are proximal (or near) to the child versus those that are more distal (or further away). Proximal inputs include the care and activities provided directly by the parents (referred to as "parenting") and the material goods they and others provide for the child (items such as food, clothing, books, and toys).

As psychologists have long recognized, however, and as sociologists and economists also emphasize, parents and their children exist in a larger context. The resources that parents are able to make available to their children depend not just on the parents' own capacities and resources but also on the larger family system, employers, and the government, as well as the community (including nonprofit and faith-based organizations). These more distal actors can help boost parental resources and may also provide resources directly to children (for example, health care, child care, and education).

These more distal sources of support are of particular interest because they are the main mechanisms through which public policy can influence children's outcomes. Are variations in these resources associated with different patterns of child development? Cross-national variations in economic, social, and policy environments can provide us with important insights into the factors that might lead to larger or smaller achievement gaps. The four countries that we consider in this book share many characteristics, but they also have substantial differences in many of the key contextual inputs to child development.

OUR FOUR COUNTRY CASES

Welfare state scholars distinguish between three main country groups: (1) social democratic countries, such as the Nordic group, where government plays a quite extensive role in providing services to families and children;

(2) continental European countries, such as Germany, where employers provide a good deal of family benefits; and (3) liberal Anglo-American countries, where families rely to a larger extent on their own and community resources before turning to employers or government for support.[9]

The United States fits squarely within the liberal Anglo-American group, and we draw our comparative cases from other countries in that group. In doing so, we are adopting a "most similar case" approach—we are trying (to the extent possible) to compare like to like.[10]

The countries we examine fit together in three important respects. First, they share similar values concerning the role of the individual and the collective. Second, they have a broadly similar sense of the role of markets versus government. Third, they each display significant diversity in ethnic and cultural backgrounds; the United States, Australia, and Canada are known for being nations of immigrants, and all four countries have a substantial immigrant presence.

The similarities across these four countries have led to substantial policy "borrowing" among them. The foundations of the U.S. welfare state, and to a large extent the Australian and Canadian welfare states, came from the English Poor Laws, and the countries in this group have looked to each other ever since. Most recently, for example, the United Kingdom's tax credit reforms of the late 1990s and early 2000s were modeled on the U.S. Earned Income Tax Credit experience, and Australia's introduction of paid parental leave in 2011 was influenced by evidence from the United Kingdom and Canada.

But of course, there are numerous differences between our countries. In particular, although all four are usually categorized as liberal welfare states, the United States best fits that model, while the United Kingdom, Australia, and Canada have more elements of the Nordic social democratic model, including universal health insurance and universal child benefits. These patterns, coupled with the greater wage dispersion in the United States, make family incomes more unequal in the United States, with the United Kingdom displaying, in turn, more income inequality than Australia and Canada.[11]

We review the overall system of support for families in each of our countries in the next section. We then provide some information about their education systems.

Support for Low-Income Families and for Working Families

All developed countries, our four included, have social insurance programs that provide income to individuals and families facing temporary or longer-term setbacks due to events such as illness, injury, disability, unemployment, or old age. But countries diverge considerably in their provisions for what are known as "social assistance" or "welfare" programs targeted to low-income families. They also diverge considerably in their support for working families. In both areas, the United States lags behind other rich countries, even when compared to its Anglo-American peers.

The U.S. welfare system was overhauled in the early to mid-1990s, right around the time the children in our sample were born. Cash assistance for low-income families is time-limited and difficult to obtain unless parents work. As a result, the major forms of income support for low-income families are the Earned Income Tax Credit (EITC), which provides an income supplement for low-income working families, and the Supplemental Nutrition Assistance Program (SNAP, formerly known as "food stamps"), which provides restricted funds that low-income individuals and families can use to buy food. Other programs for low-income families include child care subsidies and several other food and nutrition programs. Help with housing costs is limited to those who obtain a place in subsidized housing or obtain a housing voucher; there is no entitlement to a housing benefit. These provisions for low-income families are limited relative to those provided by other advanced countries.

U.S. support for working families is also limited relative to that provided in other countries. The United States is the only advanced industrialized country without a national law providing paid maternity leave. Child care support, as we discuss in more detail in chapter 4, is delivered through various piecemeal programs that do not provide universal coverage.

The U.K. welfare system provides more comprehensive support for families than the U.S. system: its provisions include a universal child benefit, a housing benefit and a sizable public housing sector, cash grants for nonworking adults, universal health insurance, and so on. The children in our U.K. sample were born under the New Labour government of Prime Minister Tony Blair and his chancellor and successor, Gordon Brown, who waged a concerted campaign to reduce child poverty during their time in office (1997–2010). Benefits for low-income families with children, and particularly young children, were made more generous. The period of paid maternity leave was doubled (from four and a half months to nine months), child care subsidies were expanded, and universal preschool for three- and four-year-olds was instituted. Other aspects of the welfare state, such as the housing benefit system, which provides an entitlement to a subsidy for low-income families, continued unchanged until the Conservative/Liberal Democrat reforms that began in 2010. Those reforms included a change to a new universal credit system in 2013, the effects of which are not yet clear as of this writing.

The Australian and Canadian welfare systems are similar to the U.K. system and hence provide a more complete safety net than is the case in the United States. Also as in the United Kingdom, supports for working families have been expanded in these two countries in recent years. The children in our Australian sample grew up in the early 2000s, a period when Australia did not yet have paid maternity leave but did have un-paid leave for new mothers. The children in our Canadian sample were born in the 1990s, when Canada offered six months of paid parental leave (doubled to twelve months in 2001) for all new parents. Child care provision in Canada varies by province, and though traditionally the private for-profit sector has played a large role—as is the case in the other countries—the role of the public sector has been growing. Child care in Australia has a similar public-private mix of provision, but with substantial federal subsidies for low- and middle-income families.

Schools

Governments also provide resources directly to children, most crucially through schools. We provide a fuller discussion of the role of schools, and what schools can do to reduce SES gaps in achievement, in chapter 5. Here it is useful to simply outline the basics of the countries' school systems so that we understand the schools that our children are attending.

In the United States, children attend local primary or elementary schools starting around age five, when they begin kindergarten. Depending on the jurisdiction, they make the transition to a middle school in fifth or sixth grade or to a junior high school in seventh grade, or they remain in one school from kindergarten through eighth grade. Children then attend high school for grades nine through twelve. Schools are funded primarily through local property taxes, and schools in more affluent areas generally have higher levels of per pupil spending, although this has been changing as a result of school finance reforms in many states in recent decades.[12] The federal role in education is quite limited; there is no national curriculum or nationally set exams.

The grade structure of the Canadian system is similar to the U.S. system. Children in Canada begin elementary school with kindergarten at age five. Depending on the jurisdiction, they make the transition to a middle school in fifth or sixth grade or to a junior high school in seventh grade, or they remain in one school from kindergarten through seventh or eighth grade, before moving to high school for grades eight or nine through twelve. However, the funding of the system is different. Canadian schools are funded by a mix of provincial and local funding, with the provinces playing an active role to ensure that lower-income communities have as much or more funding per pupil as the higher-income areas do.[13] Provinces also set the curriculum.

Children in the United Kingdom also start primary school around age five, when they begin reception, and remain there for grades one through six before moving to secondary school. The national government plays a very active role in education, setting a national curriculum and national tests that all children take at several time points (referred to as "key stages") during their school years. The national government also operates an external inspection system that monitors the performance of the schools. Funding for schools comes from the national government and is generally equal across schools, although in 2011 a pupil premium was introduced to provide extra funding to schools with more disadvantaged students.[14]

In Australia, children begin school with kindergarten around age five (depending on the state) and attend primary school until age twelve, before moving to secondary school (again, the exact age depends on the state). In addition to the state government–funded public system, there is also a large Catholic education system, as well as other independent schools. The Catholic and private schools receive federal funding allocated on a needs basis.

OUR COUNTRY DATA SETS

In this book, we both examine some key developmental outcomes for children from different social backgrounds and also document the differences in the environments and resources available to children in these four countries. Our primary information sources for both sets of results are four large child cohort studies conducted in each country. Each study followed children from school entry when they were age four (or five) through to at least age eleven (and sometimes beyond).

Though they vary in their design, each study is designed to be representative of the population of children in its country, and they are similar enough for us to start to make meaningful comparisons about the experiences of children in the primary and middle school years. Some of the features of these studies are summarized in box 3.1; more detailed information is available in our online technical appendix.

For the United States, we use the Early Childhood Longitudinal Study: Kindergarten Class of 1998–1999 (ECLS-K). This study followed a cohort of children who commenced kindergarten in the fall of 1998 up until they were in eighth grade. Information was collected from children, parents,

Box 3.1   The Child Cohort Studies

	United States	United Kingdom	Australia	Canada
	Early Childhood Longitudinal Study: Kindergarten Class of 1998–99 (ECLS-K)	Millennium Cohort Study (MCS)	Longitudinal Study of Australian Children: Kindergarten Cohort (LSAC-K)	National Longitudinal Study of Children and Youth (NLSCY)
Cohort birth dates	1992–1993	2000–2002	1999–2000	1991–1994
Sample size (balanced panel)	8,370	11,762	3,940	4,346
Age Five Wave				
Name	Fall Kindergarten	MCS3	LSAC-K4	Cycles 2 and 3
Fieldwork date	1998	2006	2004	1996–1998
Mean child age in years	5.7	5.2	4.9	4.9
Age Nine Wave (Age Seven for the United Kingdom)				
Name	Third Grade	MCS4	LSAC-K8	Cycles 4 and 5
Fieldwork date	2002	2008	2008	2000–2002
Mean child age in years	9.2	7.2	9.1	8.9
Age Eleven Wave				
Name	Fifth Grade	MCS5	LSAC-K10	Cycles 5 and 6
Fieldwork date	2004	2012	2010	2002–2004
Mean child age in years	11.2	11.2	11.2 (10.5 at national testing)	10.9

teachers, school administration, and child school records. Interviews were conducted in both English and Spanish.

While the ECLS-K sample is based on children entering school in a particular year, our other country studies are samples of children born in particular years. In these three countries, we commence our analysis when the children were of ages similar to the initial U.S. sample—though the fieldwork timing means that the average ages of the children in the other countries in the age five wave were slightly lower, averaging around five years of age compared to 5.7 in the United States.

Our U.K. data are from the Millennium Cohort Study (MCS), a study that followed children from nine months of age onwards. The sample was drawn from Child Benefit records, covering all children other than recent or temporary immigrants. We follow these children onwards from the third wave of the study, when they were around five years old. As in the ECLS-K (and our other studies), information was collected from a variety of sources, including direct child assessments. Interviews were conducted in several languages, but the child assessments were undertaken almost exclusively in English.

The Australian data are from the Longitudinal Study of Australian Children: Kindergarten Cohort (LSAC-K). This study has a similar design to the MCS, but sampled children who were age four to five in 2004 (using the universal national health insurance program for the sampling frame). Most interviews were conducted in English, but interpreters were used for around 3 percent of the interviews. For the age eleven wave, the main outcome measures come from the national school testing program, the National Assessment Program—Literacy and Numeracy (NAPLAN), when the children were on average 10.5 years old.

The Canadian data are from the National Longitudinal Study of Children and Youth (NLSCY). This is part of a long-running longitudinal study of multiple cohorts of children, with a sampling frame drawn from the household labor force survey. We draw our results from two subsets of the cycle 1 cohort—children ages either zero to one or two to three in 1994. Interviews were generally conducted in either English or French, but a small number were translated into other languages.

For the cross-national comparisons in this book (in chapters 3 to 5), our results come from a "balanced panel sample" of children who were present in all of the interview waves between ages five and eleven. This means that the results in every wave are based on the same children. (Some outcome measures have smaller sample sizes because of variable nonresponse.) Weights provided by the survey administrators are used to compensate for initial nonresponse and later dropout patterns. In chapters 2 and 6, where we do not seek to directly compare countries, we use different samples suited to each of the analyses.

A PORTRAIT OF THE RESOURCES AVAILABLE TO CHILDREN IN OUR FOUR COUNTRIES

What resources are available to children from families, employers, and the government in each of our four countries? And how unequal are those resources?

Families

Families matter for child development, in a whole host of ways. Parents and other family members influence children through the time they spend with them, the care they provide, the stimulating and nurturing activities they engage in, and the material goods they provide (such as a home in a good neighborhood, food and clothing, and books and toys). As children grow older, parents also play an important role as gatekeepers and managers for their children, engaging extended family and community resources and selecting and accessing child care programs, schools, and other out-of-home services for them.

Our key focus in this book is on how resources and outcomes for children differ by their family's socioeconomic status, so we begin with an overview of the distribution of families by SES in our countries. We then consider how other aspects of family background, parent and child health, and parenting vary by SES.

As described in chapter 2, we measure a family's socioeconomic status based on the highest level of education attained by the child's parents. Parental education matters directly for child development, since more-educated parents talk and read more to their children. It is also an indicator of family advantage: more-educated parents typically command higher salaries in the labor market and are likely to come from more-advantaged backgrounds themselves. We divide families into three groups: low-educated (the most-educated parent had a high school degree or less); middle-educated (the most-educated parent had some education beyond high school but no bachelor's degree); and high-educated (the most-educated parent had a bachelor's degree or more).

Figure 3.1 shows the distribution of parental education in our samples. The major point that emerges is that young children in Canada are less likely than children in the other three countries to be living with a parent with a low level of education (a high school degree or less). Young children in Canada are not more likely to have a parent with a college degree

Figure 3.1   Children whose parents have a high school education or less
are the largest group in the United States. This is also the case
in the United Kingdom and Australia, but not in Canada, where
parents with at least some postsecondary education make up
the largest group.

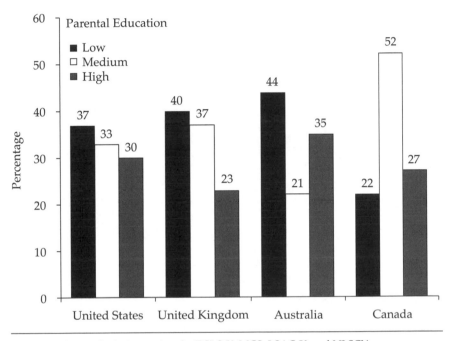

Source: Authors' calculations using the ECLS-K, MCS, LSAC-K, and NLSCY.
Notes: The education categories refer to the parent in the household with the highest education level. "High" education is a college degree or more, "medium" education is some postsecondary education (but no college degree), and "low" education is a high school diploma
or less. Parents who have trade qualifications, but did not complete high school, are in the
low category.

or more—the share in that category is highest in Australia. Instead, parents of young children in Canada are predominantly in the middle-
educated group. So the modal child in Canada (the child from the largest
group) has a parent with some education beyond high school but without
a bachelor's degree, whereas the modal child in the other three countries
has a parent with a high school degree or less.[15] The overall pattern is
similar if we define education using more detailed categories.[16]

In addition to these differences in the distribution of parental education, we find important differences in other aspects of children's family

Figure 3.2   Over one in five children in U.S. families with low-educated parents were born to a teen mother, but only three in one hundred in high-educated households.

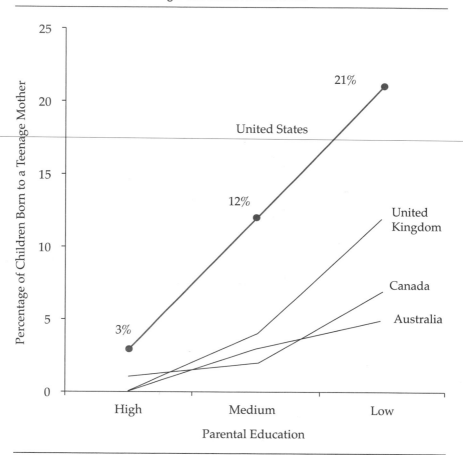

Source: Authors' calculations using the ECLS-K, MCS, LSAC-K, and NLSCY.

backgrounds across countries. In general these point to greater disparities in resources among children in the United States.

One important aspect of family background is *family structure.* In general, children fare better when they are born to more mature parents and when they are raised in stable families with both parents.[17] Across our four countries, children in the United States were the most likely to have been born to teen parents, and at age four or five children in both the United States and the United Kingdom were more likely to be living with a single

Figure 3.3   Children in the United States are the least likely to be living with both biological parents.

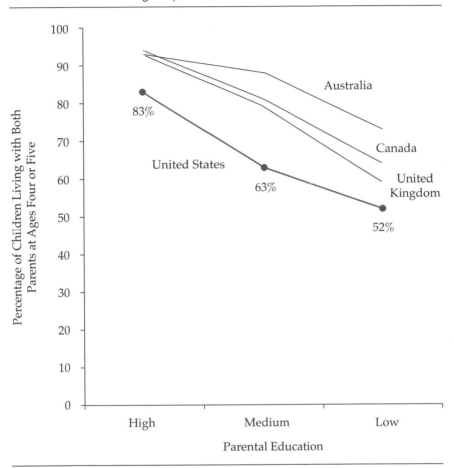

Source: Authors' calculations using the ECLS-K, MCS, LSAC-K, and NLSCY.

mother or a stepparent, and less likely to be living with both biological parents, than children in Australia and Canada. Teen motherhood and children living with a single parent or a stepparent are strongly correlated with low parental education in all four countries. But in the United States the SES differences associated with teen parenthood and low levels of residence with both parents are particularly stark (see figures 3.2 and 3.3).[18]

These family structure differences are important because they amplify the differences between children of different SES groups. In a pattern that the sociologist Sara McLanahan has called "diverging destinies," children who are already disadvantaged by having less-educated parents are further disadvantaged by having younger parents and by being less likely to live with both biological parents.[19] At the other end of the distribution, children who start life with the most highly educated parents are also the most likely to have mature parents and to live with both biological parents. Although this pattern is present in all four countries, the gap in teenage parenthood is particularly pronounced in the United States, where low-SES children, more so than in the other countries, are disadvantaged not just by lack of parental education but by parental immaturity as well. The United States also stands out for its lower overall levels of children living with both parents.

Immigrant status is another aspect of family background that might confer advantages or disadvantages for children. As mentioned earlier, all four countries have high rates of immigration. This is especially true of Australia, where more than one in three children have an immigrant parent, as compared to one in five or six in the other three countries. However, immigrant parent status displays a different SES gradient across the countries, as shown in figure 3.4. In the United States, children of the least-educated parents are the most likely to have an immigrant parent, reflecting the large share of immigrants with low levels of education in the United States. In the United Kingdom, immigrant parents are more equally distributed across the education groups, reflecting the more balanced educational distribution among immigrants in that country. And in Australia and Canada, where immigrants are often admitted on the basis of having higher education qualifications, children of the most-educated parents are the most likely to have an immigrant parent. So low parental education and immigrant status do not necessarily go hand in hand. It is only in the United States that children with the least-educated parents are also disproportionately likely to have an immigrant parent.

In the United States, family background varies not just by immigrant or non-immigrant status, but also by *race-ethnicity*. Approximately 58 percent of the children in our U.S. sample are non-Hispanic white, while 16 percent are African American, 19 percent are Hispanic, and 7 percent are of Asian or other origin. Some aspects of disadvantage (such as teen parenthood) are more common in some of these groups (and less common in others). The SES differences we find in our overall U.S. sample, however, are also present within groups. For example, if we limit our U.S. sample to just the non-Hispanic white children, we find roughly similar SES gaps on key family background variables, such as teen motherhood and single parenthood, as we find in the overall U.S. sample.[20]

So the SES disparities we find among children in the United States are not simply due to the greater racial-ethnic diversity in the United States,

Figure 3.4   Although all four countries have many immigrant parents, in the United States children of the least-educated parents are the most likely to have an immigrant parent; because of selective immigration policies, the reverse is true in Australia and Canada.

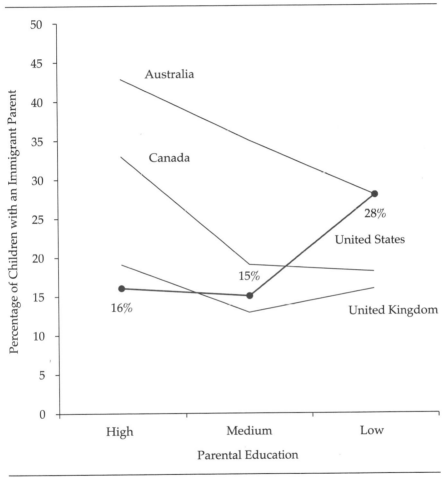

Source: Authors' calculations using the ECLS-K, MCS, LSAC-K, and NLSCY.

or to its high levels of immigration. Rather, the SES disparities in the United States are related to inequalities in key aspects of family background—in particular, parental age at birth and marital status.

Development in early childhood may also be influenced by factors related to *parent and child health*. We find that low-SES parents are more likely

Figure 3.5   In the United States children are more than four times as likely to be living with a mother in poor or fair health in households with low education compared to those living in high-educated households. Though the U.K. story is similar, this gradient is not at all as strong in Australia and Canada.

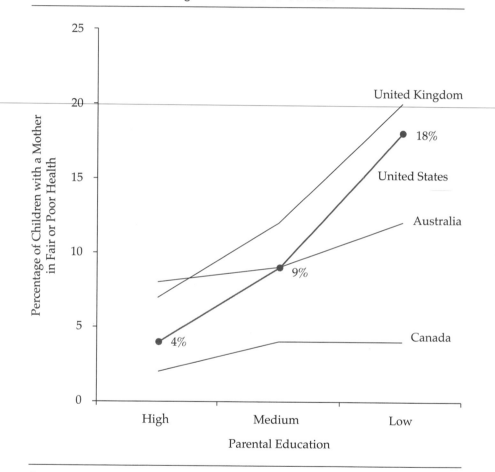

Source: Authors' calculations using the ECLS-K, MCS, LSAC-K, and NLSCY.

to face health challenges than their more highly educated peers. Mothers with low education are much more likely to be in poor or fair health than those who are more educated, particularly in the United States and the United Kingdom (see figure 3.5); they are also more likely to have mental health problems. With regard to child health, low-SES children in all four countries are more likely to have been born with a low birth weight, but are not more likely than their higher-SES peers to have a long-standing disability or illness.[21]

When considering parent and child health, it is important to note that three of our countries have universal public health insurance, which provides free or heavily subsidized access to health care. Although this coverage is far from perfect, it is qualitatively different from the U.S. model: families relying on a complicated mix of employer-provided plans and Medicaid and other public child health insurance programs for the most-disadvantaged (supplemented by public subsidies coming into effect with the Affordable Care Act for those of low and moderate income). Reflecting this incomplete coverage, about 10 percent of the children in our U.S. sample had no health insurance at age five; this share ranged from 16 percent among those with the least-educated parents to 10 percent among those with middle-educated parents, to 2.5 percent among those with the most-educated parents.[22]

So, the United States stands out from the other countries in a few respects. First, low-educated parents in the United States (and the United Kingdom) are in poorer health relative to other U.S. parents than were low-educated parents in the other countries relative to their counterparts. Second, the United States is distinct from the other three countries in having some children who lacked health insurance coverage, and once again, socially grading is present: the risk of being uninsured was highest among those whose parents were least-educated. It is interesting to note, however, that U.S. patterns in low birth weight and in childhood disabilities and long-standing health conditions are not markedly different from those in other countries.

Of course, it matters not just who a child's parents are, but also what they do. A large body of research has shown that *parenting*—what parents do—matters for child development.[23]

One important aspect of parenting is cognitive stimulation and support for learning, often measured by activities such as reading to children. Our data suggest that there is an SES gradient in these activities in all four countries, but they also reveal some interesting differences across countries (figure 3.6).[24] Most notably, the share of parents reading to their four- or five-year-old child every day was considerably higher, and more equally distributed, in Canada than in the other three countries. It is striking that the proportion of *low*-educated parents reading to their child every day in Canada (55 percent) is nearly the same as the proportion of *high*-educated parents reading to their child every day in the United States (58 percent).

We provide more data on these and other aspects of parenting in succeeding chapters, but here it is apparent that Canada stands out for hav-

Figure 3.6   Highly educated parents are much more likely to read to their children every day. However, Canadian parents with low education read to their children as often as highly educated parents from the other three countries.

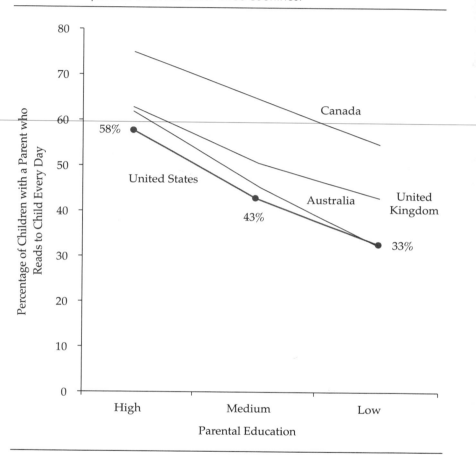

Source: Authors' calculations using the ECLS-K, MCS, LSAC-K, and NLSCY.

ing higher and more equal levels of cognitively stimulating activities with young children (as measured by reading with children). So Canada has not only more highly educated parents than the other countries but also parents who are more engaged in reading with their children, irrespective of their education.

Money is a key aspect of family resources. Although scholars have debated the extent to which money has a causal effect on child development, as opposed to simply serving as an indicator for other family attributes that matter for children, there is nevertheless good evidence that poverty and financial hardship are harmful to child development and that low-SES children are helped by additional family income.[25]

Using a comparable measure of income adjusted for family size and price differences across countries, we find that median family income (the income of a family in the middle of the income distribution) was highest in Canada ($55,700), followed by the United States ($54,100), the United Kingdom ($52,300), and Australia ($49,100).[26]

To what extent are family incomes correlated with parental education? Just as for the overall population described earlier, we find that children's family incomes are most unequal in the United States, followed by the United Kingdom (see figure 3.7). In the United States, the gap in median family income between children with the least- and most-educated parents was $66,300, and it was $57,300 in the United Kingdom; in Australia, by contrast, the gap was only $30,500, and in Canada it was $45,700 (for a family of four, in 2011 U.S. dollars). This pattern of income gaps reflects both the greater income inequality in the United States and the United Kingdom and the relatively weak association between income and education in Australia (and to a lesser extent in Canada).[27]

We also consider *homeownership*, since for most families their home is their single largest financial asset. Rates of homeownership among young families are very similar across countries (about two-thirds owned a home in the United States, the United Kingdom, and Australia, and about three-quarters in Canada), but vary a great deal within country by parental education. Inequality is greatest in the United States and the United Kingdom.[28]

So, again, the United States stands out from the other countries (as does the United Kingdom to some extent). Both incomes and assets (as measured by homeownership) are more unequal. In all four countries, children with less-educated parents live in families with lower incomes, while those with more-educated parents live in families with higher incomes, but this pattern is most stark in the United States (and the United Kingdom).

Employment

As mentioned at the outset of this chapter, family resources are augmented by those provided by employers. Indeed, parental employment is the central source of income for families in all of our countries. However, parents' engagement in the labor market is also a balancing act between their family and work responsibilities. This balancing act is different across the

Figure 3.7   Incomes of high-educated families in the United States are 1.8
times as large as in middle-educated families and three times
as large as in low-educated families. Income differentials are
markedly smaller in the United Kingdom and Canada, and
particularly in Australia.

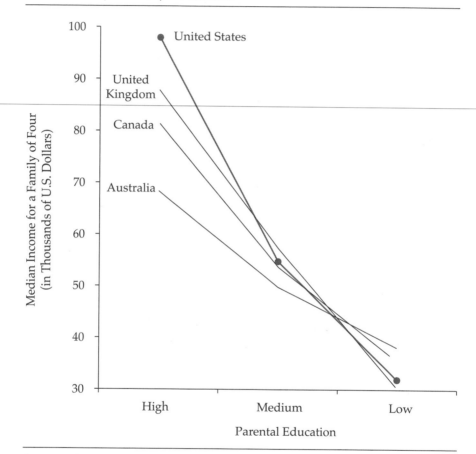

Source: Authors' calculations using the ECLS-K, MCS, LSAC-K, and NLSCY.
Notes: Income is defined as the mean of gross annual household income at ages five, seven,
and eleven. For each country, we convert each income measure to 2011 prices, using national
price indices, and equivalize for household size (N) by dividing through by 0.5*sqrt(N).
Equivalized incomes represent the income of a family of four. We convert all incomes into
U.S. dollars using purchasing power parity (PPP). The values of food stamps and EITC payments are imputed and added to the U.S. income measure. See the technical appendix for
details.

Table 3.1   Employment and weekly hours of work for parents of four- and five-year-olds vary by SES in all four countries

	United States	United Kingdom	Australia	Canada
Fathers employed (percentage)				
All	95	89	93	96
High school or less	91	78	90	93
Some postsecondary	96	93	94	97
College degree or more	97	97	96	97
Fathers' mean weekly hours (if employed)				
All	46	47	47	45
High school or less	45	46	46	46
Some postsecondary	47	48	47	45
College degree or more	47	47	47	45
Mothers employed (percentage)				
All	68	56	56	71
High school or less	63	39	48	52
Some postsecondary	72	64	59	76
College degree or more	71	72	64	78
Mothers' weekly work hours (if employed)				
All	36	25	24	32
High school or less	37	23	23	32
Some postsecondary	37	25	24	33
College degree or more	34	27	25	31
No parent employed (percentage)				
All	8	18	12	7
High school or less	13	34	21	20
Some postsecondary	7	10	7	5
College degree or more	2	1	4	2

Source: Authors' calculations using the ECLS-K, MCS, LSAC-K, and NLSCY.

countries, with U.S. mothers standing out from the rest because of their high employment rates and long work hours (see table 3.1).

More-educated fathers are more likely to be employed than less-educated fathers in all four countries, but this trend is especially marked in the United Kingdom, where the employment rate of the least-educated fathers is notably lower than for their more-educated peers. Fathers who are employed work long hours in all four countries, forty-five to forty-seven hours per week on average.

But mothers' employment patterns are strikingly different across countries. At the one extreme, mothers in the United States are among the most likely to be employed (with an average employment rate of 68 percent) and to work for the longest hours (thirty-six hours per week on average). Canadian mothers also have high employment rates (71 percent), but work somewhat shorter hours (thirty-two hours per week). At the other extreme, more than four in ten U.K. and Australian mothers are not employed at all, and the mothers who are employed work shorter hours (twenty-four to twenty-five hours per week).

In all four countries, mothers' employment is associated with SES: the most highly educated mothers are the most likely to be employed. Highly educated mothers also tend to work the longest hours (if employed), except in the United States and Canada, where the most-educated mothers have the shortest average work hours.[29]

Thus, the U.S. employment patterns stand out from the other countries in a few respects. U.S. mothers are more likely to work, and to work longer hours, than their peers in other countries. Maternal employment within the United States is socially graded, as it is in other countries, but notably, the most-educated women work fewer hours (as is also the case in Canada). We will have more to say about these employment patterns and what they imply for child development in the next chapter.

Government

The third major source of resources for children is government. In each of our countries, while families are expected to be self-reliant, with private incomes and in particular labor market earnings playing a major role, there is also an expectation that government will act as a safety net when those resources fall short. But as discussed earlier, the U.S. safety net is limited relative to that provided in other countries. Unlike the other countries, the United States does not provide unrestricted cash support for low-income families with children, nor is there an entitlement to health insurance or housing assistance.

The limited role of the U.S. safety net can be seen in statistics on *child poverty* when rates are compared before and after government taxes and transfers are taken into account. The United States has a higher child poverty rate than most other rich countries, including the United Kingdom, Australia, and Canada. But especially when compared to these other three Anglo-American countries, this higher child poverty rate is mainly due to the more limited role of government in the United States.

Figure 3.8   In the absence of government taxes and transfers, child poverty
            would be as high in the other countries as it is in the United
            States. However, government benefits do more to reduce
            poverty in the other countries than they do in the United States.

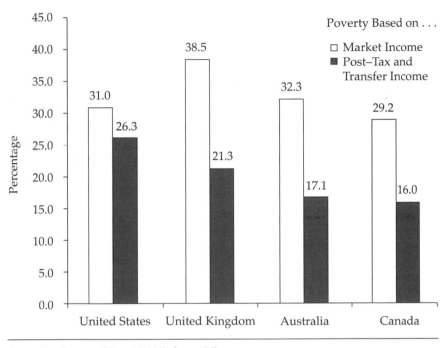

Source: Bradbury and Jäntti (2001), figure 3.7.

Figure 3.8 presents some statistics compiled by Bruce Bradbury and
Markus Jäntti, who analyzed data for the mid-1990s (when our U.S. children were toddlers). They found that government taxes and transfers reduced the U.S. child poverty rate from 31 percent to 26 percent—a five-
percentage-point reduction. In the United Kingdom, in contrast, the child
poverty rate started out much higher—at 38 percent—but was reduced by
seventeen percentage points to reach a lower level than the U.S. rate, at 21
percent. So the fact that the United Kingdom had a lower child poverty
rate was not due to family resources or employment, but rather to the
more generous social safety net. The same conclusion about the role of
government held for Australia and Canada—they started out with child
poverty rates similar to the U.S. rate, but then saw those rates fall to lower

levels after taxes and transfers, again pointing to the role of their more active safety nets.[30]

As we discussed earlier, the United States also lags behind the other three countries in *support for working families*. At the time the children we analyze were born, Australia offered new parents a year of unpaid leave (now eighteen weeks paid), Canada offered six months of paid leave (now twelve months), and the United Kingdom offered four and a half months of paid leave (now nine months). The United States, in contrast, was and still is an outlier among advanced industrialized countries, offering a paltry twelve weeks of unpaid leave to about half the workforce. Support for child care in the United States comes through various piecemeal programs that do not provide universal coverage, again in contrast to the other countries, which provide more extensive public support (Australia and Canada) or universal provision (for three- and four-year-olds in the United Kingdom). We will discuss child care in more detail in chapter 4.

The more limited safety net in the United States means that families with young children receive less overall governmental support, but also that the government plays a less active role in reducing disparities in resources between more- and less-advantaged families. The latter is particularly relevant for our story, as it suggests that we might expect to find more inequality of development among young children in the United States than in the other countries, partly because of differences in family resources but also partly because of the less active role of the government in addressing those differences.

SUMMARY OF THE RESOURCES AVAILABLE TO CHILDREN IN OUR FOUR COUNTRIES

How equal or unequal are resources for children in our four countries? What does this inequality of resources imply for equality of opportunity? We offer three main findings.

First, when we divide children by parental education (a key marker of socioeconomic status and a key input into child development), Canada stands out from the other countries in having the smallest share of low-educated parents (those with just a high school education or less). Canada's higher share of parents with medium (some college) or high (a bachelor's degree or more) levels of education is an important asset: it is not only an indicator of lower levels of inequality among the current generation of adults but also an important portent of lower levels of inequality in the next generation, since parental education and the resources that come with it are such key inputs into children's attainment.

Second, although the resources available to children differ dramatically by SES in all four countries, inequality is most marked in the United States. Children who are born to low-educated parents (those with just a high school education or less) not only have parents with less formal education but also have parents who are younger on average, who are more likely to be single at the time of the child's birth, and who are less likely to be in a stable couple during their child's early years. Less-educated parents are also more likely to have been born outside the United States and to have health problems. And families with low levels of education also have lower incomes. Although we see these gradients by socioeconomic status in all our countries, the differences tend to be sharpest in the United States, while Canada generally has the most equal distribution of resources. This finding has important implications for our analysis, because it suggests that schools and other systems that serve children have more work to do to combat initial SES inequalities in the United States (and less to do in Canada) than they do in other countries—because children come to school less equally prepared in the United States (and more equally prepared in Canada), and because the factors that produce initial inequalities are likely to continue to lead to inequalities in children's learning even after they start school.

Ironically, our third finding is that, when it comes to government policies to combat these types of inequalities in family resources, the United States does the least among our four countries. The limited role of government in the United States is seen most dramatically in the statistics for child poverty, which show that the U.S. safety net does less than those of the other three countries to reduce poverty among low-income families with children. Moreover, the United States provides less support for working families with young children because it lacks key policies such as paid parental leave and universal child care. In this respect, children from low-SES families are doubly disadvantaged in the United States—they have relatively low levels of family income and other resources *and* they receive low levels of support from compensatory government policies.

Taken together, these findings lead us to expect more inequality in school readiness among children in the United States than in the other countries (and in particular, more inequality than in Canada). They also suggest that we should expect continuing challenges with regard to inequality as U.S. children move through school, unless the differences in family resources are mitigated.

In the coming chapters, we document how, given these differences in resources in early childhood, the progress of children varies according to their family's socioeconomic status and also according to their starting point. We want to understand the extent to which children from low-SES families start out behind their higher-SES peers, and to what extent they are able to make progress over time. In particular, are those who come from low-SES backgrounds and who start out with low skills given a chance to improve? And are those who come from low-SES backgrounds but who start school with high skills given the chance to become all that they can be and achieve as much as comparably skilled children from well-to-do backgrounds?

Chapter 4 | Gaps at School Entry

As WE SAW in chapter 3, our children start life in very different families, both within and across countries. What does this mean in terms of the skills they have developed by the time they enter school? In this chapter, we use the detailed assessments of developmental outcomes undertaken in the surveys in our four countries to describe inequalities in children's skills at school entry as well as some of the factors that might help explain these inequalities.

We find that inequalities in children's cognitive skills at school entry are significantly larger in the United States than they are in the other three countries. The poor showing of the United States reflects not just a relatively large gap in skills between low- and middle-SES children, but also a large skills gap between middle- and high-SES children. These skills gaps parallel family resource gaps, which are also more pronounced in the United States than in the other three countries. At the same time, enrollment in preschool, which could offset some of these inequalities, remains highly skewed by socioeconomic status in the United States and thus plays a less equalizing role than it otherwise might.

CHILDREN'S COGNITIVE DEVELOPMENT AT SCHOOL ENTRY

Our main focus in this chapter is on children's cognitive development at or near the time of school entry. Early cognitive skills lay the groundwork for the schooling that children will receive and how much they will benefit from it. Although children who lag behind at school entry can certainly catch up, the greater the gaps among children the larger the challenges they and their classroom teachers will face. Children who are very far behind at school entry are also at risk of being labeled or tracked in such a way that their progress down the road is inhibited.

Among early cognitive skills, we focus on early language and reading

Box 4.1   Measures of Cognitive Development in the
            Four Countries

Children are assessed at or near the start of school in all four countries. In the United States, children are 5.7 years old on average at the
time of this assessment. In the United Kingdom, their average age is
5.2 years, in Australia 4.9, and in Canada 5.1.

In three of our countries, children's early language skills are assessed using tests of vocabulary. In Australia and Canada, interviewers assess children with the most widely used measure of receptive
vocabulary, the Peabody Picture Vocabulary Test (PPVT). Interviewers say a word (such as "umbrella") and ask children which of four
pictures represents that word. In the United Kingdom, interviewers
administer a widely used measure of expressive vocabulary, the British Ability Scales—Naming Vocabulary. In this assessment, the child
is shown a picture (again, something like an umbrella) and asked to
say what it represents.

In the United States, a measure especially constructed for the
ECLS-K assesses children on vocabulary along with other skills related to early language and reading. Receptive vocabulary items are
therefore included along with items that measure basic reading skills
such as familiarity with print, letter recognition, and beginning and
ending sounds. Although the U.S. assessment differs from that used
in the other countries (in measuring vocabulary along with a wider
range of language and reading skills), what is most important for
our comparative analysis is that it captures differences in early cognitive skills between SES groups in a similar way. Our analyses of
other U.S. data that offer both types of assessment suggest that this
is indeed the case.[1] For the United States only, we also have information on children's early math skills.

Here, to facilitate comparison across countries and across domains and to focus attention on the strength of the correlation between SES and outcomes, we standardize all the children's scores on
a common scale, with an average value of 0 and a standard deviation
of 1.[2] We then report differences in terms of standard deviations, as
is commonly done in psychology and education. See chapter 2 for
more discussion of standardized scores.

The test results reported here, while assessing comparable skills,
are not designed to produce scores that indicate the same level of
skills in the different countries. However, there are other studies that

have been explicitly designed to measure children's school performance using the same tests in different countries. These surveys are for older children and do not collect much information about family characteristics, but they do allow us to examine whether the variation in outcomes is different in our countries. The Progress in International Reading Literacy Study (PIRLS) has measured trends in reading comprehension at fourth grade (around age ten). The results most applicable to our cohorts are the reading scores in the United States in 2001 and the U.K. and Australian scores in 2011. The standard deviations of these scores are not significantly different from each other, suggesting that the gaps in standardized scores we report also reflect gaps in absolute reading ability (at least at fourth grade).[3]

skills, which are particularly important because they lay the groundwork for the development of reading competency, which in turn is fundamental for children's learning in other content areas. Early math skills are also an important aspect of cognitive development, and we examine these as well where data permit (see box 4.1 for details).

OTHER ASPECTS OF SCHOOL READINESS

To be ready for school, children not only need to have early cognitive skills but also need to be able to pay attention, manage their behavior and emotions, and get along with peers. Although these aspects of social and emotional development are measured in slightly different ways in our four country data sets, we draw on the available data to construct similar measures across the countries of four key aspects of early development as reported by the child's parents: (1) attention, (2) conduct problems, (3) "internalizing" problems such as anxiety and depression, and (4) ability to get along with peers.[4] "Attention" refers to a child's ability to pay attention, focus on a task, and also persist in completing a task.[5] Holding a child's starting level of school achievement constant, attention has been found to predict later school achievement, which makes sense if children who have better attention skills learn more in school.[6] Conduct problems refer to acting-out or "externalizing" behaviors, such as hitting or fighting with other children, while "internalizing" problems refer to more inward types of problems, such as being anxious or sad. Both externalizing and internalizing problems pose risks for later mental health and social outcomes but do not have strong direct effects on children's school achievement.[7] Finally, the ability to get along with peers is an important aspect of social skills. Such skills may be related to success in school as well as to success later in life.

Educators also point to physical health as an important aspect of school readiness. Children who suffer health problems may be less likely to be able to fully benefit from school activities and may also be at greater risk of missing school. We therefore consider whether the children are in poor or fair health and whether they are obese.

DIFFERENCES IN EARLY DEVELOPMENT ACROSS SES GROUPS

We begin with socioeconomic status gaps in our measure of early cognitive development—language and reading skills when children are around age five. Figure 4.1 plots the gaps between children from the three SES groups in each country: less-educated parents (high school or less); medium-educated parents (some education beyond high school, but no college degree); and highly educated parents (college degree or higher). In all four countries, children of less-educated parents have lower levels of early language and reading skills than their peers with more-educated parents. But it is also clear that this gap is largest in the United States. Comparing children from the lowest-SES group to children in the highest, the gap in mean language and reading scores is one standard deviation in the United States—significantly larger than the gaps in the three other countries (0.79 standard deviation in the United Kingdom, 0.47 in Australia, and 0.61 in Canada).[8]

While it is sometimes thought that inequality in school-readiness in the United States is driven by gaps at the bottom, figure 4.1 shows that there is as much—actually, slightly more—inequality between the high- and medium-SES students as there is between the medium- and low-SES groups, with each of these gaps being about half of a standard deviation. The medium-low gap is significantly larger in the United States than in Canada and Australia (though not the United Kingdom), while the high-medium gap is significantly larger in the United States than in any of the three other countries.[9]

The pattern for math, available only for the U.S. children, is remarkably similar (table 4.1). Again we see a gap of about one standard deviation, with about half (or slightly more) reflecting the high-medium gap and about half reflecting the medium-low gap.

SES gaps are also apparent in early social and emotional development and health, as shown in figures 4.2 and 4.3, but in general these gaps are less pronounced than the cognitive gaps.[10] The smaller gaps in these domains suggest that whatever it is about SES that is associated with school readiness does not affect all aspects of school readiness in a uniform manner.

(*Text continues on p. 75*)

Figure 4.1   Gaps in language and reading skills at age five, by parental education, are largest in the United States.

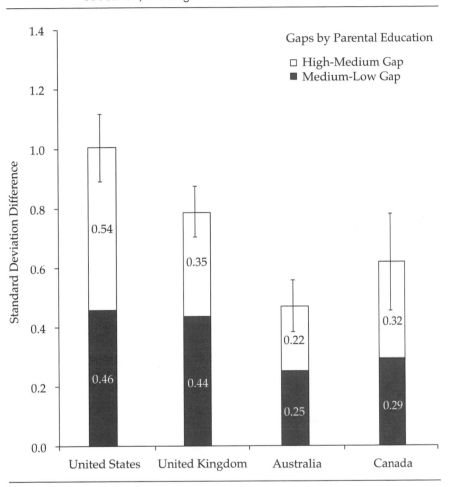

Source: Authors' calculations using ECLS-K, MCS, LSAC-K, and NLSCY.
Notes: The high-medium gap is the difference in the mean scores of children in the high- and medium-educated parental groups. The medium-low gap is the difference in the mean scores of children in the medium- and low-educated parental groups. The total height of the bar—the high-low gap—is then the difference in means between the most highly educated (college degree) and least highly educated (high school or less) groups. All outcome measures are standardized to mean zero, unit variance. Black lines mark the 95 percent confidence intervals around the estimate of the total high-low gap. See table 4.1 for pairwise significance tests.

Table 4.1 SES gaps in language and reading skills and mathematics skills at age five are largest in the United States

| | Language and Reading Skills | | | | | Mathematics Skills | | |
	United States	United Kingdom	Australia	Canada	United States	United Kingdom	Australia	Canada
High-low gap	1.00[K,A,C]	0.79[U,A]	0.47[U,K]	0.62[U]	1.02	—	—	—
	(0.06)	(0.04)	(0.04)	(0.08)	(0.05)	—	—	—
High-medium gap	0.54[K,A,C]	0.35[U,A]	0.22[U,K]	0.32[U]	0.54	—	—	—
	(0.05)	(0.03)	(0.05)	(0.07)	(0.05)	—	—	—
Medium-low gap	0.46[A,C]	0.44[A]	0.25[U,K]	0.29[U]	0.47	—	—	—
	(0.05)	(0.04)	(0.05)	(0.07)	(0.05)	—	—	—

Source: Authors' calculations using ECLS-K, MCS, LSAC-K, and NLSCY.

Notes: Standard errors are in parentheses. Superscripts indicate that the estimate is significantly different (at the 5 percent level) from the estimate for: Australia (A), Canada (C), the United Kingdom (K), and the United States (U). Language and reading scores are ECLS-K reading score theta (United States); BAS—Naming Vocabulary ability score (United Kingdom); PPVT score (Australia); and PPVT-Revised (PPVT-R) score (Canada). Math scores are ECLS-K math score theta (United States).

Figure 4.2   Gaps in social and emotional development at age five are
              largest in the United Kingdom, but in each country are smaller
              than gaps in cognitive development.

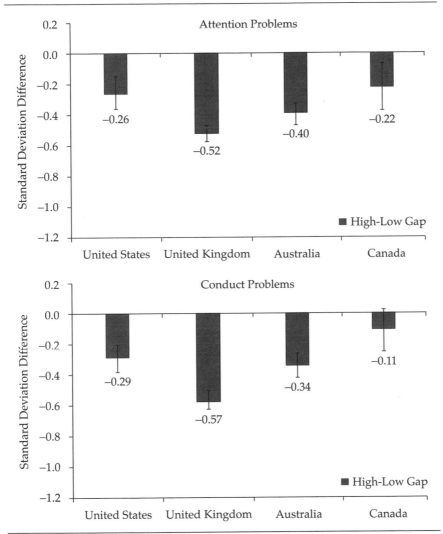

Source: Authors' calculations using ECLS-K, MCS, LSAC-K, and NLSCY.
Notes: The high-low gap is the difference in mean scores between children with the most
highly educated parents (college degree or more) and children with the least-educated parents (high school or less). Higher scores on the social and emotional measures denote more
adverse outcomes. All outcome measures are standardized to mean zero, unit variance. Black
lines mark 95 percent confidence intervals. The authors constructed the social and emotional
development measures from item-level data. See the technical appendix for details.

Figure 4.3   Gaps in health at age five are largest in the United States and the United Kingdom.

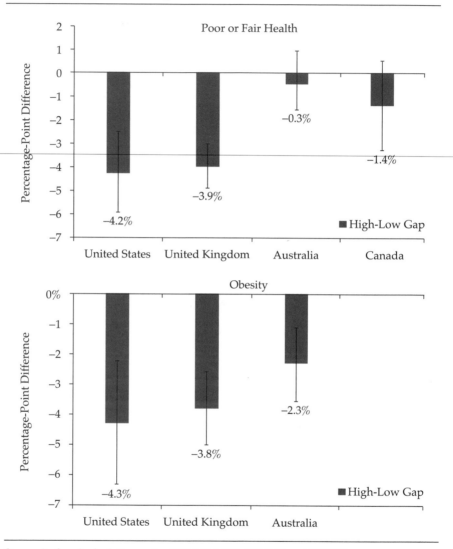

Source: Authors' calculations using ECLS-K, MCS, LSAC-K, and NLSCY.
Notes: The high-low gap is the difference in the proportion of children with each adverse health condition (poor or fair health and obesity), comparing those with the most highly educated parents (college degree or more) and those with the least-educated parents (high school or less). Black lines mark 95 percent confidence intervals. Obesity is defined by applying the cutoffs recommended by the Childhood Obesity Working Group of the International Obesity Taskforce (Cole et al. 2000) to measure body mass index. Height and weight measurements were not available for Canada.

It is also noteworthy that the patterns of inequalities in social and emotional development across countries differ from those we saw for cognitive development. For both attention problems and conduct problems, the United Kingdom has the greatest amount of disparity between children from low- versus high-SES homes—the high-low gap exceeds half a standard deviation—followed by Australia, then the United States, and finally Canada (figure 4.2). U.K. children also have the largest high-low SES gap in internalizing problems, while U.S. children display the most disparity in problems getting along with peers—although gaps in these two domains are relatively small (less than one-third of a standard deviation) (table 4.2).

With regard to child health, few children are in poor or fair health in any of the four countries, but an SES gradient is apparent in the United States and the United Kingdom and not at all, or to a much lesser extent, in Australia and Canada (figure 4.3). We also have data on obesity, based on objectively measured height and weight measurements for the United States, the United Kingdom, and Australia (such data are not available for Canada). Again, an SES gradient is apparent in the United States and the United Kingdom, but less apparent in Australia (figure 4.3).

Although we find some disparities in early child social and emotional development and child health, these inequalities are dwarfed by the much larger gaps we find in early cognitive development. These early gaps in children's cognitive skills are consequential for children's initial success in school but also are strongly related to future inequality in children's school achievement and attainment and hence life chances. We therefore focus on the cognitive gaps for the remainder of this chapter.

In particular, we focus on the relationship between socioeconomic status and children's cognitive skills and the reasons why the SES gradient in early cognitive development is larger in the United States than in the other three countries. We examine two sets of potential explanatory factors in turn: family resources (including educationally oriented items and activities as well as parenting) and patterns of parental employment and child care and early education.

THE ROLE OF FAMILY RESOURCES

As we saw in chapter 3, the United States is characterized by substantial inequalities in family resources. Children from low-SES families—those headed by parents with a high school degree or less—have parents who not only have less education but are also, to a greater extent than in other countries, younger, more likely to have been teen parents, and more likely to be single parents when their children are age four or five. The United

Table 4.2 SES gaps in social and emotional development at age five are generally smaller than the SES gaps in cognitive development

	Attention Problems				Conduct Problems			
	United States	United Kingdom	Australia	Canada	United States	United Kingdom	Australia	Canada
High-low gap	-0.26[K,A] (0.05)	-0.52[U,A,C] (0.03)	-0.40[U,K,C] (0.03)	-0.22[K,A] (0.08)	-0.29[K,C] (0.05)	-0.57[U,A,C] (0.03)	-0.34[K,C] (0.04)	-0.11[U,K,A] (0.07)
High-medium gap	-0.28 (0.05)	-0.26 (0.03)	-0.20 (0.04)	-0.26 (0.06)	-0.14 (0.04)	-0.21 (0.03)	-0.15 (0.04)	-0.19 (0.06)
Medium-low gap	0.02[K,A] (0.06)	-0.26[U,C] (0.03)	-0.19[U,C] (0.04)	0.03[K,A] (0.07)	-0.15[K,C] (0.05)	-0.36[U,A,C] (0.03)	-0.19[K,C] (0.05)	0.08[U,K,A] (0.07)
	Internalizing Problems				Problems with Peers			
	United States	United Kingdom	Australia	Canada	United States	United Kingdom	Australia	Canada
High-low gap	0.13[K,A,C] (0.05)	-0.30[U,C] (0.03)	-0.23[U] (0.04)	-0.10[U,K] (0.08)	-0.26[A] (0.05)	-0.15 (0.03)	-0.14[U] (0.04)	-0.19 (0.08)
High-medium gap	0.01[K] (0.05)	-0.10[U] (0.03)	-0.08 (0.04)	-0.04 (0.06)	-0.16[K] (0.05)	-0.04[U] (0.03)	-0.07 (0.04)	-0.02 (0.06)
Medium-low gap	0.13[K,A,C] (0.04)	-0.20[U] (0.03)	-0.15[U] (0.04)	-0.06[U] (0.07)	-0.10 (0.05)	-0.11 (0.03)	-0.07 (0.04)	-0.17 (0.07)

Source: Authors' calculations using ECLS-K, MCS, LSAC-K, and NLSCY.
Notes: Standard errors in parentheses. Superscripts indicate that the estimate is significantly different (at the 5 percent level) from the estimate for: Australia (A), Canada (C), the United Kingdom (K), and the United States (U). The authors constructed the social and emotional development measures from item-level data. See the technical appendix for details.

States is also the most unequal in terms of the income available to the three SES groups, followed by the United Kingdom and then Canada and Australia.

So inequality in family resources and, in particular, family income and family structure are perhaps the most obvious "smoking guns" that might explain the larger gaps in early cognitive development we find in the United States. But how do resources work to explain these patterns? We begin by examining two pathways through which family income and family structure might affect children's cognitive development—the provision of educationally oriented items and activities and harsh parenting. Can differences in these aspects of the home environment and parenting help explain the greater inequality of child cognitive development in the United States and, in particular, the U.S. pattern of greater gaps in cognitive outcomes both at the top and bottom of the SES distribution?

Indeed, despite the prominent consideration given to the impact of the higher poverty rate in the United States on child outcomes, one of our most distinctive findings is that of a particularly large gap between the outcomes of middle- and high-SES children in the United States. Can we find an explanation for the top-middle SES gap, as well as the bottom-middle SES gap, in the distribution of aspects of the home environment and parenting?

Differences in Educationally Oriented Items and Activities

We saw in chapter 3 that in all four of our countries children with more-educated parents are read to more often than children of less-educated parents. Previous research has found that children with more-educated parents also grow up in homes with more educationally oriented items like books and toys and are more likely to be enrolled in activities like lessons and clubs. Parents with more education have, on average, more income to spend on these kinds of items and activities, but even holding income constant, more-educated parents spend more on these items and activities than less-educated parents do.[11]

We see these patterns quite strikingly in our U.S. data. Drawing on reports from parents in the fall and spring of their children's kindergarten year, the data show that high-SES children live in homes with more children's books and are considerably more likely to be enrolled in activities such as art, music, and dance lessons as well as in organized performing arts, athletic programs, and clubs.[12] And consistent with the pattern we found for cognitive skills, there are gaps in all such items and activities not just between the bottom and the middle SES groups but also between the middle and the top SES groups. For example, parents with just some education beyond high school have nearly thirty more children's books in their home (on average) than those with a high school degree or less—but they also have nearly thirty books less (on average) than those with a college degree or more.

Where we have corresponding data in our other countries, we find that the social gradients are often (though not always) less graded than in the United States.[13] In Australia, college-educated families are slightly less likely than their U.S. counterparts to have more than thirty books in the home (93 percent of U.S. respondents, 88 percent of Australia respondents) and the middle-educated group is equally likely, but three-quarters of the least-educated Australian families have this many books, while only 55 percent of the corresponding U.S. families do. The U.K. survey uses a lower book ownership threshold but also shows a relatively small SES gap. With regard to extracurricular activities, the percentage-point gap in attendance at music lessons is less in Australia than in the United States, while the percentages attending any organized sports, gymnastics, or dance lessons are similar in each SES group in the United States and Australia. In the United Kingdom, the rates are significantly lower in all groups. For organized athletics considered on their own, for dance lessons, and for music and art lessons, the social gradient is similar in the United States and Canada. For club and recreational programs, the social gradient is flatter in Canada.

Researchers continue to debate how much these kinds of items and activities actually contribute to school readiness, but parents who invest in these items and activities believe that they do make a difference.[14] Indeed, such investments by high-SES parents have skyrocketed in recent years as returns to education have risen in the labor market and families have increasingly felt that they are competing for scarce slots in the best schools and ultimately colleges.[15] Spending has risen particularly steeply for high-SES families with young children, perhaps reflecting the growing recognition of the importance of investments in early childhood.[16]

The run-up in expenditures on educational items for children among advantaged families is seen across countries but is more pronounced in the United States than elsewhere. A recent study of the United States, Canada, and Australia by researchers Sabino Kornrich, Anne Gauthier, and Frank Furstenberg found that while inequality in spending on child care and early education has increased in all three countries since the 1970s, the increase tends to be most pronounced in the United States, with the result that the level of inequality in such spending today is higher in the United States than in the other two countries.[17]

Differences in Parenting

Another factor that may differ across families and affect children's development at school entry is the quality of parenting they receive in the home and the amount of stress their parents are undergoing. Parents who are younger, less-educated, and more hard-pressed for income may also be more stressed and harsher in their parenting. In line with this, we find that children of less-educated parents in our U.S. sample were more likely to have been spanked in the past week (in the spring of their kindergarten year) than children of more-educated parents (31 percent versus 21 percent). Children of medium-educated parents also experienced relatively high spanking rates (29 percent).

Data on spanking frequency in the United Kingdom also show an SES gradient, but less so than in the United States, and overall levels of spanking are lower. U.K. parents were asked whether they spanked their child once a month or more; 14 percent of the least-educated said that they did, versus 12 and 10 percent among the medium- and most-educated, respectively. In Canada, parents were asked about their use of physical punishment; results indicate that the use of physical punishment is rare in Canada and not significantly more common among low-SES families than in high-SES ones. (Data on spanking and physical punishment are not available for Australia.)[18]

The greater frequency of spanking in the United States, particularly on the part of low- and medium-educated parents, may be another factor that helps explain the greater inequality in early child development in the United States. A large literature in the United States has demonstrated links between frequent spanking and poorer child development; many studies find links with child behavior problems, and some studies also find connections with cognitive development.[19] These associations may reflect a direct effect of spanking or may also be a symptom of other family processes and stresses that we are not able to observe in our data and that may themselves matter for child development.

THE ROLE OF PARENTAL EMPLOYMENT AND CHILD CARE AND EARLY EDUCATION

As we saw in chapter 3, fathers, when present and employed, tend to work long hours in all four countries. But mothers' employment varies by SES in all four countries.[20] The most highly educated mothers are the most likely to be employed, but also the most likely to work part-time (between one and twenty-nine hours per week). This trend is especially pronounced in the United States, where the most highly educated mothers are less likely than their middle-educated peers to work full-time and more likely to work part-time. Part-time work, particularly when children are young, is thought to be particularly advantageous in terms of work-family balance, but of course it comes at a cost in terms of lower total earnings. Because the more-educated mothers are more likely to be married (and to be married to higher earners in the United States), they are better positioned to forgo long work hours.

If parents are working, then young children must be in some form of child care or early education. This might be parental or relative care or some other informal child care (babysitter, nanny, family day care provider), or it might be formal preschool. High-quality child care or early education can be an important input to child development, and this has rightly been a major focus of policy. The research evidence is strong that children who have attended preschool are more likely to be well prepared for school, with particularly large effects for children who come from less-advantaged backgrounds.[21] But the research also suggests that when child care or early education is not publicly provided, enrollment in preschool is strongly correlated with family SES.[22] Low-SES parents are most likely to care for their children themselves (because they are not working or, if working, cannot afford nonparental care), while at the other extreme, high-SES parents are most likely to work and to enroll their children in preschool. Indeed, high-SES parents, even if not working, typically enroll their children in some form of preschool as an enrichment activity.

We distinguish between three main types of care or early education that children might be enrolled in the year prior to starting school: (1) preschool (which includes day care centers, nursery schools, preschools, and prekindergartens); (2) no preschool, but some form of informal child care (care by a babysitter, nanny, or family day care provider); and (3) the residual category of care only by a parent or another relative.[23]

The United Kingdom and Australia exemplify the pattern seen in most OECD countries—at least some preschool is available on a universal basis to all children the year before school entry, and preschool enrollment rates are above 90 percent in all SES groups. In the United States and Canada, in contrast, preschool is less prevalent, and it is also strongly socially graded, being most common for children of highly educated parents. In the United States, for instance, 78 percent of children of highly educated parents were in preschool the year before school entry, versus only 60 percent of children with the least-educated parents. Though preschool attendance rates have continued to increase in the United States for cohorts of children after the one that we follow here, other evidence suggests that the socioeconomic status gap in preschool attendance has continued to be just as large in recent years.[24]

For children not in preschool, parental or relative care is the most common alternative (representing about one-quarter of all children in the United States and about one-third in Canada). Canadian parents are the most likely to use only informal care (a babysitter, nanny, or family day care provider) in the year before school entry. Even here, however, this only applies to 11 percent of families.

It is important to note that our data on child care and early education provide only a snapshot of the arrangements that children were in during the year prior to school entry. We know from other sources that the care and education that children experience from birth onwards varies a great deal across our four countries, and within country by SES (see box 4.2).

The Time Squeeze: Child Care and Employment Across SES Groups

Of crucial importance for children is how access to these different resources and arrangements interact. Here we look at the interaction between mothers' labor force engagement and children's preschool enrollment and the variations in this interaction across SES groups. This interaction represents the intersection of several key resources: parental time and child care or early education services (both privately provided and publicly provided).

Looking first at the horizontal dimension of figure 4.4, we can see that average maternal work hours are highest in the United States and Canada. This reflects both higher employment rates and longer hours for those working. In all four countries, the most-disadvantaged mothers work fewer hours than those in middle-educated families. In the United Kingdom and Australia, this trend continues into the highest-educated group: these mothers work the most hours. In Canada, working hours are the same in middle- and high-SES groups, while in the United States, as already noted, high-SES mothers actually work fewer hours than middle-SES mothers.

Vertically, looking at the percentage of children in preschool, patterns of enrollment reflect the different child care and early education regimes described in box 4.2. Australia and the United Kingdom are similar, with almost all children receiving at least some preschool. Nonetheless, there is still an SES gradient in preschool enrollment in Australia, an issue that has received some policy attention recently.[25]

Canada has relatively few children in formal preschool, especially

Box 4.2   Policy Provisions for Parental Leave and Child Care and Early Education in the Four Countries

As we discussed in chapter 3, the United States stands out from the other countries in not having any national paid parental leave that parents can take to provide care for a newborn. Instead, the U.S. Family and Medical Leave Act (FMLA), which came into effect in 1993 at around the same time the children in our U.S. sample were born, provides a short period (twelve weeks) of unpaid leave to the approximately half of working parents who have sufficient work hours and job tenure to qualify for coverage. Eligibility for FMLA leave, as well as eligibility for employer leave benefits, is correlated with socioeconomic status, with higher-SES workers more likely to have coverage. As a result, mothers in the United States return to work more quickly after childbirth than mothers do in the other countries, particularly if they are low-income and cannot afford a period of unpaid leave. Some child care subsidies are available to low-income parents, but there are not sufficient subsidies to cover all eligible families. Low-income families may also be able to access programs such as Head Start, which provides free preschool to three- and four-year-olds from families with incomes below the poverty line. But many low- and moderate-income families struggle to find affordable child care or early education, and the average quality of care, particularly for infants and toddlers, is not high.

The children in our Canadian sample were born in the early 1990s (between 1992 and 1994) at roughly the same time as the children in our U.S. sample. But they were born into a very different policy context. At that time, Canada provided up to six months of paid leave (extended to one year in 2001) for new mothers through its employment insurance system. Canada also offered a more extensive system of income supports for families with young children, as well as universal health insurance. However, during the period when the children in our sample were preschoolers, Canada offered relatively little in the way of support for child care. Most provinces relied mainly on private provision, with parents paying most of the costs and government subsidies and tax credits helping offset some of those.[26] Quebec was an important exception: the province offered universal child care subsidies starting in 1997 for four-year-olds and eventually extended subsidies downward to younger preschoolers, toddlers, and infants. This policy affected child care and early education arrangements for some of the children in our sample, while others had already entered school by the time it came into effect.

The children in our U.K. sample were born around 2000, at a time when supports for families with young children had been greatly expanded in the United Kingdom.[27] Nine months of paid leave was available to their mothers, as well as a short period of paid leave for their fathers. Child care subsidies helped their parents offset the cost of care if they were low-income, and at age three, they all became eligible for a free part-time preschool place. Their parents also benefited from the "right to request": the right to ask their employer for a part-time or flexible work schedule and to have that request reasonably considered. At the same time, income supports for families with young children were made more generous: the universal child allowance that goes to all families with children was increased, as were benefits for low- and moderate-income families. Families received extensive supports from the universal health care system, including universal home visits for families with newborns.

The children in our Australian sample were also born around 2000. Australia did not provide paid leave for new mothers at the time they were born (paid family leave came into effect in January 2011), but it did provide up to a year of unpaid but job-protected maternity leave, followed by subsidized child care for low- and middle-income families and then low-cost or free universal preschool (although often only part-time) starting at age four. Like Canada and the United Kingdom, Australia offers more generous income supports to low- and moderate-income families than the United States does, as well as universal health insurance.

among the least-educated families. This finding is consistent with past reports on child care and early education usage in Canada for this period. In the United States, the use of preschool is higher than in Canada and increases steadily with SES.[28]

Both employment and child care/early education are important for both parental work-life balance and child development. Higher levels of employment can increase family income but also add to time stresses on parents and children. For a given pattern of employment, access to quality child care and early education reduces parental stress and leads to positive child outcomes.[29] So the interaction between work and child care or early education is particularly important: families in which parents work

Figure 4.4   U.S. families face a "middle-class squeeze," with medium-SES
             mothers working the longest hours but having a lower share of
             children in preschool than high-SES mothers.

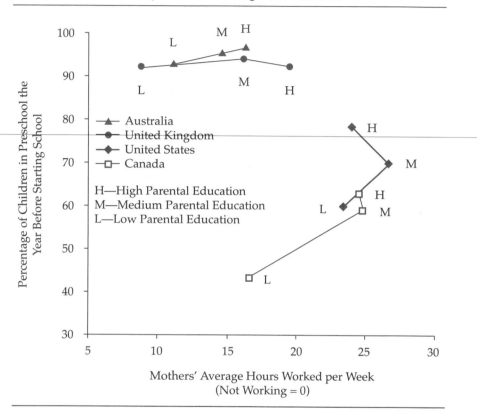

Source: Authors' calculations using ECLS-K, MCS, LSAC-K, and NLSCY.

long hours and have little access to quality child care or early education
are likely to be particularly stressed.

   In our four countries, we find three different patterns of work and child
care interaction across SES groups. In Canada, increases in work hours are
associated with corresponding increases in preschool attendance, going
from low- to middle- and high-SES groups. In the United Kingdom and
Australia, working hours increase with SES, but there is little change in
preschool attendance because, given universal provision, almost all children are attending preschool already.

   In the United States, in contrast, we observe a distinctive pattern that
we call a "middle-class squeeze." Medium-educated mothers (those with
just some education beyond high school) work the most in the United

States, yet their children are less likely to be in preschool than the children of more highly educated mothers. This preschool gap is even greater when families are grouped by income.[30] Moreover, the eight-percentage-point gap in preschool attendance that we find between middle- and high-educated U.S. parents almost certainly understates the gap in child care and early education quality. Since preschool attendance for these families is largely privately purchased (unlike in the United Kingdom and Australia), we would expect the large income gap between middle- and high-educated U.S. families to be associated with a corresponding gap in preschool quality as well as attendance.[31]

CONCLUSION

We find that socioeconomic-status inequalities in children's cognitive skills at school entry are significantly larger in the United States than they are in the other three countries. Children of the least-educated parents are a full standard deviation behind children of the most-educated parents in the United States in both language and reading skills and math skills at age five. These gaps, which are consequential not just for children's initial success in school but for their later life chances, are significantly larger in the United States than elsewhere.

Contrary to what is often assumed, the poor showing of the United States reflects not just a relatively large gap in skills between low- and middle-SES children but also a large skills gap between middle- and high-SES children. So the problem of inequality of opportunity that we find for the United States is not just a problem at the bottom—it is also a problem for the middle.

These patterns help explain why the United States has less intergenerational mobility than the other countries. Somehow, parental advantage is being transmitted to children before they start school, and more so in the United States than in our other countries. This finding is all the more striking given how comparable our data sources are, and in particular how comparably we are measuring both parental advantage and child development.

The gaps we find in early cognitive development strikingly mirror the greater degree of income inequality in the United States (and the United Kingdom to a lesser extent). These skills gaps also parallel family resource gaps, which are more pronounced in the United States than in the other three countries. These inequalities in income and family resources are in turn linked with disparities in more proximal factors such as books in the home, lessons and activities outside the home, and parents' spanking. These factors are particularly strongly correlated with SES in the United

States and may help explain how SES is linked to the development of children's early cognitive skills.

Patterns of maternal employment and use of child care and early education may also help explain the greater inequalities in child cognitive development at school entry in the United States. In particular, enrollment in preschool, which could offset some of the inequalities in family background, remains highly skewed by SES in the United States and thus plays a less equalizing role than it otherwise might. Children from low-educated families are ten percentage points less likely to be enrolled in preschool the year before school entry than children from middle-educated families, who are themselves eight percentage points less likely to be enrolled than children from high-educated families. Gaps at the bottom would be even larger if not for public programs such as Head Start and employment-related child care subsidies. But these programs are narrowly targeted to the lowest-income families and thus do not reach many in the middle-educated group, who are further squeezed by having the longest maternal work hours. This "squeeze" might be partly responsible for the particularly large gap in school-entry cognitive skills that we observe between middle- and high-SES children in the United States.

Do these early inequalities persist into later years? As we have seen, there are substantial SES gaps in cognitive skills among children at age four or five, particularly in the United States. But for the most part, these children have been assessed either before they start formal schooling or right at the start of formal schooling. To the extent that experiences during the school years are equalizing, we might expect these SES gaps to close, or at least to diminish. But we also know that "skills beget skills" and that early learning sets the stage for later learning. Are those with low skills stuck at the bottom, while those with high skills continue to excel? And what role does family background play in all this? Do low-SES children have less opportunity to attain their full potential and high-SES children more opportunity to escape from a rocky start? We turn to these questions in chapter 5.

Chapter 5 | Gaps in the School Years

As WE SAW in chapter 4, the children in our four countries come to school with very different family backgrounds—and very unequal skills—particularly children in the United States, where the early language, reading, and math skills of children from low-SES families are a full standard deviation behind those of children from high-SES families. What happens to that gap—and the gaps in other countries—if we look in on children in later grades?

Making use of the repeated assessments of the children in our four countries to describe inequalities in children's achievement by family socioeconomic status at three distinct time points from ages five to eleven, we find that children in the United States not only start primary school more unequal but also finish primary school more unequal than children in the other countries. Again, at age eleven, we find gaps of about a standard deviation between the reading and math skills of low- versus high-SES children in the United States, and again, these gaps are considerably larger than those found in the United Kingdom, Australia, and Canada.

As we discuss later, social scientists have long debated the sources of inequality in school achievement, including the question of how much might be due to schools versus factors outside of schools. We find evidence that both out-of-school and school factors are likely to play a role in the greater inequality in the United States. Inequalities in family backgrounds and resources—as indicated by measures such as access to a computer or books and participation in extracurricular and summer activities—are readily apparent at age eleven, particularly in the United States. These disparities in out-of-school resources coexist with considerable inequalities in schools, as measured by factors such as private school enrollment, exposure to high-SES peers, teacher experience, and ability grouping—again, particularly in the United States. So the fact that gaps are high—and do not narrow—during the school years in the United States is likely due to both out-of-school and school factors.

THE LEGACY OF THE COLEMAN REPORT

Analyzing inequality of educational outcomes has a long history. As we write this, the United States is nearing the fiftieth anniversary of the landmark 1966 report by the sociologist James Coleman and his colleagues, *Equality of Educational Opportunity*.[1] Analyzing the results of a survey focused on black-white gaps in educational achievement, the Coleman Report concluded that what happens in school is only one determinant of inequality in children's school achievement and that, contrary to expectation, out-of-school factors, in particular family background, play a more important role. The report found that school quality does matter, particularly for the most-disadvantaged children, but it also found that differences in school resources between schools were small at the time. The report's bottom-line message was that equalizing school resources across schools would not be sufficient to close achievement gaps because a good deal of inequality of achievement existed within schools, and because at least some portion of that inequality was due to factors outside of schools.

The Coleman Report was controversial, and almost immediately analysts began revisiting it.[2] However, the basic findings have held. Christopher Jencks and his collaborators at the Harvard Graduate School of Education, who spent three years reanalyzing the data, concluded that children are far more influenced by what happens at home than by what happens at school. And while they found that some school-level factors do matter for school achievement, they also concluded that policymakers may have little control over those factors, and hence that achieving lasting change may be difficult. The bottom-line message remained the same: schools on their own can do relatively little to close achievement gaps.

The debate about how much schools can do continues to this day. The sociologists Adam Gamoran and Daniel Long, reviewing decades of research post-Coleman, concluded that the basic challenges identified by the Coleman Report remain.[3] This sentiment was echoed by the education policy scholar Helen Ladd in her presidential address to the Association of Public Policy Analysis and Management.[4] Students come to school very unequally prepared, and the influence of out-of-school factors such as family background continues during the school years. As a result, many experts argue that schools on their own cannot close achievement gaps.[5]

But this is not to say that schools do not matter. Although much of the inequality in school achievement is due to factors outside of schools, there is ample evidence that schools also matter. In thinking about the role of schools, one immediate question is the extent to which inequality in achievement reflects inequality *between* schools versus inequality *within* them. Between-school inequality refers to the variation associated with students being sorted into different schools; this would produce inequality of achievement if the schools were of different quality and/or if students were residentially segregated such that their intake into different schools and the resulting composition of students and peers varied. Within-school inequality refers to the variation in achievement among children attending the same school. Although the relative importance of between- versus within-school inequality in achievement differs across countries and over time, a general finding is that the majority of variation in student achievement occurs within, rather than between, schools, particularly at the elementary school level (because more student sorting tends to occur in secondary school). This general finding is true for our four countries, although we do see some differences among them (see box 5.1).

Box 5.1   Estimates of Variation Between Versus Within Schools

---

International testing for the Trends in International Mathematics and Science Study (TIMSS) finds that one-third of the variation in fourth- and eighth-graders' achievement in the United States was due to variation between, rather than within, schools.[6] In Canada the proportion of variation found between schools was lower—one-fifth or less in fourth grade, and about one-quarter in eighth grade. The United Kingdom also had less variation in achievement between schools for fourth-graders (again, one-fifth or less), but more for eighth-graders (about one-half), while Australia had relatively high levels of between-school inequality at both ages; about one-third of the inequality existed between schools at fourth grade, as in the United States, and about half existed between schools at eighth grade, as in the United Kingdom.

These patterns suggest that between-school inequality may be more of a factor in some countries and age groups than in others, although as discussed earlier, this inequality may reflect differing school quality and/or student mix. But these patterns also suggest that, in general, half or more of inequality exists within schools. Previous work has found some associations between these cross-national patterns of between-school gaps and differences in achievement between socioeconomic groups. In particular, the greater between-school variation in high school achievement in the United Kingdom (compared to both U.K. primary schools and U.S. high schools) is associated with a growth in SES gaps in the high school years.[7]

Considering both between-school and within-school factors, experts on education inequalities in the United States and across countries agree on several key factors that have important effects on the achievement of disadvantaged children and inequality of achievement more generally.[8]

The first of these factors is *school quality*. If low-SES children attend systematically weaker schools, or schools with a more difficult mix of students and peers, then this sorting will contribute to systematically lower achievement for them than for more-advantaged students. There are many factors associated with school quality. Resources matter, of course, although the evidence is mixed as to how much (once they exceed a certain minimal level). Jurisdictions or countries that spend more money do not necessarily have better-quality schools. However, analyses of school finance reforms in the United States suggest that increasing school resources and making them more equal does help the achievement of disadvantaged students and thus can reduce inequality.[9]

Beyond resources, school climate and leadership clearly matter. Evidence from successful school reforms suggests that it helps low-SES children's achievement a great deal if a school has the expectation that all children can and should learn (although expectations on their own, of course, are not sufficient—they must be part of a comprehensive improvement strategy). In one reform model based on this principle, called Success for All, teachers assess student progress frequently and assign tutors to work closely with students who are falling behind.[10] KIPP (Knowledge Is Power Program) charter schools in the United States combine high expectations with several other ingredients—in particular, longer school days and a longer school year, a clear focus on goals and a no-excuses culture, and efforts to engage and involve families—to improve achievement for disadvantaged children.[11] The Harlem Children's Zone has achieved similar success using a model similar to KIPP's.[12]

The success of these models has led to renewed optimism that schools can be reformed to improve disadvantaged children's achievement and reduce inequalities. In an important recent effort to apply these principles in a large urban public school system, the economist Roland Fryer implemented what he identified as the five active ingredients of successful school reforms—frequent teacher feedback, the use of data to guide instruction, tutoring, more instructional time, and high expectations—and found that these reforms produced substantial achievement gains for disadvantaged students in the Houston public schools.[13]

Second, parents and policymakers alike believe that *teacher quality* is one of the most important determinants of student achievement, and one of the most important sources of inequality both between and within schools, and the evidence bears out this belief.[14] Measuring teacher quality is challenging. It is hard to capture with simple indicators like education or qualifications, and such indicators are not always correlated with student achievement.[15] When single indicators are used, one general finding is that less-experienced teachers are, on average, less effective.[16] There is also good evidence that teacher turnover is negatively associated with student achievement.[17]

Moving beyond single indicators, researchers increasingly have focused on comparing the gain in achievement experienced by the students of a given teacher with the gain in achievement experienced by the students of other teachers. These "value-added" analyses show that teachers can make an important difference to student learning. This should come as no surprise to parents, who often exert great effort to ensure that their children are assigned to the best teachers (or, at the very least, are not assigned to poor teachers).

Teachers not only matter for student achievement but also matter for *inequality* of student achievement. Low-SES children in the United States are more likely than their higher-SES peers to have teachers who are poorly prepared or have weak academic backgrounds; these children also encounter more inexperienced teachers and experience higher levels of teacher turnover.[18] Writing about the United States, Richard Murnane and Jennifer Steele conclude that:

> The unequal distribution of effective teachers is perhaps the most urgent problem facing American education. Poor children and children of color are disproportionately assigned to teachers who have the least preparation and the weakest academic backgrounds, and this pattern is long-standing.[19]

Teacher quality varies both between and within schools. If better teachers are located in better schools, then differential teacher quality can lead to more inequality *between* schools. At the same time, if high-SES students tend to have better teachers within a school (if, for example, more-experienced teachers are assigned the higher-ability groups), then differential teacher quality can also lead to more inequality *within* schools.

A third crucial factor, and one that can affect inequality within schools, is *ability grouping*—the sorting of children into small groups within a class, or into separate classes, based on their initial ability. Ability grouping is something of a mixed blessing. On the one hand, if sorting children by ability enables teachers to provide extra help to children who are lagging, and if that help is high-quality and tailored to their actual level of learning and their specific needs, then it might help reduce inequality. On the other hand, if sorting leads to lower standards being set for lagging students, then there is a real risk that, once behind, such students will have less chance to catch up.

A majority of elementary classrooms in the United States use within-class ability grouping, and sorting children into different classes based on ability is standard practice (particularly in math) in middle school and secondary school.[20] Both practices have been challenged on the grounds that they reinforce and indeed increase inequality: studies have found that initial gaps between low- and high-ability students tend to widen when they are taught in separate groups or separate classes.[21] Nevertheless, these practices persist because they allow teachers and schools to differentiate instruction of students who are at different levels. In some instances, both low- and high-ability children have been shown to gain from such sorting, especially when the grouping is flexible and instruction in both groups is high-quality and well-tailored to the level of the students.[22]

An extreme form of ability grouping is retention—holding children back to repeat a grade. Retention is common in the United States but remains controversial. Research on retention has tended to find that it leads to poorer outcomes for the students who are held back: their achievement levels are lower, and they are more likely to drop out.[23] But several rigorous studies have reached the opposite conclusion: in states such as Florida and Illinois, reforms to end social promotion and require failing students to repeat a grade have led to gains in achievement.[24]

The three factors we have emphasized here—school quality, teacher quality, and ability grouping—do not operate in isolation. Even highly effective teachers flounder if they are in poor schools or cannot tailor their instruction to the needs of individual students. To perform optimally, teachers need to be in schools that support collaboration across classrooms and grades and that provide opportunities for teachers to track the skills of individual students and put in place appropriate strategies for remediation and learning. And even the best schools and teachers struggle if out-of-school challenges are not addressed.

So, clearly, both out-of-school *and* school factors matter for overall levels of achievement and inequality in achievement. Thus, to understand why outcomes are so unequal for school children in the United States—and more so than in other countries—we must look at both out-of-school and school factors. And in looking at school factors, we need to consider both those that vary between schools and those that vary within schools.

MEASURING ACHIEVEMENT FOR OUR CHILDREN

Our focus is on children's school achievement at three time points bracketing their time in primary school. In the United States, these achievement scores come from tests administered to the children in the fall of kindergarten (when they are around age five), the spring of third grade (around age nine), and the spring of fifth grade (around age eleven). The ages at which children in the other three countries are tested are similar, but vary a bit depending on the test. We focus on two major domains of learning: reading (and related skills) and math (see box 5.2 for details).

Box 5.2   Measures of Achievement in the Four Countries

For our U.S. sample, we have test scores for children in both reading (English language arts) and math. These skills are important in and of themselves, but they are also critical as gateways to other fields of knowledge (such as the social sciences and the sciences).

Starting in the fall of kindergarten and continuing periodically throughout elementary school, the ECLS-K assesses English language skills with a specially constructed measure that includes items related to both vocabulary and reading. In this chapter, we use the summary label "reading" for this measure, reflecting the main focus of this measure in the later grades. (We referred to this measure as "language and reading" in chapter 4.)

Our second domain, math, is also assessed at regular intervals as children in the ECLS-K sample move through elementary school. The math assessment, also specially constructed for the ECLS-K, includes measures of core skills related to mathematics knowledge, including number sense, properties, and operations. (In later grades, the test also includes material on more advanced topics such as geometry, data analysis, statistics, probability, algebra, and functions.)

To line up scores for U.S. children with the timing of assessments in the other three countries, in this chapter we use children's reading and math test scores from the earliest test (in the fall of their kindergarten year, when children are around age five), the test from the spring of third grade (when children are around age nine), and the last test the ECLS-K administers in elementary school, in the spring of fifth grade (when children are around age eleven). (We make use of assessments of the U.S. children at additional time points in chapter 6.)

The availability of reading and math test scores in the other three countries is more limited, but in each country we have some information on children's skills at three points in time from ages five to eleven.

Box 5.2   (Cont.)

In the United Kingdom, we have measures of vocabulary or reading at age five (from the British Ability Scales [BAS]—Naming Vocabulary assessment, described in chapter 4), age seven (from the BAS—Word Reading Ability assessment), and age eleven (from the BAS—Verbal Similarities assessment). We do not have a measure of math skills at ages five and eleven in the United Kingdom, but we do have one at age seven (from the National Foundation for Educational Research [NFER] number skills test).

For Australia, we have a measure of vocabulary at ages five and nine (from the Peabody Picture Vocabulary Test [PPVT], described in chapter 4) and at age eleven (from the NAPLAN reading test, a reading comprehension test administered to all Australian children in year 5).[25] We do not have a measure of math skills at ages five and nine for Australia, but we do have math test scores at age eleven (from the NAPLAN numeracy test, which tests arithmetic and mathematics skills).

For Canada, we have vocabulary scores at ages five and seven (from the PPVT-R), but no measure of reading or language at ages nine or eleven. We have math scores for Canada at ages nine and eleven (from the CAT/2 Mathematical Operations Test [short version]).

More details on these measures are provided in the technical appendix.

As in chapter 4, we standardize all the children's scores on a common scale, with an average value of zero and a standard deviation of one, and report differences in terms of standard deviations.

As we consider gaps in reading and math scores over time, it is important to note that the achievement measures, even when they are measuring the same concept, measure different outcomes at different ages. For example, the average older child will know more words than a younger child. It is possible that genetic traits associated with SES find expression at different ages and levels of ability. So we cannot automatically assume that a constant (or changing) gap over time means a constant (or changing) association with factors associated with SES (such as family resources). However, by comparing how gaps evolve in our different countries (where we expect genetic influences to be similar), we can begin to see the influence of other policy-relevant influences.

We also note that, as we are following a single cohort in each country, changes in the gaps we observe over time may reflect both changes associated with age and progress through school and changes associated with cohort-wide factors such as the economy, education policy, and other public policies.

INEQUALITY IN READING AND MATH ACHIEVEMENT ACROSS SES GROUPS FROM AGES FIVE TO ELEVEN

Figure 5.1 summarizes the SES gaps in children's achievement at ages five, seven/nine, and eleven, drawing on both reading and math test score data (where available) and showing gaps in the average scores of children categorized by whether their parents' education was low (high school or less), medium (some education beyond high school, but less than a college degree), or high (college degree or more). (We provide more detail on the statistical significance of the differences in tables 5.1 to 5.3).

In the top graph, figure 5.1 displays the SES gaps in reading at age five across the four countries (shown earlier in figure 4.1) as well as the U.S. gaps in math scores. For both reading and math, the overall gap between children of the lowest-educated parents and the highest-educated parents in the United States is 1.00 standard deviation—significantly larger than the comparable gaps in reading in the United Kingdom (0.79 standard deviation), Australia (0.48), and Canada (0.61). Though the United States has greater gaps than the other countries at both the top and bottom of the distribution, as was noted in chapter 4, the gaps are not always significantly different in the bottom half of the distribution (table 5.1).

At age seven/nine, as shown in the middle panel of figure 5.1, the United States still has significantly larger overall gaps between the lowest- and highest-SES groups (0.98 in reading and 0.91 in math), followed by the United Kingdom (0.77 and 0.65), Australia (0.61), and finally Canada (0.70 and 0.36). As in the age five results, it is the high-medium SES gap in the United States that is most likely to be significantly different from that in the other countries, rather than the medium-low gap (table 5.2).[26]

At our last common time point, age eleven, the United States continues to stand out, with the largest overall gaps between the low- and high-SES groups (1.01 in reading, 0.94 in math). These overall gaps are significantly larger than they are in the United Kingdom (0.67 in reading) or Canada (0.57 in math), as are the high-medium gaps. Australia (with gaps of 0.74 in reading and 0.68 in math) also has notably lower gaps than the United States at this age, and the overall and medium-low gaps are significantly different (see table 5.3).

(*Text continues on p. 100*)

Figure 5.1   Achievement gaps by parental education are largest in the
United States.

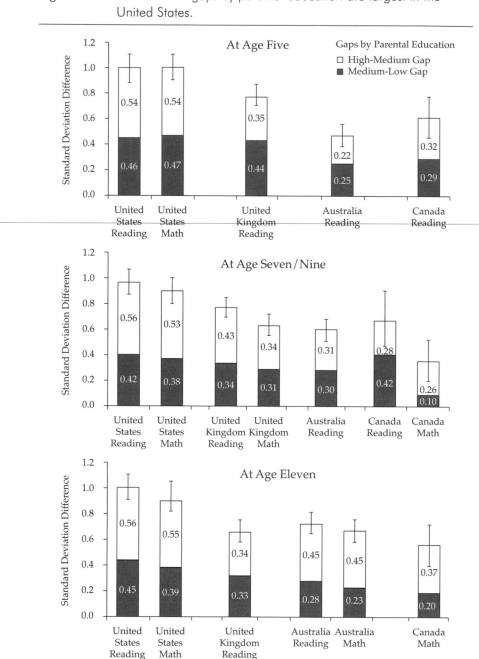

Source: Authors' calculations using ECLS-K, MCS, LSAC-K, and NLSCY.
Notes: The lower bar is the medium-low parent education gap; the higher bar is the high-medium parent education gap. Therefore, the total height of the bar is the high-low gap.
Error bars show the 95 percent confidence interval for the total high-low gap.

Table 5.1 SES achievement gaps at age five are largest in the United States

| | Reading Gap at Age Five | | | | Math Gap at Age Five | | |
	United States	United Kingdom	Australia	Canada	United States	United Kingdom	Australia	Canada
High-low gap	1.00[K,A,C] (0.06)	0.79[U,A] (0.04)	0.47[U,K] (0.04)	0.62[U] (0.08)	1.02 (0.05)	— —	— —	— —
High-medium gap	0.54[K,A,C] (0.05)	0.35[U,A] (0.03)	0.22[U,K] (0.05)	0.32[U] (0.07)	0.54 (0.05)	— —	— —	— —
Medium-low gap	0.46[A,C] (0.05)	0.44[A] (0.04)	0.25[U,K] (0.05)	0.29[U] (0.07)	0.47 (0.05)	— —	— —	— —

Source: Authors' calculations using ECLS-K, MCS, LSAC-K, and NLSCY.
Notes: Standard errors are in parentheses. Superscripts indicate that the estimate is significantly different (at the 5 percent level) from the estimate for: Australia (A), Canada (C), the United Kingdom (K), and the United States (U). Reading outcomes are ECLS-K reading score theta (United States), BAS—Naming Vocabulary ability score (United Kingdom), PPVT score (Australia), and PPVT-R (Canada). Math outcomes are ECLS-K math score theta (United States).

Table 5.2 SES achievement gaps at age seven/nine are also largest in the United States

	Reading Gap at Age Seven/Nine				Math Gap at Age Seven/Nine			
	United States (Nine)	United Kingdom (Seven)	Australia (Nine)	Canada (Seven)	United States (Nine)	United Kingdom (Seven)	Australia	Canada (Nine)
High-low gap	0.98[K,A,C] (0.05)	0.78[U,A] (0.03)	0.61[U,K] (0.04)	0.69[U] (0.11)	0.92[K,C] (0.05)	0.64[U,C] (0.04)	— —	0.36[U,K] (0.09)
High-medium gap	0.56[K,A,C] (0.04)	0.43[U,A] (0.03)	0.31[U,K] (0.04)	0.28[U] (0.08)	0.53[K,C] (0.05)	0.34[U] (0.04)	— —	0.26[U] (0.07)
Medium-low gap	0.42 (0.05)	0.34 (0.03)	0.30 (0.04)	0.42 (0.10)	0.38[C] (0.06)	0.31[C] (0.04)	— —	0.10[U,K] (0.08)

Source: Authors' calculations using ECLS-K, MCS, LSAC-K, and NLSCY.

Notes: Age seven outcomes are used in cases where age nine outcomes are not available. (See technical appendix tables A5.2 and A5.3 for separate age seven and age nine tables.) Standard errors are in parentheses. Superscripts indicate that the estimate is significantly different (at the 5 percent level) from the estimate for Australia (A), Canada (C), the United Kingdom (K), and the United States (U). Reading outcomes are ECLS-K reading score theta (United States), BAS—Word Reading Ability score (United Kingdom), PPVT score (Australia), and PPVT-R (Canada). Math outcomes are ECLS-K math score theta (United States), NFER number skills (United Kingdom), and CAT/2 Mathematical Operations Test (short-version) (Canada).

Table 5.3 SES achievement gaps at age eleven are also largest in the United States

	Reading Gap at Age Eleven				Math Gap at Age Eleven			
	United States	United Kingdom	Australia	Canada	United States	United Kingdom	Australia	Canada
High-low gap	1.01[K,A]	0.67[U]	0.73[U]	—	0.94[A,C]	—	0.68[U]	0.57[U]
	(0.05)	(0.04)	(0.04)	—	(0.06)	—	(0.04)	(0.08)
High-medium gap	0.56[K]	0.34[U,A]	0.45[K]	—	0.55[C]	—	0.45	0.37[U]
	(0.05)	(0.04)	(0.04)	—	(0.05)	—	(0.04)	(0.07)
Medium-low gap	0.45[A]	0.33	0.28[U]	—	0.39[A,C]	—	0.23[U]	0.20[U]
	(0.05)	(0.04)	(0.04)	—	(0.06)	—	(0.04)	(0.06)

Source: Authors' calculations using ECLS-K, MCS, LSAC-K, and NLSCY.

Notes: Standard errors are in parentheses. Superscripts indicate that the estimate is significantly different (at the 5 percent level) from the estimate for Australia (A), Canada (C), the United Kingdom (K), and the United States (U). Reading outcomes are ECLS-K reading score theta (United States), BAS—Verbal Similarities score (United Kingdom), and NAPLAN reading score (Australia). Math outcomes are ECLS-K math score theta (United States), NAPLAN numeracy score (Australia), and CAT/2 Mathematical Operations Test (short version) (Canada).

So, in the United States, there is no evidence that the SES gaps in children's skills close between the ages of five and eleven. Children of less-educated parents start out about one standard deviation behind the children of the most-educated parents in both reading and math, and when we look at them again at age eleven we see gaps of a similar magnitude. Children in Canada, in contrast, start out with lower gaps and seem to maintain that greater equality. In the United Kingdom, the gaps are somewhat smaller at age eleven than at age five.

In Australia, these figures suggest a trend of increasing gaps (from 0.47 at age five, to 0.61 at age nine to 0.73 at age eleven). The increase in the gap between ages five and nine is statistically significant, with the increase mainly occurring between ages five and seven. However, more detailed analysis suggests that the subsequent increase between ages nine and eleven is due to the change in the outcome measure from a receptive vocabulary measure to a test of reading comprehension. When we take this into account, the overall pattern in Australia is of stability in SES gaps after age seven.[27]

Given significant gender differences in test scores among children, we thought it important to examine whether the SES gaps in scores differ by gender. That is, do the differences in mean scores between low- and high-SES children differ if we focus solely on girls, or on boys? For the most part, we find that they do not.[28] Across all twelve outcomes examined in the United States (reading and math test scores at six different time points each), the gap in achievement between low- and high-SES girls is not significantly different from the gap in achievement between low- and high-SES boys. The story is similar in Australia—across all nine outcomes we can examine, we find no significant differences between the SES gap for girls and the SES gap for boys. In the United Kingdom and Canada, the story is slightly different. In the United Kingdom, among the four outcomes we can examine, for one (reading at age seven), the SES gap is significantly larger among boys than it is among girls. Similarly, in Canada, among the five outcomes we can examine, for one (math at age nine) the SES gap is significantly larger among boys than it is among girls (and for another, math at age eleven, it is marginally significantly larger).

What do the differences in inequality at age eleven across the four countries tell us about opportunity and inequality in the school years? We know that children from different family backgrounds start school with very unequal levels of skills in all four countries. But why do their reading and math skills continue to be so unequal at the end of primary school, and more so in the United States than elsewhere? In particular, how much of the continuing inequality in children's skills in the United States has to do with schools, and how much with factors outside of school?

DIFFERENCES IN OUT-OF-SCHOOL RESOURCES

As we saw in chapters 3 and 4, the United States is characterized by substantial inequalities in family resources. To a greater extent than in other countries, children from low-educated families not only have parents with less education but also have mothers who are younger, more likely to have been a teen parent, and more likely not to be living with the child's father. The United States is also the most unequal in terms of family income, a reflection of differences in labor markets and employer policies, as well as in government supports and policies; the second-most unequal is the United Kingdom, followed by Australia and then Canada.

And perhaps not surprisingly in light of these differences in income and other aspects of family background, the United States also has the largest gaps at school entry in children's experiences of out-of-school enrichment activities, such as reading at home and participating in lessons, organized activities, or clubs. Education scholars have long recognized that these out-of-school resources affect not just children's starting positions but also their achievement as they move through school. But it is not always clear how much these resources matter, and which ones are most consequential.[29] We focus on four types here: educationally focused inputs, extracurricular activities, summer activities, and parenting.

It stands to reason that educationally focused out-of-school inputs—such as tutoring and access to books and computers in the home—might play a strong role in educational inequality, because these inputs vary by SES and because they should boost children's achievement.[30] The relative importance of extracurricular activities like sports or music lessons is less clear. The sociologist Annette Lareau argues that such activities reflect a strategy of "concerted cultivation" that middle-class parents adopt to prepare their children for success in school and in later life.[31] In this view, extracurricular activities, while not explicitly academic, may provide children with skills that are nevertheless useful in academic and later work settings—skills such as self-control, teamwork, and so on. In addition, differential access to summer enrichment and learning opportunities may be important, and indeed there is extensive research evidence that gaps in achievement between lower- and higher-SES children in the United States tend to widen during the summers when children are not in school and when higher-SES children have more opportunities to advance their learning.[32]

Data for our U.S. children show marked differences by SES in many of the resources available to children outside of school.[33] These resources are often socially graded in all the countries we examine, but in a number of instances the United States stands out, either because levels of inputs are lower across the board or because the grading is sharper, or both.

With regard to *educationally focused inputs,* comparing children of the least- and most-educated parents, there is a thirty-percentage-point gap in the United States in the proportion who have a computer they can use at home, and there is a more than twofold difference in the number of children's books to which they have access at home (both measured as of fifth grade).[34]

In the United Kingdom and Australia, where our cohorts were born a few years later, access to a computer is nearly universal, with a very small SES gradient. In Canada, where the children were born at a similar time to the U.S. cohort, the overall rate of computer use is similar to that in the United States, but the gap between high- and low-SES groups is only twenty-one percentage points, compared to the thirty-percentage-point gap in the United States.

As we found in chapter 4 for younger children, the SES gaps in book possession are generally greater in the United States than in our other countries. The top-bottom SES gap in the percentage of children with more than thirty children's books is fifteen percentage points in Australia versus twenty-four in the United States. In Canada the size of the gap is similar to that in Australia (though for twenty-five or more books of any kind). On the other hand, the U.K. gaps look similar to those in the United States, though the measures are slightly different.[35]

With regard to *extracurricular activities,* there are large SES gaps in the participation of U.S. fifth-graders in activities such as lessons, clubs, and athletics. For example, 83 percent of high-SES children participate in some kind of organized physical activity, compared with 54 percent of low-SES children; 43 percent of the high-SES group take music lessons, but only 16 percent of the low-SES group do; and while 38 percent of the high-SES group belong to a club or recreation program, only 19 percent of low-SES children participate in such activities. These U.S. patterns are generally echoed in the other countries, although there are variations in the specific activities for which the other countries have data.[36]

One source of educational inequality that appears less salient in the United States than in some other countries is participation in tutoring outside of school. Measured as of third grade, out-of-school tutoring is relatively rare in the United States, and it is actually more common among low-SES children than among their higher-SES peers, in contrast to the United Kingdom, where tutoring is more common and tilted toward the higher-SES group. The overall rate in Australia is similar to that in the United States, but with a flat social gradient. In Canada, few children of this age are tutored outside of school, but as in the United Kingdom, those with more-educated parents are more likely to receive tutoring.

With regard to *summer learning,* our results show that SES gaps in participation in enrichment activities in the summer before first grade are prominent in the United States.[37] Fully one-third of high-SES children attended camp before first grade, as opposed to only 8 percent of the low-SES group. And 56 percent of the high-SES group were taken to a museum over the summer, compared with only 22 percent among the low-SES group. We do not have data on summer activities for the United Kingdom or Australia, but available evidence for Canada (in the summer before fifth grade) suggests that SES gaps in summer activities are not limited to the United States. Nevertheless, gaps in summer activities are likely to matter more in the United States than in the other countries because the summer holidays are longer.

It is also important to consider the role of *parenting.* In the previous chapter, we looked at spanking when children were age five. We also have some information in our surveys about parents' use of spanking when children were age eleven, which may shed some light on the type of parenting that school-age children are receiving and the level of parental stress in their home. Although spanking is less commonly used as children grow older, one-quarter of parents in the United States say that they would spank their eleven-year-old child in a hypothetical situation ("If your child got so angry that he/she hit you, what would you do—Would you spank him/her?"), and this proportion is much higher (28 percent) among the less-educated than among the highly educated (16 percent). Though the data for our other countries are not comparable, there is no SES gradient in spanking in the United Kingdom, and rates of spanking at this age for all SES groups in Canada are very low.[38]

The rules and family routines established by parents, such as regular meal and bed times and limits on TV watching, are also thought to be important for child development at this age. The United States stands out among our countries for having the highest rate of frequent TV watching (children watching three or more hours of TV on a weekday) and the largest SES differential in frequent TV watching among the four countries (figure 5.2). We have fairly detailed data for the United States on other family routines, but our data for the other countries are patchier. These data indicate that children from low-educated families in the United States miss two more days a year of school on average than those from highly educated families, and that they eat breakfast with their family one fewer day per week on average than children in highly educated families. In some respects, however, low-SES children experience environments similar to those of their higher-SES peers. The vast majority of children of low-educated parents (89 percent) have a regular bedtime (compared with 94 percent of children of high-educated parents), a pattern virtually identical to the United Kingdom. Most families also said that they eat dinner to-

Figure 5.2　Primary school children in the United States watch more television than children in other countries, and this is most marked among those of lower socioeconomic status.

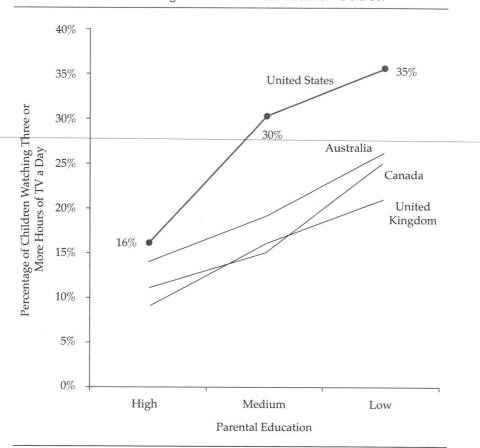

Source: Authors' calculations using ECLS-K, MCS, LSAC-K, and NLSCY.
Note: Data come from parental reports on children at age nine in Canada and children at age eleven in the other three countries.

gether most nights of the week, and this is equally true for low- and high-SES children.[39]

Parental involvement—talking with their child, helping with homework, and monitoring their child's activities and school progress—is also thought to be an important contributor to child development for school-age children. Less-educated parents are just as likely as more-educated parents to say that they talk with their child about what he or she does with friends every day, although they are slightly less likely to talk about school (79 percent versus 86 percent) or to have someone in the home who is able to help with math homework (93 percent versus 98 percent). Similar questions asked in the non-U.S. surveys reveal that high levels of parental involvement, differing only slightly with SES, are common across all our four countries.[40]

So the majority of less-educated parents establish family routines and interact positively with their children on a daily basis (although we are not able to capture the content and quality of those interactions in our data). But are their aspirations and expectations for their children's futures as high as those of more-educated parents? Our data reveal that in this area there are large disparities between SES groups. In the United States, only 57 percent of low-SES parents expect their child to complete a four- to five-year college degree or more, versus 93 percent of high-SES parents. This expectations gap is not unique to the United States; in Australia, the comparable proportions are 49 and 84 percent, and the gap is only slightly smaller in the United Kingdom. Similar patterns can be seen in all four countries when parents are asked about whether they hope or expect their child to receive any education beyond high school.[41] These numbers are worrying for all of our countries, as parental aspirations and expectations are known to be strongly associated with student achievement for school-age children and adolescents.

So clearly, there are quite large SES differences in a number of aspects of children's out-of-school experiences, such as books in the home, participation in out-of-school activities, and parental aspirations, and in some cases, such as with spanking and TV watching, these differences are more pronounced in the United States than in the other countries. But what about the role of schools in the United States, and how does their role compare with the role of schools in other countries? Students learn during their time in school, and if children are having systematically different school experiences, such differences could play an important role in gaps in their achievement, in addition to or in concert with the role played by differences in out-of-school factors. We therefore need to also consider differences in schools that might be related to the SES gaps in achievement that we find.

DIFFERENCES IN SCHOOLS

We begin with the *quality of the schools* that low- and high-SES children attend. Although we do not have direct measures of quality, we do have a number of different indicators of the composition and characteristics of children's schools and classrooms (at around fifth grade).

Class size has been much discussed as a measure of school quality, although the extent to which it matters is disputed, and its importance is likely to decline as children age.[42] Interestingly, the United States has the smallest average class size of the countries with available data—twenty-three compared with twenty-six to twenty-seven in the United Kingdom and Australia—and in none of these countries is class size socially graded. Smaller average class sizes therefore do not appear sufficient to narrow the U.S. differential in achievement gaps. (We do not have data for Canada on class size and several other factors we discuss later, owing to differences in survey design.)

One factor that is strongly graded, as we might expect, is attendance at a private school. In the United States, 20 percent of children in high-SES families attend private schools, compared with only 4 percent in low-SES families. This pattern is similar in the United Kingdom, where private school enrollment, while less frequent overall, is also strongly socially graded. (Fourteen percent of high-SES children attend private school versus 1 percent of their low-SES counterparts.) Australia and Canada also have social gradients in private school enrollment, but they are less steep than in the United States and the United Kingdom.[43]

Children of more-educated parents in the United States also attend schools with higher-SES peers, a factor that has been found, from the Coleman Report onwards, to be important for student achievement.[44] While high-SES children in the United States attend schools where on average 23 percent of children have low enough incomes to be eligible for free school meals, low-SES children are in schools where on average half of the children are eligible. And high-SES children are in classes with a lower proportion of children with limited English proficiency (2 percent for high-SES children versus 9 percent for their low-SES counterparts). The United Kingdom also has a gradient in exposure to limited-English-proficient peers (although a less steep one than in the United States), while Australia is notable for not having a social gradient at all on this factor.[45]

We next consider *teacher quality*, which parents know is the single most important input to children's learning, and which parents also know can vary considerably, both between and within schools. What do we know about teacher quality in our four countries, and to what extent does it vary by SES? In particular, are low-SES children being doubly disadvantaged by starting out with lower levels of readiness and then having the weakest teachers? Or are schools assigning teachers equally by student SES, or even in a way that compensates for disadvantage, by ensuring that low-SES children have the strongest teachers?

Focusing on teacher experience, which is the best indicator of teacher quality available in our data, we find that low-SES children in the United

Figure 5.3   Low-SES children in the United States are more likely to have a
             novice teacher than their higher-SES peers, and the differential
             is greater than in other countries.

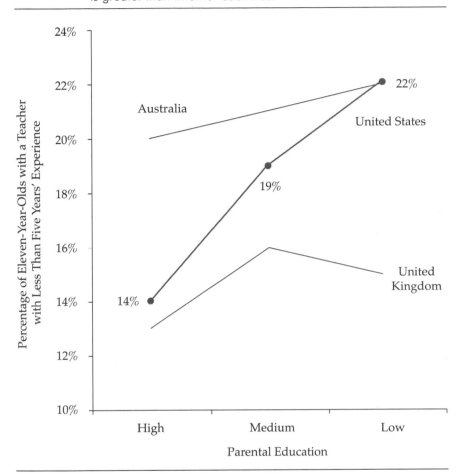

Source: Authors' calculations using ECLS-K, MCS, LSAC-K, and NLSCY.
Note: Data for the United Kingdom refer to England and Wales only. No data are available
for Canada.

States are more likely to have inexperienced teachers than their more-
advantaged peers: 22 percent have a teacher with less than five years of
experience compared to 14 percent among their higher-SES peers (figure
5.3). The distribution of novice teachers is more equal in the United
Kingdom (where the comparable percentages are 15 percent and 13 per-

cent, respectively). Australia again is notable for having little or no social gradient.[46]

A third factor that varies considerably within and across countries and that matters for achievement is the use of *ability grouping*. (As discussed earlier, ability grouping can entail either assigning students to different classes based on ability or teaching students within a class in small groups based on their ability level.)

In our U.S. sample, teaching children in small groups based on their achievement level is a fairly common practice, but it is reported more frequently by teachers of low-SES children than by teachers of high-SES children. For example, about two-thirds of math teachers of low-SES children say that they use ability groups, compared to just over half of teachers of high-SES children. This gradient is not evident in the United Kingdom or Australia, where children are almost equally likely to experience ability grouping regardless of their parental education.

Whether because of ability grouping or differences in the characteristics of children within schools, low-SES children in the United States are in classes with fewer children who are classified as gifted and talented (on average, 6 percent of their classmates), and there are more children who have special needs in their classrooms (on average 15 percent of their classmates) than there are in the classrooms of their higher-SES peers (for whom the comparable figures are 12 percent and 10 percent, respectively). Data for the United Kingdom and Australia indicate that fewer children are identified as having special needs than in the United States, and that such children are more equally distributed across classrooms.[47]

As discussed earlier, retention—holding children back to repeat a grade—is another type of ability grouping. Retention by age eleven is quite common for the children in our U.S. sample (19 percent had been retained in the overall sample), and children of less-educated parents were much more likely (26 percent) to have been held back than children of the highly educated (11 percent) (figure 5.4). Retention is much less common in Australia and Canada (5 percent on average in the overall sample); it is not socially graded in the former, but is in the latter.[48]

It is perhaps unsurprising that many aspects of the school environment in the United States are socially graded, but the key contribution of our analysis here is to provide specific examples from other countries in which these gaps have been eliminated or avoided completely: these include peer group composition, teacher experience, use of ability groups, and grade repetition. Our finding that U.S. schools have managed to avoid placing low-SES children in larger classes holds out the possibility that this kind of equality could be extended to other aspects of the school environment.

Figure 5.4   Rates of grade repetition are much higher in the United States
than elsewhere and are noticeably greater among low-SES
children.

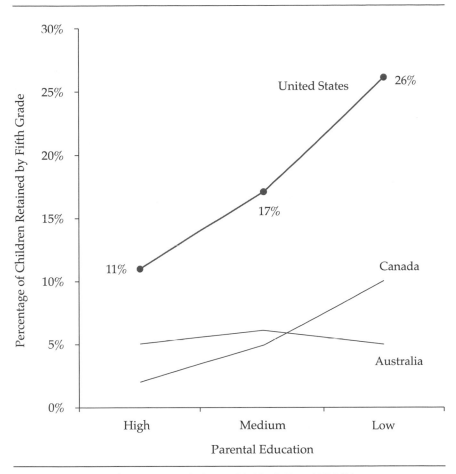

Source: Authors' calculations using ECLS-K, MCS, LSAC-K, and NLSCY.
Note: No data are available for the United Kingdom (where grade repetition is rarely used).

CONCLUSION

Making use of the repeated assessments of children in our four countries
to describe inequalities in children's achievement by parental education at
three distinct time points from ages five to eleven, we find that children in
the United States not only start primary school more unequal but also finish primary school more unequal than children in the other countries.

Low-SES children lag behind their high-SES peers by a full standard deviation in both reading and math at age five, and those gaps remain about as large at age eleven, when children are nearing the end of primary school.

What accounts for the greater inequality in eleven-year-old children's achievement in the United States? Both out-of-school and school factors are likely to play a role.

With regard to out-of-school factors, we find pronounced inequalities among primary school students in their family backgrounds and in their access to resources that are likely to boost learning—resources such as computers and books, extracurricular activities, and summer enrichment activities. We also find significant differences in some (but not all) aspects of the parenting that low- and high-SES children receive, as measured by indicators such as spanking and TV watching. Inequalities in out-of-school factors are a common challenge in all of our countries, but in a number of dimensions these inequalities are largest in the United States.

These disparities in out-of-school resources coexist with considerable inequalities in schools—as measured by factors such as private school enrollment, peer group composition, teacher experience, and ability grouping. On each of these factors, low-SES students are in poorer-quality or more challenging settings than their high-SES peers. Again, these inequalities tend to be largest in the United States.

Thus, it appears that disparities in the family backgrounds and home environments between low- and high-SES children are being compounded by disparities in their school experiences and environments. Certainly, there is little evidence that schools are playing a compensatory role by providing higher-quality services to low-SES children. On the contrary, it appears that, if anything, school resources are tilted toward the more-advantaged children. This situation contrasts with the other countries, where school resources tend to be less socially graded and, in some cases, are equally distributed.

The patterns we have observed in this chapter pertain to average outcomes for children in each of our SES groups. How do the patterns we have seen in this chapter play out for more specific groups of children? Among those with a low-educated parent, is it the children with low ability who are particularly disadvantaged, while those with higher ability are able to do well? Or does low SES limit opportunity regardless of a child's initial ability? If we can better understand these processes and how they play out for more specific groups of children, can we better pinpoint the degree of inequality in the United States and the factors that might be involved? These are the questions to which we turn in the next chapter.

Chapter 6 | Diverging Progress Through School

WE SAW IN chapter 5 that SES gaps in children's school achievement are large at school entry and after several years of school, and that these gaps tend to be larger in the United States than in the other three countries. But the snapshots of children's average achievement by SES at ages five, seven/nine, and eleven cannot tell us about their trajectories after they begin school and the role of SES in their school-age development. One possibility is that the role of SES operates entirely through its influence on a child's level of achievement at school entry. In this scenario, a low-SES child who manages to "buck the odds" and enter school well prepared would be at no disadvantage moving forward relative to a similarly prepared high-SES child. An alternative possibility is that SES influences a child's progress, over and above its effect on his or her initial achievement level. In this scenario, the advantage of high-achieving low-SES kindergarteners would be eroded over time relative to their high-SES counterparts, and inequalities would widen further over the school years.

Discerning which of these possibilities holds in practice is crucial for thinking about policy interventions to reduce inequality. In the first scenario, closing gaps at school entry would be sufficient to secure equality at school completion, and an exclusive focus on the early years would be warranted. In the second scenario, elimination of initial gaps would not solve the problem, as low-SES children would still systematically fail to live up to their potential. In reality, gaps for adolescents are almost certain to reflect some combination of both inequality in initial achievement and inequality in progress given initial achievement. Knowing how these two factors combine and their relative importance is important for thinking about policy interventions and their timing. Yet attempts to untangle the relative importance of the two influences have been rare, most likely because the data requirements to do so are stringent.

In this chapter, we make use primarily of our U.S. data set, which uniquely measures outcomes in a comparable metric for a large sample of children on six occasions between kindergarten and eighth grade and thus provides the detailed data we need to examine individual children's trajectories. We find that the majority—60 to 70 percent—of the SES gap in achievement at age fourteen in the United States can be attributed to differences already present at school entry. But a substantial portion—30 to 40 percent—emerges during the school years. So there is a role for policy interventions in both periods.

The United States is the only country in which a common achievement test was administered over the full range of the school years, and for this reason the trajectory analyses that are possible for our other countries are not the same as those for the United States. At the end of the chapter, we provide some brief estimates from similar analyses for the United Kingdom and Australia, but we must be cautious in drawing direct comparisons. The available evidence does suggest, however, that low-SES children also make less progress than their higher-SES peers during the primary school years in those two countries, though, as we have seen, the overall SES gaps are still smaller than those in the United States by age eleven.

HOW ACHIEVEMENT GAPS CHANGE DURING THE SCHOOL YEARS

As we discussed in chapter 3, the economist James Heckman has laid out a model of "dynamic complementarity" in which early skills lay the groundwork for a child to benefit from later learning opportunities. In this model, "skills beget skills" and "learning begets learning," providing a mechanism by which early disadvantages impede a child's later learning, while early advantages provide a boost. The result is to magnify initial SES differences, leading to increasing skills gaps over time. Remedial intervention, whereby disadvantaged children receive extra services to help them catch up, is intended to counteract this tendency to widening gaps. Conversely, if children with initial advantages also receive more resources as they move through school, and children with initial disadvantages have access to fewer resources, the trend in this model toward widening gaps is reinforced.

A number of studies have examined whether SES gaps in achievement widen or narrow as children age.[1] In one example, Pedro Carneiro and James Heckman, analyzing data on children from the National Longitudinal Survey of Youth (NLSY): Child Supplement, concluded that "socioeconomic differences in cognitive and non-cognitive skills appear early and, if anything, widen over the lifecycle of the child."[2] Looking at children's math scores, they found that children from the lowest-income quartile group (the bottom fourth of the income distribution) started out with average scores just above the fortieth percentile at age six and had average scores just below that percentile by age twelve, in contrast to children from the highest-income quartile group, who started at around the fifty-fifth percentile at age six and were on average close to the sixty-fifth percentile by age twelve—so the gap between the two groups widened from about fifteen percentile points to nearly twenty-five.[3]

Evidence on how and when SES gaps evolve among children who start with the same initial achievement levels is more limited. Using British cohort data, Leon Feinstein found that the trajectories of children with similar levels of initial achievement depended strongly on their SES background.[4] High-SES children who started at low levels of achievement tended to overcome their early difficulties by mid-childhood, while those who started as high-performers maintained their position. But the opposite was true for low-SES children: initial low-performers remained at the bottom of the distribution as they grew older, while initial high-performers saw their position eroded until they ended up somewhere near the average.[5] These results are intriguing, but up until now a similar analysis has not been carried out for the United States.

THE ACHIEVEMENT TRAJECTORIES OF U.S. CHILDREN

To analyze children's trajectories in the United States, we make use of the repeated assessments available for the children in the ECLS-K, which tests children in reading and math in the fall of their kindergarten year and at five subsequent time points between the spring of kindergarten and the spring of eighth grade. The start and end points of the trajectories analyzed in this chapter therefore differ from those in previous chapters, as we are no longer constrained to use only measurement occasions common to the data sets of all four countries.[6] As in previous chapters, we divide children into three SES groups—low (parents with a high school education or less), medium (at least one parent with some college), or high (at least one parent with a college degree or more)—and compute the test score of the average child in each group at different ages. But then we go on to distinguish between children based on their initial test scores as well as their SES background. This allows us to examine how, on average, children with identical initial test scores but from different SES groups proceed through school.

In a similar spirit to the analyses from earlier chapters, figure 6.1 plots

Figure 6.1   Average reading scores of children from different SES groups—
and the gaps between them—change relatively little between
kindergarten and eighth grade.

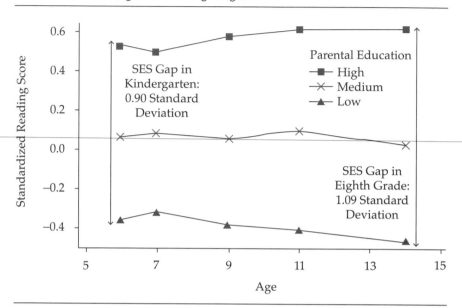

Source: Authors' calculations using the ECLS-K.
Notes: The chart plots the average standardized reading score of children from the three parental SES groups at kindergarten (spring, age six), first grade (age seven), third grade (age
nine), fifth grade (age eleven), and eighth grade (age fourteen). Sample sizes (rounded to the
nearest 10 in accordance with NCES reporting rules) are about 17,170, 14,240, 12,160, 9,650,
and 7,960, respectively. All estimates are weighted using cross-sectional weights to be representative of the underlying national population.

the reading test scores of the average child in each SES group at different
ages between the spring of kindergarten and eighth grade. We begin our
analysis with spring kindergarten scores rather than fall kindergarten
scores so that we can address possible measurement error in children's
initial test scores (see box 6.1 for details). As before, we standardize children's test scores so that we can express gaps in standard deviation units.[7]

At first glance, the widening of overall inequality over this period appears relatively minor. There is a gap of just under one standard deviation
between the average low- and high-SES child in the spring of kindergarten, which rises to just over one standard deviation by the spring of eighth
grade. The great majority of the gap we observe in eighth grade, therefore,
is already present in kindergarten. A similar plot for average math scores

Box 6.1   Addressing Measurement Error

In our analysis of children's trajectories, it is important to address the problem of possible measurement error. Simply put, we cannot be certain that the test scores children obtain on their first assessment, in the fall of kindergarten, are an accurate measure of their true ability. Discrepancies between what we aim to measure and the child's actual test score can arise for a variety of reasons: children may differ in their response to the testing conditions; they may exert different degrees of effort; they may make lucky or unlucky guesses; or they may by chance be familiar or unfamiliar with certain test items in a way that it is not representative of their wider knowledge or ability.

If we fail to address this issue, we will underestimate the degree of persistence in an individual's achievement over time and observe a "spurious" regression to the mean that does not reflect a real outcome trajectory.[8] Moreover, the interaction of such measurement error with an SES effect can lead to an appearance of diverging trajectories of children who have equal initial ability levels but are from different SES groups when in fact no difference in trajectory exists.[9] This latter effect arises because SES is associated with initial outcomes, and so the average low-SES child who is observed with an initially high outcome score will have a greater measurement error component to his or her initial score than the average high-SES child with the same score.

To correct for bias due to potential measurement error, we start our analysis with the children's second test score, from the spring of kindergarten, using the information from the first (fall) test score to refine our estimates through a statistical procedure known as *instrumental variables analysis.* The use of instrumental variables is a well-known solution to the problem of measurement error.[10]

(not shown, but available in the technical appendix) also reveals a large SES gap that is even more stable over time.

It seems, then, that very little is happening in terms of the development of further SES inequalities after school entry. It is tempting to conclude that the influence of SES on children's achievement is largely "all over" by school entry.

But the story is not as simple as it first appears.

THE PHENOMENON OF
REGRESSION TO THE MEAN

The complication in the story is related to the fact that there is a great deal of movement up and down the achievement distribution for children over time. As Leon Feinstein has shown, using British data, it is far from the case that a child's position in the distribution is frozen at the time of school entry.[11]

We can see this in table 6.1, which uses children's reading scores in the spring of kindergarten and in eighth grade to illustrate how much movement there actually is. The rows in the table show where children who scored in different quartiles (fourths) of the reading test score distribution in the spring of kindergarten ended up in the distribution of reading test scores in the spring of eighth grade. The (bold) diagonal cutting across the table shows the children who ended up in the same ability group that they started in.

The first point to note is that fewer than half of the children (44 percent) ended up in the same ability group as the one they started in. The proportion of nonmovers is slightly over half (53 percent and 52 percent, respectively) in the lowest- and highest-achieving groups, but only around one-third for those who began in the middle two groups. Among the remaining 56 percent of children, half (or 27 percent of all children) moved into a higher ability group over the period, while the position of the other half deteriorated. So there is a lot of movement between kindergarten and eighth grade.

The second point to note is that the likely direction of a child's move is related to where he or she started. The lower the child's initial position, the more likely he or she was to move up; the higher the child's initial position, the more likely he or she was to move down. This relationship is, of course, mechanical when it comes to the top and bottom groups. The lowest achievers can only move up or stay the same—they cannot fall further—and conversely, the highest achievers can only move down or stay the same. But the pattern is also apparent for the middle two groups. The consequence of this inverse relationship between children's kindergarten scores and their progress over time is that we would not expect them to end up with the same score in eighth grade as they started with in kindergarten. Part (but only part) of this movement reflects the imprecision of ability measurement in kindergarten. Even after we take account of this possible measurement error (see box 6.1), however, we would still expect to see some movement in relative ability over time.

Table 6.1 is useful for illustrating the point that there is quite a bit of movement in children's relative positions over the school years. But it pro-

Table 6.1   Many children change their position in the distribution of reading scores between kindergarten and eighth grade: almost half of the lowest achievers early on escape the bottom quartile over the period, and a similar proportion of the highest early achievers drop out of the top quartile by eighth grade.

| Quartile of Reading Score in Kindergarten | Quartile of Reading Score in Eighth Grade | | | | |
	1 (Lowest)	2	3	4 (Highest)	Total
1 (lowest)	**53**	25	15	7	100
2	29	**36**	22	13	100
3	14	24	**34**	28	100
4 (highest)	4	15	29	**52**	100
All children	25	25	25	25	100

Source: Authors' calculations using the ECLS-K.
Notes: The table shows the percentage of children from a given reading quartile group in kindergarten scoring in each quartile group in eighth grade. The numbers highlighted in bold on the diagonal are the percentage of children in the quartile group in kindergarten who are still in the same group in eighth grade. N = about 7,960 children. Weighted estimates and sample sizes are rounded to the nearest 10 in accordance with NCES reporting rules.

vides only a general picture, and it also ignores gradations in achievement and movement within a particular ability group. In fact, each child has his or her own achievement score in kindergarten, and this can be used to predict the child's most likely achievement score in eighth grade on an individualized basis.

Therefore, we use the detailed individual data in the ECLS-K to estimate the most likely eighth-grade reading score associated with each value of the kindergarten score. Figure 6.2 shows some examples of typical trajectories found in our data for a range of different starting scores.

Figure 6.2 is a visual representation of the phenomenon of "regression to the mean."[12] Children who start with above-average scores tend to follow downward trajectories, and children who start with below-average scores tend to follow upward trajectories. There is, of course, variation around these lines in terms of the paths followed by individual children—certainly there are some children who start high and become even stronger, and some children who start poorly and fall even further behind. But on average, children's scores tend to converge over time.[13]

What is driving this regression to the mean? The answer lies in the tran-

Figure 6.2   Children with very high reading scores in kindergarten tend on average to "regress to the mean"—to fall back slightly—by eighth grade. Conversely, children with very low scores in kindergarten tend to improve their relative position over the period.

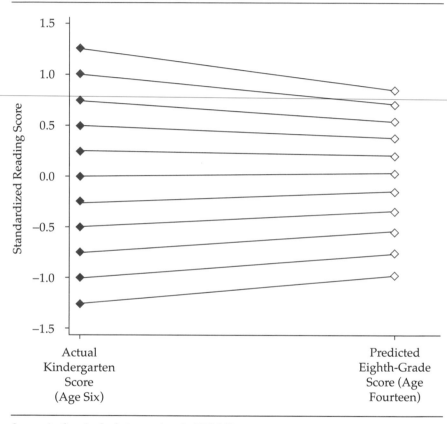

Source: Authors' calculations using the ECLS-K.
Notes: Eighth-grade reading scores are predicted solely on the basis of reading scores in the spring of kindergarten. We allow for a nonlinear (quadratic) relationship between the scores at the two time points and instrument the spring kindergarten score with the fall kindergarten score to correct for measurement error. The relationship between the scores estimated from the data is: $Read_{8G} = -0.03 + 0.73 \times Read_K - 0.07 \times Read_K^2$. The chart takes a selection of possible scores in kindergarten and shows how children who began with each score were, on average, predicted to perform in eighth grade. N = about 7,960 children (sample size rounded to nearest 10 in accordance with NCES reporting rules).

sitory influences on children's achievement that fluctuate randomly from year to year. We can think of these as "lucky" or "unlucky" influences that affect the speed of a child's development at a particular point in time but do not persist (unlike SES differences) over the longer term. There are many possible examples. Children experience "growth spurts" at different points in time, so that their development temporarily lags behind or surges ahead of other children of the same age. Children may have a particularly good or bad teacher one year (or one who is particularly well or ill suited to a child's learning style), but then get a different "draw" from the pool of teachers the next year. Peer groups, physical health, and family circumstances can also fluctuate and affect the course of a child's achievement in the short term. By their nature, the impact of these random influences tends to even out over time. Children will not be systematically lucky or unlucky year after year.

The regression to the mean we see in figure 6.2 reflects the fact that some portion of the scores of the highest-achieving children in kindergarten resulted from a temporary positive circumstance that would not persist over time, such as a growth spurt. Those who were luckiest at the start would tend to be less lucky later on. Similarly, children who experienced a short-term negative influence early on—one that depressed their kindergarten score—would tend to see their luck improve. Of course, luck is only one component of the factors that determine a child's achievement in any given year, and it is unlikely to be the most important. Children who start with very high scores are still expected to score well above the mean by eighth grade, and children who are not ready for school in kindergarten do not tend to make it back to average achievement by the end of the period. But there is *some* role for transitory influences in early achievement, and it is this component that tends to wash out over time.

Figures 6.1 and 6.2 depict simple associations between variables estimated from the same underlying data. But there is an apparent inconsistency in the story they tell. The left-most points in figure 6.1 say that low-SES children began with below-average scores and high-SES children began with above-average scores. Figure 6.2 says that the position of children who began with below-average scores tended to improve over time, while the position of initially high-scoring children tended to deteriorate over time. Together these statements seem to imply that average scores of low-SES children should be moving up toward the mean, while those of high-SES children should be moving down toward the mean—so the gap between the two should be narrowing over time. Yet as figure 6.1 shows, this was clearly not the case; if anything, the SES gap widened slightly over the period.

Figure 6.3   Only 60 percent of the SES reading gap we observe in eighth
grade can be attributed to differences in ability present in
kindergarten: 40 percent is due to the fact that children from
different SES groups do not follow common trajectories after
kindergarten.

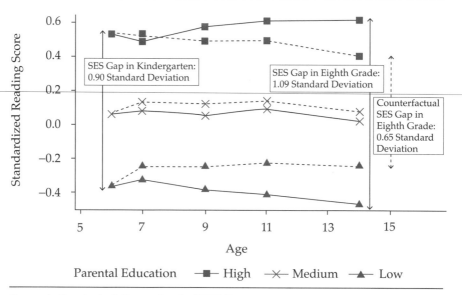

Source: Authors' calculations using the ECLS-K.
Notes: Solid lines plot the average scores of children in each SES group at different ages.
Dashed lines trace the trajectories associated with the three average SES-group scores in
kindergarten from a common trajectories model (that is, one in which the outcome depends
only on initial score and not on SES). The counterfactual SES gap in eighth grade is the gap
predicted by the common trajectories model. Common trajectories models at ages seven,
nine, eleven, and fourteen (first, third, fifth, and eighth grades) are estimated using instrumental variables in the way described in the note to figure 6.2.

How can we reconcile this paradox? The answer comes when we recognize that the trajectories depicted in figure 6.2 are for the average child at
each initial ability level, with no disaggregation by SES. They depict a
world in which SES has no impact on a child's progress given his or her
initial starting position. The dotted lines in figure 6.3 simulate how the
gaps would evolve under this counterfactual of common trajectories by
SES. We can contrast these dotted lines with solid lines plotted using the
same technique as in figure 6.2 to predict where children with three differ-

ent starting scores—the scores of the average high-, middle-, and low-SES child in kindergarten—will end up in each of the later grades. If the common trajectories assumption is valid, regression to the mean should operate to close some of the initial gap between these children, and our estimates imply that we should see an SES gap of 0.65 points in eighth grade. The difference between this and the gap of 1.09 we actually observe (0.44 points, or 41 percent of the total) is a measure of the failure of the common trajectories assumption—or the extent to which achievement diverged by SES for children who started with the same ability in kindergarten.

This measure of postkindergarten divergence is considerably larger, at 0.44 points, than the increase in the average gap between the SES groups of 0.19 points. It reveals that a simple comparison of the average gaps over time will overstate the portion of the eighth-grade gap that can be attributed to initial differences, and understate the portion due to later widening, because it does not account for the tendency to regress to the mean.

DIVERGING TRAJECTORIES

The results presented so far provide indirect evidence that low-SES children systematically fall behind high-SES children who begin school with the same level of achievement. Initial differences in average scores between SES groups are large, and their consequences persist strongly through the school years, but they are not sufficient to account for the levels of inequality we see as children prepare to enter high school. We now show directly how the "low-SES penalty" continues to operate during the school years.

As we have done so far, we estimate statistical models that predict the expected, or most likely, score at later ages for a child with a particular score in kindergarten (as before, using an earlier test score as an instrumental variable to correct for measurement error). Now, however, we allow the trajectory associated with a given starting score to differ across SES groups. The results of this analysis for reading achievement are shown in figure 6.4. Our statistical model enables us to calculate the expected outcomes in grades 1 through 8 for a child from each SES group with any initial score we choose. To illustrate the results, in figure 6.4 we predict outcomes for children with three specific starting values, one high, one average, and one low (scores of +1, 0, and −1 standard deviations above the mean, respectively).

What we can see clearly in figure 6.4 is that trajectories diverge based on SES. Low-SES children who started out with high scores lost ground relative to their higher-SES peers. The achievement of high-SES children

Figure 6.4   Over time, achievement gaps emerge between low- and high-SES children who started school with the same level of reading ability. High-SES children always develop an advantage, whether they started with high, average, or low ability in kindergarten.

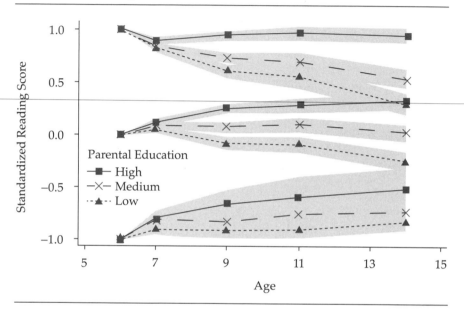

Source: Authors' calculations using the ECLS-K.
Notes: Lines depict the predicted scores in grades 1 through 8 of children with three specific reading test scores in kindergarten (+1, 0, and −1 standard deviations above the mean, respectively). The predicted scores associated with a given initial score were allowed to differ with SES. A quadratic relationship between the spring kindergarten score and the later test score was calculated separately for each group (with fall kindergarten scores used as instruments to correct for measurement error), and predictions were generated from these models. Shaded areas are 95 percent confidence intervals that indicate the precision with which we can predict later outcomes.

who began with average achievement tended to rise above the average over time, while the opposite was true for low-SES children who had the same reading skills in kindergarten. High-SES children who began with the low reading score shown in the figure went a long way toward recovering by eighth grade, while low-SES children with the same initial low score remained at the bottom. The gray shaded areas in the figure are confidence intervals that reflect the degree of uncertainty of our estimates. Even taking this uncertainty into account, the vertical gaps between the scores of the high- and low-SES children are statistically significant from first grade (age seven) onwards for all three of the starting test score values shown in the figure. The reading achievement of low-SES children systematically improved less, or deteriorated more, than the achievement of high-SES children who had the same ability in kindergarten, and this is true whether we focus on the brightest, the weakest, or the most ordinary children.

Figure 6.4 makes it clear that the challenges faced by low-SES children are not "all over" by school entry. Although it was obscured by the relatively constant average SES gaps shown in figure 6.1, something is happening to low-SES children during the school years that seriously hinders their ability to live up to their potential. Compared to their higher-SES peers who start school with the same initial ability, low-SES children are being left behind.

Figure 6.5 presents results of the equivalent analysis for trajectories of children's math scores. The degree of divergence is somewhat less than in reading scores, but it is still clearly apparent for children starting with average levels of achievement or higher. In contrast to the pattern for reading, however, high-SES children who started with very low math skills appear to have been no more able than their low-SES counterparts to recover in the years up to fifth grade, although by eighth grade they had gained a statistically significant, if small, advantage. Perhaps for this reason, when we calculate the common trajectories counterfactual for SES gaps in math, we find that a smaller proportion of the eighth-grade gap is attributed to postkindergarten divergence: 29 percent, or 0.32 points of the overall 1.08-point eighth-grade gap. Even for math, however, when we account for regression to the mean, the portion that cannot be attributed to differences at school entry is noticeably larger than the 0.12-point increase in the average SES gap between kindergarten and eighth grade. So in math as well, low-SES children are being left behind.

WHAT HAVE WE LEARNED ABOUT WIDENING SES GAPS?

We have seen that *average* SES gaps in U.S. children's math and reading do not change much overall between kindergarten and eighth grade. At first sight, we might infer from this pattern that the environments to which children are exposed after school entry—whether in school or in the home—either differ relatively little by SES or, if such differences exist, do not matter greatly for achievement. But this conclusion is contradicted by our finding that, whatever their initial ability level, low-SES children's

Figure 6.5   Diverging trajectories are found in math as well as reading. Low-SES children who start school with average or advanced math skills do not progress at the same pace as their high-SES counterparts.

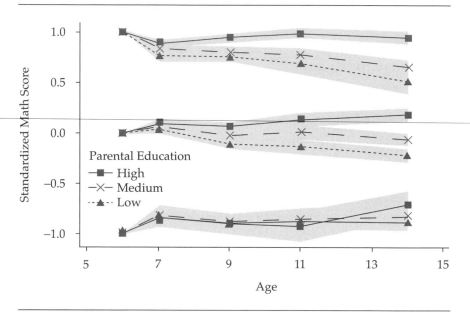

Source: Authors' calculations using the ECLS-K.
Note: See note to figure 6.4.

achievement systematically deteriorates more (or improves less) than high-SES children's over the period. How can the unchanging gaps in figure 6.1 coexist with the diverging trajectories shown in figure 6.4? The answer is that there are two countervailing forces operating on SES gaps over time.

Regression to the mean—the tendency of "luck" to even out over time—works to narrow gaps as children age. But systematic SES differences in factors that influence children's achievement—schools, something outside of school, or both—continue to exist after school entry, and these factors lead to widening gaps between low- and high-SES children of identical starting ability. Particularly in math, the effect of these inequality-widening factors seems to fall more heavily on those with higher or average ability at school entry than on those with low ability. So potential is being lost at both the top and in the middle—low-SES children in those starting positions are not achieving up to their full potential.

WHY DO CHILDREN'S TEST SCORES DIVERGE OVER TIME?

While it might be tempting to conclude that this divergence in children's test scores during the school years must be all due to schools, that conclusion would be too simplistic. As we discussed in earlier chapters, children start school with large SES gaps in achievement, and the out-of-school genetic and environmental factors that produce those gaps might continue to affect achievement as children move through school. Parents who are talking and reading more to their children before they start school may also be doing more homework and other activities with them during the school years. And the same children whose parents sent them to high-quality preschool programs may also have more opportunities to attend enriching after-school and summer programs. Out-of-school factors not only affect what children learn outside of school but can also affect how much children learn in school. If children come to school hungry, sleepy, ill, or stressed, they may not learn as much as other children. Children's learning can also be affected by repeated absences and frequent moves, both of which are more common in low-SES families.

Although we cannot pin down with certainty the specific factors that are widening SES achievement gaps, we can use the U.S. data to shed light on one potential explanation—that low-SES children attend schools that are of poorer quality than the schools attended by higher-SES children, and that it is this experience that hampers their progress, whatever their initial ability.

We know there are systematic differences in the quality of schools attended by low- and high-SES children in the United States. We know also that being in a good school and having good teachers and peers can make a world of difference to a child's achievement. But because of residential segregation in the United States, even in the elementary school years the schools that children attend differ considerably depending on their family's socioeconomic status.

It is important to note that differences across schools can reflect several different types of factors. Some schools may have more experienced and more capable teachers, or they may have stronger leadership. Or schools may differ not because of the quality of their teachers and leaders but because of differences in their student populations (if students are sorted into schools based on factors we cannot observe). Yet another factor that would help explain differences across schools is the effect of differences in the composition of students' peers, which can make it harder or easier for children to make progress even if their own initial abilities—and their teachers and school principals—are equivalent.

Children in our U.S. sample were clustered within schools, with an average of about twenty children per school in kindergarten. This feature of the data allows us to disentangle how much of the gap in achievement between low- and high-SES children is associated with the different schools they attended, and how much of the gap exists even comparing children who attended the same school.[14]

When we do this, we find that about half the divergence in reading achievement we saw in figure 6.4 is associated with differences between schools, and around half is due to differential achievement within schools by SES. For math, the role of between-school differences is somewhat smaller, accounting for around one-quarter of the gaps. The gaps we find even after controlling for the school the child attended reflect within-school inequality in how children from different backgrounds progressed and suggest that simply ensuring that low- and high-SES children attend more equal schools would not fully close the gaps.

IS THE ACHIEVEMENT OF LOW-SES CHILDREN IMPEDED BY POOR BEHAVIOR?

Another possible explanation, which we can examine with our data, is that even when low-SES children and high-SES children have identical academic ability in kindergarten, the low-SES children might tend to lack the social and emotional skills that matter for progress through school. To assess this possibility we draw on teacher reports of the four domains of child social and emotional development we introduced in chapter 4: attention, conduct problems, internalizing behavior, and prosocial behavior.

First, we test whether social and emotional differences in kindergarten—measured at the same time as initial academic achievement—can help to explain why low-SES children make slower progress than higher-SES children. We find that while some of these measures are modestly associated with achievement beyond kindergarten, they do not account for any of the SES divergence in achievement from a given starting score that we saw in figures 6.4 and 6.5.[15]

Second, even if initial differences in social and emotional skills at school entry are not consequential, it is possible that low-SES children develop poorer behaviors as they become older and that it is these behaviors that adversely affect their achievement in later grades. We explore this by controlling for social and emotional skills measured at the time of the achievement test, instead of in kindergarten. The predictive power of these contemporaneous measures of behavior for achievement is somewhat stronger, but they contribute little to the divergence in trajectories. Around 10 percent of the gaps that emerge in reading after kindergarten are accounted for by the emergence of differences in social and emotional skills, but none of the gaps in math. So we conclude that differences in children's behavior cannot explain the patterns of SES gaps in reading and math that we find in the school years.

HOW DO CHILDREN'S ACHIEVEMENT TRAJECTORIES DIVERGE IN OTHER COUNTRIES?

Although the data for the other countries do not consistently measure the same skills at different ages, and children are measured at different time points than U.S. children, we can still use these data to sketch out a version of children's trajectories over time. As in the United States, we focus on three SES groups, defined by parental education, and further distinguish children by their initial starting ability. As before, we do not begin with the earliest test score because of concerns about measurement error but instead start with the second test score (and use the first one to refine our estimates using the instrumental variables procedure mentioned earlier).

For the United Kingdom, we explore trajectories between ages five and eleven, and for Australia between ages seven and eleven. In both countries, initial ability is measured using a vocabulary test (and this is corrected for measurement error using results on the same test administered two years previously). The age eleven outcomes are the verbal similarities test for the United Kingdom and the national reading test for Australia (discussed in chapter 5). To provide as much comparability as possible, we present these results alongside the U.S. age eleven results from figures 6.3 and 6.4 rather than the age fourteen end-points emphasized previously.

Unfortunately, we were unable to carry out this analysis for Canada because of inconsistency in the Canadian outcome measures over time (early vocabulary scores versus later math scores).

We summarize the trajectory results for gaps to age eleven for the United States, the United Kingdom, and Australia in table 6.2. The decomposition of the age eleven high-low SES gap uses the same method as in figure 6.3. The component attributed to initial differences is the gap we would predict if children starting with the average score for their SES group followed a common trajectory to age eleven. The component attributed to subsequent divergence therefore captures the degree to which children with an identical starting score progress at rates that differ with SES.

As explained, we must be cautious in drawing comparisons between

Table 6.2   The United States is not alone in seeing divergence by SES among children who had the same ability levels earlier in childhood. SES-group differences in initial achievement are very important in all three countries, but they cannot account fully for the gaps we observe in reading at age eleven.

	United States	United Kingdom	Australia
Initial ability age	Six (spring kindergarten)	Five	Seven
Instrument age	Five (fall kindergarten)	Three	Five
Initial top-bottom education gap	0.90	0.76	0.56
Age eleven top-bottom education gap	1.03	0.69	0.68
Of which:			
Attributed to initial differences	0.72 (70%)	0.40 (57%)	0.45 (66%)
Attributed to subsequent divergence	0.31 (30%)	0.29 (43%)	0.23 (34%)
N	9,650	10,717	3,333

Source: Authors' calculations using the ECLS-K, MCS, and LSAC-K.
Notes: The figure reports analyses that split the observed high-low SES gap in reading at age eleven into two components, using the common trajectories framework illustrated in figure 6.4. The component attributed to initial differences is the gap predicted to exist if all children with a given initial test score make the same progress, on average, by age eleven. The component attributed to subsequent divergence therefore reflects systematic differences in the progress from a given start made by children from different SES groups. Gaps are reported in standard deviation units. The magnitudes shown here may differ from those reported elsewhere in the book owing to estimation sample differences. See the technical appendix for details. The sample size for the United States is rounded to the nearest 10, in accordance with NCES reporting rules.

the countries. But it is clear that similar processes are operating in all of them. Initial SES gaps in ability, whether they are measured at ages five, six, or seven, are sufficient to account for more than half the gaps observed at age eleven in all three countries, but they do not account for the whole. Even though the size of the gaps increases little over the periods covered (and actually falls in the United Kingdom), a substantial portion of inequality at age eleven is due to influences operating *after* the initial measurement of achievement.

Table 6.2 also highlights again that much of the larger U.S. SES gap at age eleven is due to the gap at school entry as opposed to the portion that develops during the primary school years. At age eleven, low-SES children in the United States are 1.03 standard deviations behind their high-SES peers, in contrast to much smaller gaps of 0.69 and 0.68 standard deviations in the United Kingdom and Australia, respectively. Although, as discussed, we must be cautious given that the data and timings of measurement are not strictly comparable, when we divide these gaps into the portion present at school entry versus the portion that develops subsequently, it appears that where the United States most strongly differs is in the early gap—which is 0.72 standard deviations in the United States versus 0.40 and 0.45 standard deviations in the United Kingdom and Australia, respectively. In contrast, the portion that develops during the school years is broadly similar in the three countries (0.31 standard deviations in the United States as opposed to 0.29 and 0.23 in the other two countries).

CONCLUSION

So we now know quite a bit about the progress of children from different SES groups through the school years in the United States. Low-SES children start nearly one standard deviation behind their high-SES peers in reading. Without additional downward pressures on the achievement of low-SES children, we estimate that by eighth grade that gap would have narrowed to about two-thirds of a standard deviation, owing to regression to the mean. The fact that the gap in eighth grade is actually slightly larger than in kindergarten is evidence that socioeconomic status continues to exert a considerable influence on achievement throughout the school years, propelling high-SES children ahead and leaving low-SES children with identical initial ability behind.

Analysis by children's initial ability level indicates that low-SES children are making less progress than their high-SES peers with the same initial starting ability, especially those who started out with high or average scores (in math). So low-SES children are not achieving their full potential—the talent of these children is being, at least partially, wasted.

These patterns are not unique to the United States. In both the United Kingdom and Australia, we also find evidence of substantial divergence in children's language and reading trajectories during the primary school years by SES. (We were not able to carry out similar analyses for Canada owing to data limitations.) But importantly, the SES gaps at age eleven are significantly lower in the United Kingdom and Australia than they are in the United States; in combination, these findings suggest that lower inequality at eleven in these two countries may be due to their significantly smaller SES gaps at school entry.

We have shown that it is easy to underestimate the importance of SES for achievement after school entry by focusing only on changes in the *average* gaps. But this should not obscure the fact that initial differences in achievement remain the biggest predictor of inequalities for children on the cusp of entering high school. Early childhood development is the first bottleneck in life—and a very consequential one. Children who do not negotiate it successfully suffer the consequences far into the future. But it is also not the only point at which inequality develops. Inequality of opportunity manifests itself from the day a child is born and then cumulates continuously throughout childhood and adolescence.

Our analysis of the detailed U.S. data—offering an unprecedented picture of children's progress from kindergarten to eighth grade—has also thrown some light on the reasons for the continued divergence of achievement by SES during the school years. The inequality that is present at eighth grade is due both to inequality within schools and to inequality between schools, suggesting that simply ensuring that children attend more equal schools would not fully address the problem. We also examined the possibility that this differential progress is due to differences in children's behavior, but found little support for that explanation. Social and emotional development does differ by SES, but such differences do not explain children's differential progress in reading and math.

To more fully understand the influences that drive the greater inequality in the United States and what might be done to combat them, we must turn to other sources of evidence. A vast body of work is devoted to evaluating an array of competing explanations and, most importantly, to identifying what can be done to promote opportunity and reduce inequality. We turn to this work in the next chapter.

Chapter 7 | What the United States Can Do to Reduce the SES Gap in Achievement

THE PRECEDING CHAPTERS have made clear that the United States has a problem with equality of opportunity.

Our data show the United States to have the least equality of opportunity across our four countries. Gaps in cognitive development between children from less- versus more-advantaged families are large already at school entry, and they remain large as children move through school. These gaps signal greater inequality among children in the United States both in early childhood and in the school years.

These childhood gaps have lifelong consequences. Other data show this greater inequality continuing into later adolescence and adulthood, and indeed, the patterns we find across our four countries are consistent with patterns found for teenagers and adults in international test score data (see box 7.1). They also are consistent with what we know about income inequality among adults. This makes sense, since one important source of income inequality is inequality in the underlying distribution of skills. If young people in the United States are coming into the labor market with more unequal skills, then this will be reflected in greater inequality of earnings.

The childhood gaps we have documented also have intergenerational consequences. If low-SES children attain lower levels of schooling, their disadvantage is more likely to be passed on to the next generation through low levels of resources, low incomes, and so on. Conversely, boosting the skills of low-SES children today would help produce more equality of family background and opportunity in the next generation.

As we have seen, unequal skills begin early in life. These early gaps are large in the United States, and they persist. Indeed, our results show that even if environments during the school years were equal by SES, there would still be large gaps for U.S. children at age fourteen simply because the gaps in preschool readiness persist. Since any policy response that leaves these initial inequalities unaddressed can be only a partial solution at best, early years policy must be a key part of any strategy to reduce the achievement gap for U.S. children.

But this is a long way from saying that schools and other factors that affect achievement in the school years are not also an important part of the solution, for three reasons. First, our results show the United States does have inequality during the school years, as trajectories continue to diverge (a pattern that would not be clear if we simply inspected the aggregate data). So policies that affect inputs during this period (both in and out of school) are still needed to work directly on the sources of the ultimate achievement gaps. Our school fixed-effects results show that up to half of the post–school entry divergence in the United States can be traced to the different schools attended by low- and high-SES children. So it is important to even out school quality and address the ways in which children are sorted into disparate schools. Second, the elimination of SES differences in school quality is not the upper bound on what school reforms could achieve. School policies could be *compensatory* and actually help to offset some of the initial disadvantages of low-SES children, as happens in other countries (through policies such as the pupil premium in the United Kingdom). And third, although families matter, schools may be much more malleable from a policy perspective, so gains via this route might be easier and less costly for a government to achieve.

Our analysis shows that the SES gaps at least in part reflect demographic differences between different SES groups, in factors such as young parenthood. This is a reality of U.S. society as well as others—not all families are created equal. But is it inevitable that an unequal society such as the United States must have less equality of opportunity for the next generation? We would argue that it is not—as witnessed by the evidence of smaller achievement gaps in our other countries, each of which is also unequal in at least some respects.

We have documented many of the potential channels for the greater inequality of achievement in the United States—instances where the SES gradient in key inputs to child development is greater in the United States and where the different economic resources of families at the top, middle, and bottom of the distribution are likely causes of these associations. We discuss in this chapter which of these factors looks to be most important in explaining the greater inequality of achievement in the United States and what policy might do to address them.

We recognize that, in more unequal societies, not only do parents have

Box 7.1   Cross-National Results for Teens and Adults Also Point
to Greater Inequality in the United States

The Program for International Student Achievement (PISA) tests nationally representative samples of fifteen-year-olds across a host of
countries. In all countries in which PISA is administered, students
from low-SES families have lower average test scores than students
from higher-SES backgrounds. But the PISA data also show that the
SES gap (the gap in achievement between students from low- and
high-SES families) is much larger in some countries than others.

Canada and other top performers—Finland, Japan, Korea—have
not only high overall achievement levels but also relatively high
scores among their low-SES students. The United States, in contrast,
has not only mediocre average scores but also notably low scores for
its low-SES children, while its high-SES children fare relatively well
by international standards.[1] As a result, the association between SES
and student achievement is stronger in the United States than in
many other countries.[2] In PISA 2009, for instance, about 17 percent of
the variance in student achievement in the United States was explained by SES—twice the share explained by SES in Canada (or Finland and Japan).[3] Equity in U.S. test scores improved in PISA 2012,
but the United States remained less equal than Canada (or Finland
and Japan).[4]

The United States also has a larger SES gap in adult achievement
than other peer countries. This is seen in data from the Survey of
Adult Skills conducted by the Organization for Economic Cooperation and Development (OECD).[5]

When we focus on our four countries, the cross-national test score
data confirm that the SES gap in student achievement is relatively
large in the United States and relatively small in Canada. For example, an analysis of data from the Trends in International Math and
Science Study (TIMSS) from 1995 and 1999 found that the United
States was in the most unequal quarter of OECD countries, while
Canada was in the most equal group.[6] A similar pattern is seen in
adult literacy: the United States and, to a lesser extent, the United
Kingdom stand out for having low average literacy levels and large
SES gaps in literacy, in contrast to Australia and Canada, which have
higher average literacy and lower SES gaps in literacy.[7]

More recent evidence from PISA 2012 shows that average levels of

Box 7.1   (Cont.)

math and science achievement for fifteen-year-olds are lower in the United States than in our other three countries, while average reading achievement is lower in both the United States and the United Kingdom than in the other two countries.[8] Canada, in contrast, stands out not just for its better average performance but also for its high rank in terms of equity, as measured by the strength of the association between SES and achievement. SES accounts for 9.4 percent of the variance in math achievement among fifteen-year-olds in Canada and for 12.3 percent in Australia and the United Kingdom, but it accounts for 14.8 percent of this variance in the United States.[9] Canada also has a higher share (8.4 percent) of "resilient" students—youth from the lowest-quartile SES group whose achievement puts them in the highest-quartile group of math performance. In contrast, 6.3 percent of youth in Australia, 5.8 percent in the United Kingdom, and 5.2 percent in the United States could be classified as resilient on this basis.[10]

unequal access to resources, but the unequal opportunities they see ahead in their children's lives give them all the more incentive to push harder to obtain the best outcomes for their children. It is unrealistic to expect parents not to want the best for their children, and if parents' abilities to attain the best vary, then we should not be surprised if children's outcomes vary also. This is the "problem of the family" we referred to earlier.

But while the role of the family must remain a constraint on equality of opportunity in the United States, as it is in other countries, this does not mean that nothing can be done to improve the outcomes of the most-disadvantaged children. There is also scope to improve outcomes for children in the middle. Indeed, the evidence we review in this chapter offers considerable proof that there is much that can be done.

WHAT CAN FAMILIES, SCHOOLS, AND OTHER ASPECTS OF SOCIETY DO?

The challenge is clear. SES gaps in achievement exist in all four of our countries but are most pronounced in the United States. Moreover, these gaps begin in early childhood and act as a bottleneck on children's development, limiting future opportunities. What can families, schools, and other aspects of society do not only to reduce these gaps and bottlenecks but to promote greater equality of opportunity?

To answer this question, we draw on the best available evidence about policies and programs that might be effective at narrowing SES gaps in achievement, whether by addressing such gaps directly or by addressing factors that our research suggests are associated with the gaps. In particular, we draw on an extensive body of research in the United States that provides rigorous estimates using random assignment to treatment or control groups or taking advantage of "natural experiments" brought about through policy or other reforms.

We also draw on evidence about what other countries do. As we have discussed, Canada and several other countries (such as Finland, Japan, and Korea) stand out in international comparisons of high school students for the cohorts and time period we examine by having not only higher average achievement than the United States but also more equal achievement. In our analysis, Australia also seems to have more equal achievement patterns in early childhood and primary school; Australia's greater equality is also found in international data on its adult literacy scores. The United Kingdom too is an interesting case, since our analysis—in conjunction with other reports—suggests some narrowing of inequality in the primary school years in that country.

These other countries provide proof that the strong associations we see between SES and children's achievement in the United States are not inevitable. The SES gap does not have to be as large as it is in this country. So that is why our main focus in this chapter is on learning what the United States can do to reduce its (too large) gap in achievement. The lessons we draw should be useful to other countries looking to reduce their achievement gaps as well.

We are mindful that we must be cautious in drawing lessons across countries, given the differences in systems and the larger contexts, but we also see international comparisons as offering a unique chance to look at reforms at scale. Much of the evidence about school reforms in the United States comes from small-scale experiments or pilot programs, but skeptics often ask whether such reforms really could be implemented and be successful at scale. In this regard, lessons from other countries' systems can be very useful.

What does the research tell us about what families, schools, and other aspects of society can do to reduce SES gaps in achievement? What do our four countries do, and is there something to be learned from the best performers among them, and from other top performers internationally?

As we have emphasized throughout the book, schools are not the only factors affecting gaps in children's school achievement. Families play an important role, particularly but not exclusively in the preschool years, and so too do other aspects of society. So we organize our discussion in this chapter accordingly—starting with family resources, then schools, and finally other aspects of society.

At each of these levels, we identify policies that could help reduce the sizable SES gaps in achievement in the United States. The evidence suggests that most important among these are: (1) policies to provide more support for children's early learning through more widespread availability of evidence-based parenting programs for families with infants and toddlers and through universal preschool for three- and four-year-olds; (2) policies to improve the quality of teaching and learning in schools by recruiting, supporting, and adequately compensating more effective teachers, implementing more rigorous curricula, and setting higher expectations and providing more support for low-achieving students; and (3) policies to raise family incomes for poor and near-poor families through provisions such as an increased minimum wage and a more generous Child Tax Credit and Earned Income Tax Credit.

THE ROLE OF THE FAMILY

As we saw in earlier chapters, children's family backgrounds and out-of-school experiences vary widely, both before they start school and while they are in school. Teachers report that their instruction is limited by out-of-school factors, more so in the United States than in the other three countries.[11] For example, in an international survey of fourth-grade teachers in 2011, three out of four teachers in the United States said that their instruction was limited by students lacking sufficient sleep, and two out of five said that their instruction was limited by students lacking basic nutrition; these are higher shares than in our other three countries. Interestingly, U.S. teachers did not see their students as more disruptive than teachers in other countries, but they did say that their students were more likely to be uninterested. In the same survey, U.S. fourth-graders reported having fewer home learning resources than did their peers in the other three countries.[12] They were the least likely to have more than one hundred books in their home (only 28 percent) and to have their own room and an Internet connection (64 percent). As we saw earlier, not only do children in the United States have fewer books in the home on average, but there is also more inequality among them in the number of books in their home.

What family-level factors drive the lower average achievement of U.S. students and the greater inequality in achievement among them, and what might policymakers be able to do about them?

Family Demographics

As we saw in chapter 3, compared to the other three countries, the United States has more children living with young parents and fewer children living with both biological parents, particularly among low-SES families. So children in these families not only have less-educated parents but also parents who are less mature and have less stable living arrangements.[13] Such demographics are an obvious "smoking gun" that might help explain the SES gaps we find in school-readiness and achievement, but they are not easy to address with policies. The United States has had some recent success in slowing teen birth rates, and our analysis suggests that further reductions would be beneficial. The existing evidence on preventing teen parenthood and unplanned pregnancies points to a role for improved methods of contraception as well as a role for the media in helping to convey messages to youth.[14] Changing trends in marriage would be beneficial in terms of promoting family stability, but this factor is likely to be more challenging to address, given that marriage promotion policies have had a poor track record of success.[15] Many scholars argue that until low-income men's employment and earnings prospects increase, the United States will not see more marriages in low-income communities.[16]

Perhaps surprisingly, we found that the racial-ethnic makeup of the U.S. population is not a large factor in explaining the greater SES achievement gap in the United States relative to other countries. When we excluded racial and ethnic minorities and limited the analysis to non-Hispanic white children, we still found a very large SES gap in achievement in the United States. So the SES achievement gap is not driven by racial-ethnic achievement gaps—these are distinct phenomena. Nor is the share of immigrant children an important factor explaining differences across countries. Most of the countries we analyzed have substantial numbers of immigrant families. And as with race-ethnicity, immigrant-native achievement gaps are distinct from SES achievement gaps.

Parenting

If we take the demographics of low-SES families as given—at least in the short term—what factors associated with low SES and low achievement might be more malleable? One set of potentially relevant factors has to do with parenting behaviors, and in particular the aspects of parenting that are known to be associated with children's cognitive development and school-readiness. Researchers have documented the "word gap"—the gap in the number of words that children in low-SES versus high-SES homes hear as they are growing up.[17] There is also ample evidence, as we have seen, of what we might call a "book gap" and a "reading gap": children in low-SES homes grow up with fewer books and are read to less often than their higher-SES peers. We have also seen an SES gap in harsh parenting, as evidenced by the use of spanking (which is associated not just with worse child behavior but also with poorer cognitive development).[18]

Our earlier research on this topic indicated that such differences in parenting are the single largest factor associated with SES gaps in school-readiness in the United States (and the United Kingdom).[19] There is also research showing that a central reason why low-SES parents talk less to their children and read less with them is a lack of knowledge about the extent to which these kinds of activities are beneficial for children.[20] So there is good reason to believe that providing more information to low-SES parents about what they can do to help their children learn could make an important contribution to reducing SES gaps in school-readiness.[21]

Researchers are studying how to communicate this kind of information to parents and the extent to which such communication influences parents' behavior and children's development. Although the evidence base on parenting programs is not as strong as we would like—many programs have not been rigorously evaluated, and those that have been evaluated often have been found wanting—there are a few parenting programs that, in rigorous evaluations, have been found to be effective in changing parents' behavior and improving children's early development, although the effects on child development are often not large.[22] For example, a randomized study of Early Head Start, which works with low-income families with children from birth to age three, found that it achieved modest improvements in parenting as well as in early child cognitive and behavioral development.[23] Building on this promising evidence, Early Head Start is now being expanded to serve a greater share of low-income infants and toddlers in the United States.

Another example is the health-oriented Nurse Family Partnership Program, which provides home visiting by nurses to high-risk first-time mothers during pregnancy and the first two years of a child's life. Tested in three randomized trials, this program was found to not only reduce harsh parenting but also to modestly improve the quality of the home environment, parents' literacy activities, and children's early vocabulary.[24] This program is now being implemented across the United States as well as in the United Kingdom.[25]

Another promising program—Play and Learning Strategies (PALS)—has had success in improving children's early language development by using videotapes to teach parents of infants and toddlers to provide more sensitive and responsive care and to better encourage their children's language development.[26] Also using a videotape approach to improve parenting, the behavior-oriented Family Check-Up program recruits low-income families in health settings and provides specific feedback about what they could do to better foster their child's growth and development.[27]

Some evidence-based programs target early reading more directly. In the United States, Russ Whitehurst and his colleagues developed an approach that they call "dialogic reading," which teaches parents (or teachers) how to foster children's emergent literacy by talking with them during shared book reading; in a series of evaluations, this approach has successfully raised children's literacy skills both in home-based programs and in child care and school-based programs.[28] In the United Kingdom, the Peers Early Education Partnership (PEEP) program increased children's literacy skills by providing parents with age-appropriate literacy materials and supporting them in using the materials with their children (in both group sessions and home visits).[29]

These parenting and early reading programs are promising because the evidence suggests not only that they change parents' behavior but also that they improve children's vocabulary, early literacy, and other aspects of cognitive development.[30] Although the gains in children's development are often modest, these programs nevertheless provide evidence that it is possible to work with parents to reduce SES gaps in children's school-readiness during the crucial early childhood period.

Preschool

A substantial SES gap in preschool enrollment in the United States was another striking finding in our data, with both low- and middle-SES children lagging behind their high-SES counterparts in attending preschool in the year or two before starting school.[31] So, in the U.S. context, universal provision of high-quality preschool is another important tool to reduce SES gaps in early childhood school readiness. This is all the more important in light of the long working hours of low- and middle-SES mothers in the United States.

Researchers and policymakers generally agree that the evidence base on preschool is very strong. Randomized studies of model programs in the United States have shown that high-quality preschool can lead to dramatic gains in school readiness for disadvantaged children.[32] The question really has been whether such gains are also possible when small model programs are implemented at scale. We now know that the answer is yes. Universal prekindergarten programs in the United States have a solid track record of boosting achievement, and typically more so for disadvantaged children than for their more-advantaged peers.[33] Although we do not have experiments where children are randomly assigned to attend prekindergarten or not, we do have natural experiments where birthday cutoffs lead to some children being offered a prekindergarten place, while other, very similar, children are not. A series of studies in Tulsa, Oklahoma, using this natural experiment approach, found that children given the chance to attend prekindergarten gained in school readiness, and more so if they were disadvantaged.[34] These results have since been replicated in several other states.[35] Most recently, a comprehensive study of Boston's universal prekindergarten program found that it not only raised students' cognitive readiness but also yielded gains in children's behavioral readiness.[36]

Universal preschool is the norm in most other industrialized countries, and in many cases we now have many years of data on the effects of such programs. Reviewing that evidence, Christopher Ruhm and Jane Waldfogel concluded that "expansions of early education generally yield benefits at school entry, adolescence, and for adults, particularly for disadvantaged children."[37]

Recognizing the potential of preschool to reduce gaps in school readiness, U.S. cities and states are moving to expand universal prekindergarten, whether by offering such programming directly in the schools or by supporting prekindergarten in other community-based settings.[38] In the cohort that we studied (children who started school in the fall of 1998), only one in six had attended prekindergarten, but by the fall of 2011, one in four entering kindergarteners had.[39] Nevertheless, this share pales by comparison to most of our peer countries, where enrollment rates in the equivalent of prekindergarten are generally 95 to 99 percent.[40] And in spite of recent expansions, the SES gap in preschool enrollment in the United States persists, reflecting the fact that it is still only a minority of children who have access to publicly funded programs.[41]

Family Income

A final family-level factor that may be implicated in SES gaps in early school readiness (as well as later school achievement) is family income. As we saw in the earlier chapters, income inequality is higher in the United States than in our other three countries, and the incomes of low-SES families lag further behind the incomes of their high-SES counterparts. We cannot know with certainty how much income matters in children's school achievement. Experiments that randomly give some families more income and then assess their children's development are very rare. There are some natural experiments that take advantage of policy variation. Such natural experiments provide some evidence that raising the incomes of low-SES families reduces parental stress and leads to better outcomes for children.[42] There is also evidence from behavioral economics that when individuals are consumed with worrying about financial scarcity, their cognitive performance is impaired.[43] We note that it is difficult to capture the full role of income, since income is linked to many of the mechanisms we have highlighted in earlier chapters (such as investments in children, enrichment activities, and residential location and segregation), as well as factors we highlight in this chapter (such as family breakdown and parental stress, which in turn matter for parenting and behaviors like spanking). Because income can affect so many of the different pathways that matter for achievement, even modest associations with each one could add up to a substantial impact. A further reason to focus on income is that it is malleable from a policy perspective, and poverty acts as a brake that can undermine the effectiveness of other interventions.

Thus, while policies to raise family incomes for the poor and near-poor are certainly not the only or even primary remedy for SES gaps in achievement, we think there is a role for such policies as part of a broader policy package. In particular, we see promise in building on recent efforts in the United States to increase incomes for the poor and near-poor through measures such as increasing the minimum wage and increasing the generosity and reach of income supports such as the Child Tax Credit and the Earned Income Tax Credit.

Several other policies could help address the gaps in resources families can invest in their children. For example, we have stressed that parents in the United Kingdom, Australia, and Canada now all have up to a year of paid parental leave, while parents in the United States—under the federal Family and Medical Leave Act (FMLA)—have only twelve weeks of unpaid leave (and half of working parents are not even eligible for that). Three states (California, New Jersey, and Rhode Island) have implemented paid family leave, and the evidence so far is very promising—both in terms of benefits for families and children and in terms of impacts on employers.[44] More generally, there is a role for policies that provide more flexibility for working parents through measures such as flexible work hours, paid sick leave, and paid time off for family obligations such as parent-teacher conferences.

We have also seen that families in the United States, to a larger extent than in other countries, are engaged in what we have called an "arms race" of investments in out-of-school enrichment activities. This is a race that low- and even middle-SES families are poorly equipped to compete in, because they do not have the time and financial resources to arrange and pay for the array of activities that high-SES families are providing.

Subsidies to help lower- and middle-income families purchase such activities, or greater public provision of such opportunities, would help level the playing field. In the United Kingdom, for example, our data show that the gap in having the chance to learn a musical instrument is reduced considerably when schools provide music lessons and children do not have to rely exclusively on private lessons. Local nonprofit agencies, religious organizations, and other state and local groups could play a similar role in providing access not only to music but also to organized physical activity, clubs, summer enrichment, and other opportunities.

THE ROLE OF SCHOOLS

As we have seen in prior chapters, low-SES children in the United States are more concentrated in schools with other low-SES children than is the case in other countries. They are also more likely to have inexperienced teachers. And they are more likely than their higher-SES counterparts to be taught in groups by ability and to be retained (held back), in contrast to other countries where the use of ability groups is less stratified by SES and where grade retention is less common.

What can be done to address these factors? We begin with policies that might address the problem of children attending systemically different schools, and then we turn to policies that have to do with other aspects of inequality that might arise both between and within schools.

Sorting and Segregation

We begin with school sorting and the concentration of low-SES children with others from low-SES families. A considerable body of research, from the Coleman Report onwards, has found that both low- and high-SES students do better when they are in schools with more high-SES peers and fewer low-SES peers.[45] But U.S. students are less likely to attend a socially integrated school than students in other countries. According to international data from PIRLS 2011, 51 percent of U.S. fourth-graders were in schools where more than one-quarter of students were from economically disadvantaged homes and fewer than one-quarter were from affluent homes, in contrast to 35 percent in the United Kingdom, 27 percent in Australia and 28 percent in Canada.[46]

Students are sorted between schools for various reasons, and so policy remedies to address sorting can also vary. Particularly at the secondary level, it used to be common for school districts to sort children into different schools on the basis of ability (with higher-achieving students sorted into more academically oriented high schools and less-proficient students sorted into more vocationally oriented high schools). The research is clear that greater, and earlier, use of such between-school sorting leads to increased inequality of achievement.[47] There is also good evidence that when countries eliminate separate secondary schools and replace them with more standardized comprehensive schools (as Finland and Poland have done), inequality of achievement narrows.[48] The equalizing effect arises because more-integrated schools particularly benefit the achievement of low-SES students, thus leading to reduced SES gaps.[49]

But nowadays, with the decline of separate high schools, sorting is more commonly driven by residential segregation. Thus, policy remedies might involve housing reforms to reduce residential segregation, or school reforms to weaken the link between location of residence and location of school (reforms such as busing, magnet schools, and so on). However, such reforms are unlikely to completely equalize the schools that children attend, given residential segregation and the strong desire of parents to have their children attend local schools, particularly at the primary level. Moreover, many current reforms that increase choices for parents might even exacerbate inequalities, since those with the most resources might be in the best position to take advantage of these choices.[50] Attention has therefore focused on policies that might improve quality in the lowest-performing schools and help reduce inequality between schools.

Improving School Quality in Low-Performing Schools and Reducing Inequality Between Schools

To improve quality in the lowest-performing schools and reduce inequality between schools, a great deal of emphasis in the United States has been placed on increasing external accountability, both through state reforms and through the 2001 federal law, No Child Left Behind (NCLB). NCLB was not very popular because it was seen as raising expectations without providing funding to help meet them. It was also criticized for placing undue emphasis on testing and evaluating both students and teachers. But it does seem to have been effective in at least somewhat improving achievement among disadvantaged students, according to research by education economists. Tom Dee and Brian Jacob find that states with no or weaker prior accountability saw greater gains on the National Assessment of Educational Progress (NAEP) tests in at least some grades and subjects after NCLB was introduced, while Randall Reback, Jonah Rockoff, and Heather Schwartz find that NCLB had generally positive or neutral effects on student achievement in reading, math, and science.[51]

More recently, interest in common standards has grown in the United States as a remedy for variation in quality between schools. While not as binding as a national curriculum (such as is in place in many countries), common standards do set guidelines as to what all students should be taught and should learn. Between 2009 and 2014, forty-three U.S. states voluntarily adopted a set of common standards, known as the Common Core State Standards (or "Common Core" for short). Developed through an initiative led by state governors and state education commissioners, the Common Core is intended to lead to improvements in the quality of instruction and learning. In math, for example, the Common Core places greater weight on conceptual understanding than on mere competence with procedures. At the time of this writing, however, political debate as to whether the content of the Common Core is correct for all localities and states was ongoing.[52]

External inspection is a third approach to addressing low quality and evening out quality across schools. This approach is used in many countries, although not in the United States. For example, as discussed later, the United Kingdom has an external inspection service, OFSTED, that regularly visits all schools and makes more frequent visits to struggling schools. The intent is to make sure that schools are performing to sufficiently high standards and to identify and support schools that are not.

Compensatory funding, which directs more resources to schools serving more-disadvantaged children, is a fourth approach. While the United States stands out from other countries in spending a relatively high level of resources on its education system, it also stands out in being one of only three OECD countries that have *fewer* average resources in schools serving disadvantaged children than in schools serving more-advantaged ones.[53] Existing research from the United States is unclear on the extent to which more equal resources, or compensatory resources, would help reduce achievement gaps. The United States does have Title I, a federal program that directs additional funding to schools with low-income children. However, the programs offered through Title I do not appear to be very effective in improving achievement among low-income children.[54] Research on state school finance reform in the United States finds that when states take steps to equalize spending on education, this does lead to reduced gaps in student achievement.[55] At the same time, analysts point out, implementing more equal funding in the United States might be very challenging, given the political constraints and also given the large amount of funding that might be needed to overcome gaps in out-of-school factors such as family incomes and other resources.[56]

Can we learn something from other countries about how to use these kinds of measures to improve low-performing schools and equalize quality between schools? Recent education reforms in England provide an interesting case study. (In the United Kingdom, education policy is set at the "country" level—that is, by the English, Scottish, Welsh, or Northern Ireland government. We focus here on England, which represents about five in six U.K. schoolchildren.)

England has a national curriculum, national exit exams, and a national external inspection system. It also has national funding for the schools, including a tradition of compensatory funding for districts with higher numbers of disadvantaged students. Although these policies do not eliminate variation between schools, they do reduce it, particularly at the primary level, where children tend to attend local schools (in contrast to the secondary level, where children may test into schools or attend schools out of their area).

Under the New Labour government, which was in office from 1997 to 2010, a series of measures were introduced to raise overall achievement and to reduce SES gaps in achievement. These included reductions in class sizes in primary schools and the introduction of required literacy and numeracy hours (an hour a day dedicated to English instruction and an hour a day dedicated to math instruction). The reforms were costly—education spending increased by 40 percent between 2000 and 2007—but average achievement rose and gaps between low-income children and their higher-income peers narrowed, particularly in primary schools.[57]

These education reforms were a core part of the New Labour government's agenda to fight child poverty and were strongly pushed by Prime Minister Tony Blair, who emphasized "education, education, education," as well as by his chancellor Gordon Brown, who succeeded Blair as prime minister.[58] The goal of raising educational attainment, especially for disadvantaged students, resonated strongly with the public, and the Conservative–Liberal Democrat government that succeeded Blair and Brown in 2010 introduced further measures to reduce gaps, including a pupil premium that directs more resources to schools serving more-disadvantaged children.[59] Schools have flexibility as to how they use the extra resources, but the government provides guidance through its support for the independent Education Endowment Foundation, which gathers and posts evidence on the most effective policies and programs to improve achievement for disadvantaged students.[60]

The experience of Ontario—Canada's largest province—is also interesting. Like the United States, Canada places primary responsibility for education at the provincial (state) and local level. Provinces set the curriculum, and since 1997 they have also provided 100 percent of the funding, including additional funds to ensure that schools in poorer districts are as well funded as schools in other districts. International experts point to Ontario as an exemplar of a province that has raised achievement and reduced achievement gaps.[61]

During a series of reforms from 2003 to 2010, Ontario, like England, emphasized improving literacy and numeracy in the primary schools, as well as improving achievement in the lowest-performing secondary schools. Ontario's reforms, like England's, were focused on achieving success for all students, but they were less prescriptive in terms of what schools and teachers were required to do. Schools and teachers were given a clear message about raising literacy and numeracy levels in primary schools and preventing dropout in secondary schools, but they were also invited to participate in figuring out how to accomplish these goals and then given time and support to do so. The results of the reforms have been very impressive—improved literacy and numeracy at the primary level, improved graduation rates at the secondary level, and a decrease in the number of low-performing schools.[62]

Improving Teacher Quality and Reducing Inequality in Teacher Quality

Teacher quality is an important aspect of school quality, and an important factor in the variation in the quality of education that children receive both between and within schools. How do our four countries compare in terms of teacher quality? Perhaps the most straightforward way to assess teacher quality is to examine how well paid teachers are. In countries where teachers are relatively highly paid, it would stand to reason that they would be more highly qualified than in countries where teachers are relatively poorly paid. Data from OECD on how primary school salaries compare to earnings for all college-educated workers show a striking pattern (see figure 7.1): teacher salaries are above (105 percent) those of comparably educated workers in Canada, nearly on par (99 percent and 92 percent, respectively) in the United Kingdom and Australia, but seriously behind (67 percent) in the United States.

Moreover, as we saw in chapter 5, not only are teachers less well qualified in the United States, but they are also more unequally distributed. Using teacher experience as a marker of quality, we found that low-SES children in the United States are disproportionately likely to have inexperienced teachers (teachers with less than five years of experience). This was not the case in our other three countries, where novice teachers are more equally distributed.

There is ample evidence that improving teacher quality does help raise the achievement of disadvantaged students.[63] For example, a study in New York City found that as teachers became more equally distributed across schools owing to changes in teacher recruitment and selection policies between 2000 and 2005, student achievement rose in low-SES schools.[64]

Figure 7.1   Salaries for primary school teachers are above the salaries of comparably educated workers in Canada and nearly on par in the United Kingdom and Australia, but they are seriously behind in the United States.

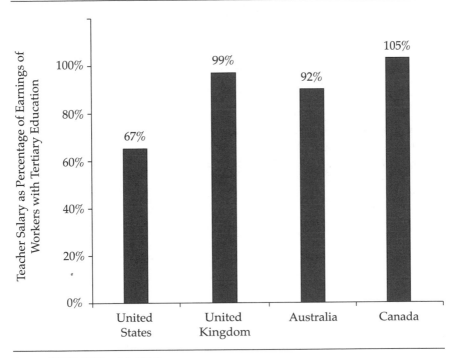

Source: OECD (2012, table D3.1).
Note: The figure shows the mean primary school teacher salary as a percentage of earnings for workers with tertiary education.

There is also evidence that school reforms that bring in more committed teachers improve achievement for disadvantaged students; this is true both in successful charter schools and in applications of successful charter school models in public schools.[65]

Raising teacher quality is challenging but not impossible, and the pay-offs for the United States would be large.[66] In fact, an ambitious national campaign is under way in the United States to raise the quality of the teaching workforce. In particular, researchers and policymakers are working to develop better methods to train and mentor teachers and to identify effective (and ineffective) ones.[67]

What can we learn from other countries about raising the quality of teachers and achieving a more equal distribution of teachers? Education researchers often point to the example of Finland, which has very high standards for teachers and attracts the most-qualified young people to the profession.[68] In Finland, teachers are not only highly trained (and well paid), but also have very good working conditions. The average Finnish school teacher is in the classroom delivering lessons three hours a day, in contrast to five hours a day for the average U.S. school teacher.[69] This schedule gives Finnish teachers more time for preparation and also more time to meet with colleagues to talk about teaching strategies and pupil progress.

Closer to home, Canada also has a high-quality teaching workforce. A 2011 OECD study reported that Canadian teachers are drawn from the top 30 percent of college graduates.[70] One Canadian teacher explained that it was hard to get into a teachers college in Canada but added that "there was a loophole—you could always cross the border to the United States. Anyone can get credentialed there."[71]

Of course, having a teaching workforce of high average quality does not necessarily ensure that teachers are equally distributed. The coordinated pay and promotion structures of centralized teaching systems (as in the United Kingdom, Australia, and Canada) at least ensure that teacher salaries are not *lower* in disadvantaged areas. A further step would be to pay teachers higher salaries to teach in more-disadvantaged areas or schools.[72]

Reforms to Ability Grouping and Retention Policy

There is also a good deal of research under way on using ability grouping and grade retention more effectively—that is, to help raise achievement among struggling students rather than to set them on a path to near-certain failure. A key factor seems to be the role of aspirations and expectations. If the goal of ability grouping or other remedial programming is to help ensure that all children learn the age-appropriate material, then such programming can be very effective in reducing achievement gaps. This model is in contrast to one in which children in different groups are taught different material, which merely serves to reinforce or even widen gaps; with this latter model, those who are lagging never catch up, and indeed, they often fall further behind. So the issue is not so much whether or not schools use ability grouping, but how they use it. OECD analysts point out, for example, that Canadian schools use ability grouping about as much as U.S. schools do but have more equal achievement outcomes because of how they use ability groups.[73] In the United States, the Success for

All school reform model provides other examples of how to use ability grouping in a positive way to improve achievement for struggling students.[74]

Similarly, grade retention can have quite different effects depending on its purpose and how it is implemented. A good deal of the research has found that retention leads to poorer outcomes—in particular, lower levels of achievement and a greater likelihood of dropping out—for the students who are held back.[75] But several rigorous studies have reached the opposite conclusion: recent reforms (in states such as Florida and Illinois) to end social promotion and require failing students to repeat a grade have led to gains in achievement.[76]

Raising Aspirations and Expectations

As mentioned earlier, a key factor in using ability groups and retention more effectively is the role of aspirations and expectations. *Whole school reforms* attempt to change the entire culture of a school, and in particular to increase the academic focus of the school and instill the expectation that all children can and should learn.[77] In schools adopting the Success for All model, for instance, the goal is to have all students achieve success in reading; to that end, teachers assess students frequently and assign tutors to work closely with students who are falling behind.[78]

The Knowledge Is Power Program (KIPP) charter schools in the United States provide another example of a whole school reform that emphasizes raising aspirations and expectations.[79] KIPP schools have a good track record of raising disadvantaged children's achievement—through a clear focus on goals and a no-excuses culture, in tandem with longer school days and years and efforts to engage and involve families.[80] The Harlem Children's Zone schools, using a similar model, have achieved similar success in raising the achievement of low-SES children.[81]

The economist Roland Fryer, who directs the Education Lab at Harvard University, emphasizes the role of high expectations in whole school reform, along with four other active ingredients: frequent teacher feedback, the use of data to guide instruction, tutoring, and more instructional time. He tested these five elements in a set of reforms implemented in the Houston public schools and found that the package led to substantial achievement gains for disadvantaged students.[82]

As mentioned earlier, Finland has greatly improved its performance both in terms of average achievement and equality of achievement. In addition to highly qualified teachers, another key ingredient in the Finnish story is the fact that students are held to a uniformly high standard. All students are taught the same curriculum, even students who may require extra help to learn the material. (In fact, nearly half of Finnish students do receive extra help at some point during their school years.)[83]

Extending the School Day or Year

Extending the school day or year is another school-level policy that holds promise as a means to reduce SES gaps in achievement. As mentioned earlier, this is one of the elements that Roland Fryer identified in successful schools, and one that also characterizes KIPP schools and the Harlem Children's Zone schools.

The United States differs from other countries in the length of its school year. U.S. schools are open thirty-six weeks a year, compared to thirty-seven weeks in Canada, thirty-eight weeks in the United Kingdom, and forty weeks in Australia.[84] Not only is the school year shorter in the United States, but the summer break is particularly long. There is a good deal of evidence that SES gaps in achievement widen during the long summer holiday in the United States, then narrow again when children are back in school.[85] There is also good evidence that educational programs offered during the summer can help counter summer learning loss among disadvantaged children.[86] Many school districts have achieved learning gains for disadvantaged students through summer school programs (whether mandatory or voluntary).[87] In addition, several experimental studies have found that home-based summer programs that provide books to children lead to reading gains for low-income children.[88]

There may also be a role for extending the school day. As of 2012, more than one thousand schools in thirty-six states had extended the school day and were offering a range of programming, including both additional lessons and extracurricular activity time.[89] It makes intuitive sense that the opportunity to learn should matter—that children will learn more when they are taught for longer periods of time. And research shows that more time on task is beneficial. For example, disadvantaged children make greater gains in math in elementary school when their teachers spend more time on math and teach them more advanced math content.[90] But research to date on extended days is somewhat mixed. As mentioned earlier, Roland Fryer, in his analysis of school reforms, identified a longer school day or year as one of the key elements of success. But a large evaluation of an extended learning time initiative in Massachusetts had disappointing results.[91] The key is likely to be how the extended time is used and in particular the extent to which it is connected to the regular school day programming and to individual student needs. What probably differentiates the successful schools that Fryer studied from more run-of-the-mill extended day programs is that the former tightly linked their extended day program to their regular program and focused on addressing the learning needs of struggling students.

In-School Tutoring

A host of experimental studies have shown that in-school tutoring—extra instruction provided in school for struggling students—is an effective way to boost student learning.[92] But having teachers provide such tutoring is costly. For this reason, there is a good deal of interest in the role of other types of tutoring that schools might provide to raise the achievement of low-performing students.

Peer tutoring—students tutoring each other—looks to be very promising. Research has shown that even low-performing students can effectively tutor their peers, if given proper training and materials, and that both the tutors and tutees gain from the experience.[93] There is also a growing evidence base on paraprofessional tutoring—adults who are not trained teachers working with students individually or in very small groups. The Match program, which pairs paraprofessional tutors with pairs of struggling students for an extra hour a day of tuition, has produced impressive achievement gains in Boston, Lawrence (Massachusetts), Houston, and Chicago.[94]

Other Supports Within Schools

There is probably also a role for other supports within schools. The education policy scholar Helen Ladd cites evidence on the effects of elementary school guidance counselors on student test scores.[95] She and others have also argued that there is a role to be played by school-based health clinics, given that health problems are more prevalent among low-SES students and that such problems may be a barrier to learning.[96]

Reducing Class Size?

The patterns in our data also help shed light on school-level factors that do *not* seem to be strongly implicated in the SES gap in achievement. For example, when we looked at data on class size, we found that SES disparities in class size in the United States were minimal. We also found that the United States had, if anything, smaller class sizes than our comparison countries. This is consistent with evidence from the OECD, which found in 2010 that primary school classes on average had twenty students in the United States, compared to twenty-three students in Australia and twenty-six in the United Kingdom.[97] (The OECD does not have data on Canadian class sizes, which vary by province, but in recent years these have averaged twenty or more.[98]) So class size does not emerge as a clear "smoking gun" in the way that other factors do.

This is not to say that class size does not matter for student achievement. There is a good deal of evidence that reducing class size can lead to better overall achievement and more equal achievement.[99] The strongest evidence comes from the Tennessee STAR experiment, which found that class size reductions led to gains in student achievement, particularly in the early grades and particularly for disadvantaged children.[100] Tennessee STAR also led to higher college enrollment, and researchers have found that the benefits of the program outweighed the costs.[101] However, some class size reforms have produced smaller effects, and given the relatively high cost of class size reductions, many analysts have concluded that other school reforms might be a more cost-effective way to reduce inequality.[102]

THE ROLE OF OTHER ASPECTS OF SOCIETY

As indicated earlier, there is also a role for government and other aspects of society in helping to address the family- and school-level factors that are linked to SES gaps in achievement. For example, the evidence supports a role for more government funding for proven parenting and preschool programs and for legislative action to improve incomes for low-income families. There is also clearly a huge challenge ahead for all levels of government, as well as the nonprofit sector, to raise the quality of the teaching workforce and improve and equalize the quality of schools.

In addition, there may be a role for community organizations and civil society. Although we do not know precisely how important out-of-school activities and summer programs are for children's achievement, we do know that high-SES families in the United States believe that they are important and are investing in them more heavily than ever before, while low- and middle-SES families do not have the resources to keep up. The political scientist Robert Putnam, in his book *Our Kids,* argues that these disparities create an important "opportunity gap."[103] So there may be a role for community and civic organizations to play, either in offering such activities and programs directly to less-advantaged children or in helping to raise and provide funds to enable them to take part. This is certainly an area where more experimentation and evidence is needed.

CONCLUSION

We draw two main conclusions from the work we have carried out for this book and from the analysis and review of evidence in this chapter.

First, and most important, the strong associations we see between socioeconomic status and children's achievement in the United States—and the resultant inequality of opportunity—are not inevitable. The evidence from other countries makes clear that the SES gap does not have to be as large as it is in the United States. This country is leaving too many children behind—and it can do better.

Second, there are some concrete steps that the United States could take to reduce the SES gap in achievement. We reviewed many promising policies, but among them, three are worth highlighting:

1. *Policies to provide more support for children's early learning* through more widespread availability of evidence-based parenting programs for families with infants and toddlers and through universal preschool for three- and four-year-olds

2. *Policies to improve the quality of teaching and learning in schools* by recruiting, supporting, and adequately compensating more effective teachers, implementing more rigorous curricula, and setting higher expectations and providing more support for low-achieving students

3. *Policies to raise family incomes for poor and near-poor families* through provisions such as an increased minimum wage and more generous Child Tax Credits and Earned Income Tax Credits.

The challenge facing the United States is not a simple one. The SES gap in achievement is large, and it has many causes. But it is not intractable. The evidence from our peer countries indicates clearly that the United States can do better. The evidence is also clear that making headway on this challenge will yield multiple benefits. Improving the achievement of today's children will pay off in many ways, not least in raising the education level of tomorrow's parents and the opportunities for their children—America's collective future.

Notes

CHAPTER 1   INTRODUCTION

1. The discussion of "good luck comes to those who work hard" as a mantra is informed by "Mantra of the Day: Luck Comes to Those Who Work Hard," Last Voices Channel, uploaded July 12, 2009, available at: http://www .youtube.com/watch?v=n-2Z1lP8fR0 (accessed March 2, 2014).

2. The public opinion poll, conducted in 2009 by the Pew Charitable Trust, was based on responses from 2,119 Americans chosen according to acceptable statistical methodology. The exact wording of the question was: "Some people use the term ECONOMIC MOBILITY to describe the ability of individuals to move up or down the income ladder over a lifetime or from one generation to the next. I am going to read you a list of factors that may contribute to a person's economic mobility, that is, their ability to improve themselves financially and get ahead in life. For each one I read, please tell me if this is essential, very important, somewhat important, not very important or not important at all?" See Pew Charitable Trust (2011).

3. Nicholas Kristof, "When Even the Starting Line is Out of Reach," *New York Times*, February 22, 2014.

4. There is a very large and developed literature on the theory of the structure and development of the human brain, and particularly its plasticity. One book that outlines the major findings but also frames them in terms of public policy implications is Keating and Hertzman (1999). Professor Heckman has also written extensively on these topics using an economic framework. The discussion in the text draws on some of his more policy-oriented publications on readiness to learn, skills development, and the returns to investment in education, especially Heckman (2008) and Knudsen et al. (2006). See also James J. Heckman, "Lifelines for Poor Children," *New York Times*, September 14, 2013.

5. The information on the growing gap in enrichment expenditures between rich and poor families (families in the top and bottom fifths of the income distribution, respectively) controls for inflation and is measured in 2014 con-

stant dollars. The first set of figures consider expenditures by families in 1972 and 1973; the latter figures are drawn from 2005 and 2006. See Duncan and Murnane (2011), figure 1.6.

6. For an article on the causal impact of money on child development that also cites a number of related studies, see Moises Velasquez-Manoff, "What Happens When the Poor Receive a Stipend?" *New York Times,* January 18, 2014. Additional research on the same theme includes Dahl and Lochner (2012) and, more generally, Mayer (1998).

7. Kristof, "When Even the Starting Line is Out of Reach." Kristof's article received a number of comments from some of the newspaper's readership, some of whom suggested that Johnny's circumstances were not the result of his bad luck but of choices made by his mother; Kristof summarizes and responds to these comments in "The Compassion Gap," *New York Times,* March 1, 2014.

8. Katherine Bouton, "A Son's Deafness Prompts a Scientific Journey," *New York Times,* April 15, 2014.

9. NCLB called for "closing the achievement gap between high- and low-performing children, especially the achievement gaps between minority and nonminority students, and between disadvantaged children and their more advantaged peers"; see U.S. Department of Education, "Laws & Guidance: Elementary and Secondary Education: Title I—Improving the Academic Achievement of the Disadvantaged," available at: http://www2.ed.gov /policy/elsec/leg/esea02/pg1.html (accessed July 3, 2014). Historically, research on the achievement gap in the United States focused on the black-white test score gap (Jencks and Phillips 1998; Magnuson and Waldfogel 2008). More recently, attention has turned to the gap between low- and high-socioeconomic status (SES) children. Important recent research by Sean Reardon (2011) has shown that the gap in achievement between the poorest and wealthiest children has been growing in the United States and now exceeds the gap between black and white children.

10. The PISA tests are organized by the Organization for Economic Cooperation and Development (OECD); see OECD, "About PISA," at: http://www.oecd. org/pisa/aboutpisa/. In the United States, the tests are administered by the National Center for Education Statistics (NCES); see NCES, "Program for International Student Assessment (PISA)," at: http://nces.ed.gov/surveys/ pisa/. The PISA tests are specifically designed to be comparable across countries and are very widely cited by researchers and policymakers (although some U.S. analysts criticize them for not being fully comparable; see, for example, Carnoy and Rothstein 2013; Loveless 2012).

11. See chapter 7 for more details.

12. Throughout the book, we define parents' SES as follows: low-SES parents have a high school degree or less, medium-SES parents have some education

beyond high school but no college degree, and high-SES parents have a bachelor's degree or higher.

13. For an example of the methods used to formally evaluate causal impacts of school reforms, see the analysis of the Harlem Children's Zone by Will Dobbie and Roland Fryer (2011). This study suggests that, when proper methods mimicking an experimental design with random assignment are used, the Harlem Children's Zone schools increase student performance to the point of closing the black-white gap in mathematics and language.

14. Specific examples of high-performing kindergarten and elementary classrooms are described in chapters 5 and 6 of Duncan and Murnane (2014). See also the three school-based initiatives described on the associated website, available at: http://restoringopportunity.com/ (accessed March 27, 2014).

CHAPTER 2   THE MEANING AND MEASUREMENT OF EQUAL OPPORTUNITY

1. More information on the U.S. data set, the Early Childhood Longitudinal Study: Kindergarten Class of 1998–99, is provided in the technical appendix. See also National Center for Education Statistics (NCES), "Early Childhood Longitudinal Study (ECLS-K): Kindergarten Class of 1998-99 (ECLS-K)," available at: http://nces.ed.gov/ecls/kindergarten.asp (accessed June 24, 2014).

2. Amanda Ripley, the noted journalist, built upon this research in her book *The Smartest Kids in the World: And How They Got That Way*. She casts a critical light on the American education system by telling the story of some particularly motivated American teenagers who spent a year abroad navigating high schools in countries where students get the highest test scores.

3. Roemer and Trannoy (2013), 3.

4. In other words, the fraction of the differences in outcomes reflecting differences in opportunities as opposed to differences in "effort" depends on how finely grained we make the categories used to define the groups. These divisions are an empirical representation of the value judgment the researcher brings to the analysis.

5. Roemer and Trannoy (2013), 45.

6. Ibid., 55.

7. Fishkin (2014a).

8. Esping-Andersen (2004) and Jencks et al. (1972). Drawing on work by James Fishkin (1983), John Ermisch, Markus Jäntti, Timothy Smeeding, and James Wilson (2012) refer to a "liberal trilemma"—the tension between the principles of merit, equality of life chances, and autonomy of the family.

9. As is clear from figures 2.3 and 2.4, this perspective implies that there is not just one gap but many. The gaps for children ranked exactly in the middle of

the distribution for their group, at the fiftieth percentile, are 0.64 standard deviation units between the high- and medium-SES groups, and 0.44 units between the medium- and low-SES group, giving a total of a 1.08 gap between the "median" child from the most- and least-advantaged groups. The gap is somewhat larger or smaller if we instead select children who do particularly well (or badly) relative to other children in their group. The high-low-SES gap in math at the ninetieth percentile, for example, is smaller at 0.94 units, while the gap at the tenth percentile is larger at 1.14.

10. Fishkin (2014b).

11. See, for example, Goldin and Katz (2008), and Garfinkel, Rainwater, and Smeeding (2010).

12. Lemann (1999), 48–49.

13. Garey Ramey and Valerie Ramey (2010) document a "rug rat race" in the time U.S. parents spend with their children and show that this is not the case for Canadian parents. See also Duncan and Murnane (2011), Kornrich and Furstenberg (2013), and Kaushal, Magnuson, and Waldfogel (2011) for documentation of wide and growing SES gaps in investments in children, particularly in the United States. The media have also reported an "educational arms race" in the United Kingdom; see, for example, Aditya Chakrabortty, "Why School Trips to New York Mean an Educational Arms Race for Parents," *The Guardian*, April 14, 2014; and Libby Page, "Auctioning Off Unpaid Internships Is Wrong," *The Guardian*, May 8, 2014. Interviews and fieldwork with parents in the United States indicate the importance that middle- and upper-class parents place on extracurricular activities for their children; see Lareau (2003), Levey (2009), and Luthar and Becker (2002).

14. See, for example, Davies and Hammack (2005). There has been a good deal of interest in expanding such opportunities for youth in the United States and the United Kingdom. U.S. policymakers have long been concerned about youth who do not complete a college education and have called for the development of alternative opportunities for these youth; see, for example, President Barack Obama's State of the Union Address of January 28, 2014, available at: http://www.whitehouse.gov/the-press-office/2014/01/28/president-barack-obamas-state-union-address (accessed July 21, 2014). In the United Kingdom, policymakers have also been concerned about this group and have called for expanded education and training opportunities for them; see, for example, the May 21, 2012, address by Labour Party leader Ed Miliband, "Speech to the Sutton Trust on Social Mobility," available at: http://archive.labour.org.uk/ed-miliband-speech-on-social-mobility-to-the-sutton-trust.

15. For example, Boudarbat, Lemieux, and Riddell (2006) show that the college wage premium has risen by much less in Canada than in the United States.

CHAPTER 3   RESOURCES FOR CHILDREN

1. John Watson, *Behaviorism* (1925), quoted in Ridley (2003), 256.
2. Francis Galton, "The History of Twins, as a Criterion of the Relative Powers of Nature and Nurture," *Fraser's Magazine* 12(1875): 566–76, quoted in Ridley (2003), 73.
3. Matt Ridley provides an overview of the work on gene-environment interactions in his 2003 book *Nature Via Nurture*.
4. Frances Champagne (2010) provides an overview of epigenetics across the life span.
5. There is a large and contested body of literature on genes, environment, and gene-environment interactions and their implications for differences in intelligence. Nisbett (2009) and Nisbett et al. (2012) provide a helpful overview and give particular attention to differences by socioeconomic status.
6. Waldfogel (2006) provides a more detailed overview.
7. See, for example, Shonkoff and Phillips (2000).
8. Steinberg (2011).
9. This welfare state typology was originally put forward by Gøsta Esping-Andersen (1990) and has since been updated by him and other scholars to include a wider range of countries and to take fuller account of the role played by gender and other factors.
10. For more information on the "most similar case" approach, see Seawright and Gerring (2008).
11. The Luxembourg Income Study (LIS) database reports Gini coefficients of equivalized household disposable income of 0.36, 0.34, 0.31, and 0.32 for the United States, the United Kingdom, Australia, and Canada, respectively, in 2003–2004. See Luxembourg Income Study, "Inequality and Poverty Key Figures," at: http://www.lisdatacenter.org/data-access/key-figures/inequality-and-poverty/.
12. For an overview of recent reforms and estimates of their impact on spending and student outcomes, see Jackson, Johnson, and Persico (2014).
13. Herman (2013).
14. Department for Education (2013).
15. The low-educated group is made up of those who did not complete high school and those who completed high school but acquired no further education. Among the non–high school graduates, some may have obtained other certificates or qualifications. This group was particularly large in Australia, where 45 percent of the parents in our sample were in the low-educated group: 13 percent did not complete high school and had no other qualification; 19 percent did not complete high school but had some other certificate or qualification; and 12 percent completed high school but had no further

education. We code the "other certificate or qualification" group as low-educated because their incomes were similar to incomes for other low-educated parents, and lower than for the middle-educated group.

16. See appendix table A3.1.

17. Isabel Sawhill (2014) provides a review of the evidence on teen parenthood; for a review of the evidence on single-parent families, see McLanahan, Tach, and Schneider (2013).

18. For additional details, see appendix table A3.6. As the sociologist Andrew Cherlin (2014) points out, a distinctive feature of the U.S. situation is the instability of nonmarital living arrangements, with high rates of single parenthood and repartnership among the nonmarried.

19. McLanahan (2004).

20. See appendix table A3.9.

21. See appendix table A3.7.

22. Fortunately, most U.S. children receive medical care regardless of SES: 92 percent of kindergarteners with the least-educated parents in our sample had been seen for routine care in the past year, and 95 percent of those with middle- or high-educated parents had received care. But SES is associated with gaps in the receipt of dental care: 78 percent of kindergarteners of the least-educated parents had been seen by a dentist in the last year, compared to 84 percent of children of middle-educated parents and 89 percent of children of the most-educated.

23. Jeanne Brooks-Gunn and Lisa Markman (2005); Ariel Kalil and Tom DeLeire (2004); Meredith Phillips (2011); Phillips et al. (1998); Waldfogel (2006) and Waldfogel and Washbrook (2011a).

24. See also appendix table A3.8.

25. Susan Mayer (1998) argued that the causal effects of income for children had been overstated, but there is now good causal evidence showing that children benefit from exogenous increases in family income. See, for example, Dahl and Lochner (2012), Evans and Garthwaite (2010), Milligan and Stabile (2008), and Strully, Rehkopf, and Xuan (2010).

26. Family income changes over time as parents mature and make gains in the labor market, or perhaps encounter setbacks or negative shocks. To better approximate the "permanent income" available to children, we average the income that families report at three different points in time—when the child is approximately ages five, seven, and eleven). Our measure of family income includes government benefits. These are included in reported income in the data we use for the United Kingdom, Australia, and Canada. Some important benefits (for example, food stamps and tax credits) are not included in the U.S. data, so we impute them. However, our income measure does not reflect taxes paid. To make income figures comparable across countries, we express all income amounts in 2011 U.S. dollars (adjusting them across countries us-

ing a measure that reflects purchasing power parity, or PPP). It is important to note that time differences across the cohorts will affect this comparison, if incomes have grown in real terms over time. The U.S. sample comes from the earliest year (born roughly 1993); however, incomes have been relatively stable at the bottom over this period. We provide more detailed information about incomes in our samples in the technical appendix (including information on mean income and income at the tenth and ninetieth percentiles; see appendix table A3.2). This more detailed information confirms the pattern of greater inequality of income in the United States and the United Kingdom than in Australia and Canada.

27. For example, 45 percent of Australian children are in the lowest parental education group, but among Australian children who are in the bottom income quintile, 68 percent are in this lowest-educated group—a concentration ratio of 1.5 (= 68/45). The corresponding ratios in the other countries are 2.0 or greater. Australia is also an outlier at the top of the income distribution, where the difference is partly due to the high education but low income of immigrants. See the technical appendix for more details.

28. Appendix table A3.2.

29. We can also characterize households by whether any parent is employed or whether the household is "workless" (no parent employed). We find that this phenomenon was most common in the United Kingdom (followed by Australia) and was strongly socially graded in all four countries. However, despite these cross-national variations in worklessness, the income levels of families in the most-disadvantaged SES groups were quite similar because of cash transfer programs.

30. Bradbury and Jäntti (2001), figure 3.7.

CHAPTER 4   GAPS AT SCHOOL ENTRY

1. We have compared the SES gaps in vocabulary and reading for children from the Early Childhood Longitudinal Study: Birth Cohort (ECLS-B), which followed U.S. children born around 2001 from birth to school entry. (The results are in the technical appendix, section A4.2.) The high-low education gaps are very similar for vocabulary and reading. The ECLS-K measures used in this book are primarily a combination of vocabulary and reading scores, and so we conclude that they will provide estimates of high-low gaps that are comparable to the vocabulary scores in the other countries.

2. We adjust scores for the child's age at the time of the assessment (since children were tested at various ages). All our estimates take account of the survey weights to best reflect the population characteristics. Our estimates of statistical significance similarly take account of the design features of the surveys. We do not make any adjustments to take account of possible reliability

differences between the tests. In the technical appendix (section A4.1), however, we show that for plausible patterns of reliability the significant differences in high-low SES gaps that we observe here would still remain.

3. See the technical appendix for details about the source of the PIRLS data and our analysis of it. The technical appendix also provides more discussion of the data in other years and other measures.

4. See the technical appendix for details. Depending on the age of the child and the country, in some instances we also have measures of the child's behavior as reported by the teacher. Because teacher and parent reports differ, and because it is parents' reports that we have consistently available across our four countries at around age five, we use the data from parents' reports here.

5. Some aspects of attention skills overlap with constructs such as conscientiousness and "grit" (a shorthand term for skills related to effort and persistence); see Duckworth and Eskreis-Winkler (2013) and Tough (2012).

6. Duncan et al. (2007); Greg Duncan and Katherine Magnuson (2011). Adolescents who score higher on "grit" go on to have higher grade point averages and watch fewer hours of TV (Duckworth and Quinn 2009). And adolescents who have more self-discipline have higher school achievement; indeed, there is evidence that self-discipline predicts school performance more strongly than IQ does (Duckworth and Seligman 2005). Both grit and self-discipline are related to conscientiousness, which develops throughout childhood and reflects self-control, industriousness, responsibility, orderliness, and other factors (see, for example, Eisenberg et al., in press).

7. Duncan et al. (2007).

8. Results by income quintile show once again that the United States has the largest top-bottom gap, followed by the United Kingdom, Australia, and Canada (see the technical appendix). These results echo the similar patterns we found in analyses of more recent cohorts of children in the United States, Australia, and Canada (and the same cohort of U.K. children) (Bradbury et al., 2012).

9. If we limit the U.S. sample to non-Hispanic whites, we continue to see a larger high-low gap in the United States than in the full populations of the other three countries, although the overall gap is reduced from 1.00 standard deviation to 0.86 standard deviation. (The high-medium gap remains at about half of a standard deviation, but the medium-low gap falls to 0.36; see technical appendix figure A4.2.)

10. See table 4.2 and technical appendix table A4.9 for details.

11. Kaushal, Magnuson, and Waldfogel (2011).

12. See technical appendix table A4.12 for details.

13. These results are in some cases assembled from multiple questions. See the technical appendix for details.

14. See discussion in Kaushal, Magnuson, and Waldfogel (2011).

15. Kornrich and Furstenberg (2013).
16. Ibid.
17. Kornrich, Gauthier, and Furstenberg (2011).
18. For details, see technical appendix table A4.13.
19. See, for example, MacKenzie et al. (2013).
20. See technical appendix table A4.10 for details.
21. Ruhm and Waldfogel (2012) and Yoshikawa et al. (2013).
22. Magnuson and Waldfogel (2014).
23. See technical appendix table A4.11 for details.
24. Magnuson and Waldfogel (2012).
25. See, for example, Brennan and Fenech (2014).
26. Doherty, Friendly, and Beach (2003).
27. Waldfogel (2010).
28. When we disaggregate by income quintile rather than parental education, the bottom three quintiles have similar levels of preschool use and the increase is found only among the top two quintiles. The percentages in preschool are 62, 64, 62, 71, and 83 for the lowest to highest income quintile groups, respectively.
29. See, for example, Smolensky and Gootman (2003) and Waldfogel (2006).
30. The middle-quintile group worked an average of twenty-seven hours per week, with 62 percent of their children in preschool, while the top quintile worked twenty-five hours per week and had 83 percent of their children in preschool.
31. See, for example, Kornrich et al. (2011), Kaushal, Magnuson, and Waldfogel (2011), and Magnuson and Waldfogel (2012).

CHAPTER 5   GAPS IN THE SCHOOL YEARS

1. Coleman et al. (1966).
2. See, for example, Mosteller and Moynihan (1972) and Jencks et al. (1972). Gamoran and Long (2007) provide a review of other reanalyses of Coleman et al. (1966).
3. Gamoran and Long (2007).
4. Ladd (2012).
5. See, for example, Ravitch (2010).
6. These statistics and those that follow are from the TIMSS administered between 1995 and 2007. We emphasize the years and grades closest to the cohorts we analyze. Note that TIMSS data for the United Kingdom are for England only. Note also that other studies provide lower estimates of the proportion of variation between schools for the United States; see Hedges and Hedberg (2007). See the technical appendix for more details.

7. Magnuson, Waldfogel, and Washbrook (2012) and Ermisch and Del Bono (2012).
8. For the United States, see Dobbie and Fryer (2013) and Jacob and Ludwig (2009). Looking across countries, OECD (2013a) highlights four policy approaches that it sees as leading to improved performance *and* improved equity: (1) targeting students and schools with low achievement (regardless of their SES); (2) targeting disadvantaged children; (3) adopting universal policies to raise standards for all students; and (4) including marginalized students in mainstream schools and classes. Andreas Schleicher (2009), who leads the comparative program of educational research at OECD, offers a detailed set of prescriptions: (1) limit early tracking and selection; (2) manage school choice;)3) prevent dead ends and dropout in secondary school; (4) offer second chances; (5) provide early help to those who are falling behind instead of relying on grade repetition; (6) strengthen links between home and school; (7) take active steps to engage children of immigrants and minority groups; (8) prioritize funding for early childhood education and basic education; (9) provide extra resources to areas and schools with the greatest need; and (10) set specific targets for equity (see also Field, Kuczera, and Pont 2007).
9. Jackson, Johnson, and Persico (2014, 2015).
10. See the overview in Nisbett (2009) and a review of the evidence in Borman et al. (2003).
11. Angrist, Pathak, and Walters (2013). For an overview of KIPP and its approach, see Matthews (2009).
12. Dobbie and Fryer (2011) and Tough (2008).
13. The five policies are discussed in Dobbie and Fryer (2013). The Houston reforms are described in Fryer (2014).
14. See, for example, Aaronson, Barrow, and Sander (2007); Kane, Rockoff, and Staiger (2008); Rivkin, Hanushek, and Kain (2005); Rockoff (2004); and Sanders and Rivers (1996).
15. An example of a study that did find that teacher math SAT scores and certification status were predictive of student achievement is Boyd et al. (2008).
16. Rivkin et al. (2005), Kane et al. (2008), and Rockoff (2004).
17. See, for example, Ronfeldt, Loeb, and Wyckoff (2013).
18. Betts, Reuben, and Danenberg (2000); Clotfelter, Ladd, and Vigdor (2006); Hanushek, Kain, and Rivkin (2004); Lankford, Loeb, and Wyckoff (2002); Murnane and Steele (2007). Even within schools, low-achieving students are assigned less-experienced teachers; see Kalogrides, Loeb, and Béteille (2013).
19. Murnane and Steele (2007).
20. Loveless (2013).
21. See reviews by Adam Gamoran (2010) and Herman Van de Werfhorst and Jonathan Mijs (2010). For example, Christy Lleras and Claudia Rangel (2009), analyzing data from ECLS-K, find that, in the first few years of school, stu-

dents placed in low-ability groups learn substantially less and students placed in high-ability groups learn slightly more; thus, overall achievement is lower, and inequality is higher, than for students who were not grouped. Takako Nomi (2010) finds that these effects are particularly pronounced in the low-SES and high-minority schools that are most likely to use ability grouping (whereas ability grouping can have more benign or even positive effects in more-advantaged schools).

22. Courtney Collins and Li Gan (2013), for example, find gains for both low- and high-ability students in their study of sorting in the third and fourth grades in the Dallas school system.

23. See review in Jacob and Lefgren (2004).

24. Ibid.; see also Greene and Winters (2007) and Winters and Greene (2012). Retention may also have effects on the students who are not retained—by changing the peer groups with whom they are taught or the allocation of school resources. One study that examined the effects of retention on entire cohorts found benefits of retention (as measured by adult wage gains) across the whole distribution, suggesting that benefits accrued to both the retained and the nonretained (Babcock and Bedard 2011).

25. NAPLAN is also administered in year 3 (around ages eight and nine), but it is not available for a substantial fraction of the sample because the test program only commenced in the year after they had passed through year 3.

26. The middle panel of figure 5.1 and table 5.2 use the most comparable data available from ages seven or nine. Tables A5.2 and A5.3 in the technical appendix show the detailed data at ages seven and nine, respectively.

27. A subset of the sample has results for both these tests at the same age. Comparing these, we find that the latter test has a larger SES gap. The difference is almost exactly the same as the increase in the top-bottom gap between ages nine and eleven shown here. See the technical appendix, section A5.4, for more details.

28. See the technical appendix, section A5.6, for details.

29. For example, parent involvement with the school varies by parental SES, but how it affects student achievement appears to depend on the nature of the involvement. For example, is the parent advocating for the child to have a better teacher or to be placed in a different class, or is the parent simply attending school meetings?

30. See the review in Kaushal, Magnuson, and Waldfogel (2011).

31. Lareau (2003).

32. Benson and Borman (2010), Burkam et al. (2004), Downey, von Hippel, and Broh (2004), Entwistle and Alexander (1992), Heyns (1978, 1987), and Murnane (1975).

33. See technical appendix tables A5.6–A5.16 for detailed results for both out-of-school resources and school resources.

34. See technical appendix table A5.4.
35. The large U.S. gaps in computer use and book ownership are made all the more salient when we consider other data from the 2011 Progress in International Reading Literacy Study (PIRLS) (Mullis et al. 2012), which reports a lower average level of home learning resources in U.S. families (as shown in table A5.4).
36. See technical appendix table A5.6.
37. See technical appendix table A5.7.
38. See technical appendix table A5.8.
39. See technical appendix table A5.9.
40. See technical appendix table A5.10.
41. See technical appendix table A5.11.
42. See, for example, Krueger and Whitmore (2001).
43. See technical appendix table A5.12.
44. Gamoran and Long (2007).
45. See technical appendix table A5.13.
46. See technical appendix table A5.14.
47. See technical appendix table A5.15.
48. See technical appendix table A5.16.

CHAPTER 6   DIVERGING PROGRESS THROUGH SCHOOL

1. Early research in the United States reported that inequality between SES groups narrows during the first few years of school (Stipek and Ryan 1997), but more recent large-scale studies in the United States have found that SES gaps widen during the school years (Carneiro and Heckman 2003; Rathbun, West, and Hausken 2004). Recent U.K. studies also find that inequality widens after school entry (DCSF 2009; Feinstein 2003, 2004; Goodman and Gregg 2010; Goodman, Sibieta, and Washbrook 2009). We are aware of only one prior comparative study. Analyzing SES gaps from school entry to age fourteen in the United States and one region in the United Kingdom, and using rich longitudinal data, Katherine Magnuson, Jane Waldfogel, and Elizabeth Washbrook (2012) find that patterns differ across the two countries: in the United States, SES-related gaps diminish somewhat in the first few years of school but then widen (although patterns vary depending on whether standardized or raw scores are used); in the United Kingdom, in contrast, gaps are relatively constant through primary school but then widen in secondary school. (This latter finding is consistent with evidence in Ermisch and Del Bono 2012.) Researchers have also studied how racial/ethnic gaps change during the school years (see, for example, Fryer and Levitt, 2004; Murnane et al., 2006; Reardon et al., 2012; Waldfogel, 2012a).
2. Carneiro and Heckman (2003), 163.

3. Ibid., 130, figure 2.9.
4. Feinstein (2003).
5. The Feinstein and Carneiro-Heckman studies focus on different aspects of SES inequality. Feinstein explores whether gaps emerge at later ages *holding initial ability levels constant,* while the gaps presented in Carneiro-Heckman (and in our previous chapters) reflect the combination of SES differences in both initial achievement and any subsequent development. Both studies seem to point to a worsening of SES inequality as children age. But interpretation of these findings is complicated by two factors. The first is the difficulty of measuring young children's true ability—the problem of "measurement error." The second is the fact that transitory influences on children's achievement tend to even out over time—a phenomenon known as "regression to the mean," which works to decrease between-group differences over time. We will have more to say about each of these in the next section.
6. In particular, the use of the spring rather than fall kindergarten score results in somewhat smaller estimates of the SES gaps on the first measurement occasion, while the use of the eighth-grade rather than the fifth-grade score tends to result in larger gaps on the last measurement occasion. Hence, the overall widening of inequality appears greater when measured over the particular time span considered in this chapter. The results reported here also use different sample sizes and weights than the comparative analyses of previous chapters. Detailed comparisons of estimates for the United States at all time points and under different sampling rules can be found in the technical appendix.
7. We use standardized scores for reasons discussed in chapter 2. It is important to note that trends in the size of the gaps as children age are sensitive to the metric used to measure achievement (see, for example, Bond and Lang 2013).
8. Underestimating the association between an earlier test score measured with error and a later score—persistence—is a classic example of *attenuation bias;* see, for example, Wooldridge (2002), section 4.4.2.
9. Jerrim and Vignoles (2013).
10. See, for example, Wooldridge (2002), section 5.3, and Reardon (2008) for a discussion in the context of black-white achievement gaps. The instrumental variables procedure involves the prediction of the spring achievement measure (and its square) using the fall test score (and its square). The predicted estimates of achievement in spring of kindergarten obtained from this first-stage regression are then used in place of the actual values in a second-stage regression to predict later achievement. The intuition is that the fitted values of initial achievement have been "purged" of their measurement error component and now reflect a true signal of ability that was present in both the spring and fall test scores. See the technical appendix for further details.

11. Feinstein (2004).

12. Regression to the mean was first described by Sir Francis Galton in the late nineteenth century in the context of the transmission of height across generations: children of tall parents tend to be shorter than their parents, and children of short parents tend to be taller than their parents (Galton 1886).

13. The estimates in figure 6.2 and subsequent estimates in this chapter control for any "spurious" regression to the mean due to measurement error (see box 6.1).

14. The results reported here are derived from school fixed-effects models, which effectively adjust for a common effect of the quality of the school attended by the child, one that is assumed to be the same for all children in the school, regardless of their socioeconomic status or initial achievement level. Because only a subset of children who changed schools were followed by the ECLS-K, the school a child "belonged to" is specified as the one he or she attended at the start of kindergarten. This means that the school effect picks up influences that are common to children who began school together, even if some of them subsequently moved to different schools. To assess the sensitivity of our results to student mobility we reestimated the models on the subsample of children who remained in the same school from kindergarten through fifth grade. See the technical appendix for further details.

15. Greg Duncan and his colleagues (2007) explored the relationship between teacher-reported behavior problems and early and later achievement in the ECLS-K (among other data sets). Although the behavior measures we use are not identical, we find similar results. Attention skills are significantly (if modestly) associated with later achievement when early test scores are held constant, but this is generally not the case for other domains of behavior.

CHAPTER 7   WHAT THE UNITED STATES CAN DO TO REDUCE THE SES GAP IN ACHIEVEMENT

1. See, for example, Ladd (2012) and Schleicher (2009).

2. Schleicher (2009), Paine and Schleicher (2011), and Hanushek and Woessman (2011).

3. OECD (2011), 16, table 1.1.

4. OECD (2013a), 27, figure II.1.2.

5. OECD (2013b).

6. Schütz, Ursprung, and Woessman (2008).

7. OECD (2013b), figure 3.8c and table A3.8.

8. Kelly et al. (2013). The lower averages in the United States reflect both higher shares of children with low scores and lower shares of children with high scores. In math, for instance, 12, 15, and 16 percent of U.K., Australian, and Canadian youth have high proficiency, respectively, versus only 9 percent of

U.S. youth, and only 14, 20, and 22 percent have low proficiency, versus 26 percent of U.S. youth.

9. OECD (2013a), table II.A. Note that the U.S. performance in 2012 was better than in 2003 on this metric: the share of the variance accounted for by SES fell by over four percentage points over that period.

10. OECD (2013a), table II.A.

11. See technical appendix table A7.1 for details.

12. See technical appendix table A7.2 for details.

13. On teen parenthood, see Furstenberg, Brooks-Gunn, and Chase-Lansdale (1989) and Hoffman and Maynard (2008). On the detrimental effects of family instability, see McLanahan and Sandefur (1997), McLanahan (2011), and Waldfogel, Craigie, and Brooks-Gunn (2010).

14. On the role of contraception, see Haskins and Sawhill (2009) and Sawhill, Thomas, and Monea (2010). On the role of the media, see Kearney and Levine (2014).

15. Cowan, Pape-Cowan, and Knox (2010).

16. See, for example, Edin and Kefalas (2011).

17. In a well-known study, Betty Hart and Todd Risley (1995) found that children of professional parents heard 30 million more words by the age of four than children of parents on welfare. For a discussion of this and related research, See Clinton Foundation and Next Generation (2014).

18. MacKenzie et al. (2013).

19. Waldfogel and Washbrook (2011a, 2011b). See also Duncan and Brooks-Gunn (1997) and Lee and Burkam (2002).

20. Rowe (2008) and Cunha, Elo, and Culhane (2013).

21. This is the working assumption behind the Too Small to Fail Initiative (Clinton Foundation and Next Generation 2014).

22. For an overview, see Waldfogel and Washbrook (2011a).

23. Love et al. (2013).

24. The Nurse Family Partnership Program was tested in three sites: Elmira, New York; Memphis, Tennessee; and Denver, Colorado (see Eckenrode et al. 2010; Kitzman et al. 2010; Olds et al. 2014). Although results differed somewhat across sites, significant effects were found in at least two sites on improvements in children's school readiness, as well as improvements in prenatal health, reductions of childhood injuries, reduction and slowing of subsequent pregnancies, and increases in maternal employment; see Nurse Family Partnership, "Proven Results," at: http://www.nursefamilypartner ship.org/proven-results (accessed June 11, 2014). Cost-benefit analyses have found that the program, which currently costs $9,500 per family (Olds et al. 2007), saves on average $17,000 per family, with larger effects for high-risk families than lower-risk ones (Aos et al. 2004; see also Karoly et al. 1998; Karoly, Kilburn, and Cannon 2005).

25. As of March 2014, the Nurse Family Partnership Program was serving fami-

lies in forty-three U.S. states (Nurse Family Partnership 2014). There is also a large trial under way in the United Kingdom, where the program is known as Family Nurse Partnership (Department of Health 2013). Ron Haskins and Greg Margolis (2014) provide an extensive discussion of home visiting programs, including the U.S. Nurse Family Partnership, in their book on evidence-based policymaking.

26. Landry, Smith, and Swank (2006), Landry et al. (2008), and Landry (2008).

27. Brennan et al. (2013) and Lunkenheimer et al. (2008).

28. See the review in Whitehurst and Lonigan (1998). See also Whitehurst et al. (1994).

29. Evangelou et al. (2005) and Evangelou and Sylva (2003).

30. There are also programs that have had success in helping parents better manage difficult child behavior that might also interfere with children's early learning. One is the Incredible Years Program (see Jones et al. 2007; Sonuga-Barke et al. 2001; Webster-Stratton 1994). Another is the Triple P-Positive Parenting Program (see Sanders 1999).

31. The disparities we find in preschool enrollment mirror those found in other studies of U.S. children. See, for example, Magnuson and Waldfogel (2008, 2012, 2014). As a group, children of immigrants are particularly likely to miss out on formal preschool; see Magnuson, Lahaie, and Waldfogel (2006) and Crosnoe (2007).

32. See the reviews by Almond and Currie (2011), Duncan and Magnuson (2013), Heckman and Musso (2014), Karoly et al. (1998), and Karoly et al. (2005).

33. See the reviews by Ruhm and Waldfogel (2012) and Yoshikawa et al. (2013).

34. Gormley et al. (2005) and Gormley, Phillips, and Gayer (2008).

35. Wong et al. (2008) and Barnett et al. (2010). There has been some debate recently about findings from an evaluation of Tennessee's prekindergarten program. The evaluation found that benefits at the end of the pre-K year were mostly not sustained into kindergarten and first grade (Lipsey et al. 2013). Some argue that these results undermine the case for universal pre-K (Whitehurst 2013), while others argue that the results may be biased by differential attrition and should therefore be given less weight than those from other studies (Bartik 2014). If we put the Tennessee study aside, the remaining evidence on universal pre-K in the United States is uniformly positive.

36. Weiland and Yoshikawa (2013).

37. Ruhm and Waldfogel (2012), 23. Research in progress that is evaluating the effect of the United Kingdom's recent expansion of universal preschool for three- and four-year-olds has found modest effects overall, but considerably larger benefits for children in disadvantaged areas and children with English as an additional language; see Blanden and Ben-Galim (2014).

38. One way to think about universal preschool is that it effectively enables children to start school a year or two earlier. Research on school starting age sug-

gests that starting school earlier should lead to less inequality of achievement. In the United States, the starting age for school is set by the states. Most states require that a child be five years old by October to enter kindergarten, but that cutoff ranges from as early as August 1 to as late as January 1. Research within the United States suggests that a later school starting age leads to more inequality of readiness at school entry, because when young children are not in school, higher-SES children are more likely than their low-SES peers to be in high-quality, educationally oriented preschool. A later school starting age is also associated with more inequality of eventual attainment, because low-SES children are more likely than their higher-SES peers to drop out when they reach the legal school-leaving age. School starting ages are not fully binding; in particular, parents may choose to wait to enroll a child later than when he or she is age-eligible, an option referred to as "red-shirting." Red-shirting is most common among high-SES boys and is thought to confer advantages for them because they enter school more mature and hence better able to succeed academically and behaviorally. See Deming and Dynarski (2008) and Bassok and Reardon (2013).

39. Authors' estimates from ECLS-K 1998 and ECLS-K 2010.

40. OECD (2013c).

41. Magnuson and Waldfogel (2012, 2014).

42. Recent studies have shown positive effects of the EITC on maternal health, mental health, biomarkers (Evans and Garthwaite 2010), birth weight (Strully, Rehkopf, and Xuan 2010), and child test scores (Dahl and Lochner 2012). Researchers have also found positive effects of the Canadian child benefit program on child test scores and aggression and on maternal depression (Milligan and Stabile 2008).

43. Mullainathan and Shafir (2013).

44. Bartel et al. (2014).

45. Gamoran and Long (2007).

46. Mullis et al. (2012), exhibit 5.2, p. 142.

47. See the reviews in Hanushek and Woessman (2011) and Van de Werfhorst and Mijs (2010).

48. OECD (2011) and Kerr, Pekkarinen, and Uusitalo (2013).

49. Hanushek and Woessman (2011).

50. Lareau and Goyette (2014).

51. Dee and Jacob (2011) and Reback, Rockoff, and Schwartz (2014). Internationally, there is evidence that students in countries that have external exit exams (or standardized tests) have higher achievement than students in countries without such exams; see Hanushek and Woessman (2011).

52. The Common Core State Standards were developed by the governors and education officers from forty-eight states and were voluntarily adopted by forty-three states (see the website for Common Core State Standards Initia-

tive at: http://www.corestandards.org/). But at the time of this writing in 2015, several states had taken a step back from the Common Core, and others were discussing doing so.

53. OECD (2011).
54. See, for example, van der Klaauw (2008).
55. See Card and Payne (2002).
56. See the discussion in Ladd and Fiske (2011) and in Wilson, Lambright, and Smeeding (2006).
57. Holmlund, McNally, and Viarengo (2010) and Waldfogel (2010). The U.K. government monitors progress on inequality in English state schools by comparing the outcomes of children eligible for free school meals (FSM) with those of children who are not eligible. (Around one-fifth of children are eligible for FSM, which are conditional on eligibility for means-tested benefits.) When our cohort took the national Key Stage 1 assessments in 2008, at age seven, 87 percent of non-FSM children reached the expected standard in reading, but only 69 percent of FSM children did—a gap of eighteen percentage points. The gap in writing at the same age was twenty percentage points. Four years later, when the same cohort took the Key Stage 2 assessments at age eleven, the gap in English (which combines reading and writing assessments) had fallen to fourteen percentage points. See the technical appendix for further details.
58. For further details, see Waldfogel (2010).
59. Department for Education (2013).
60. The evidence is posted in a toolkit that is available at the Education Endowment Foundation website, http://educationendowmentfoundation.org.uk/toolkit/. For an overview, see Lee Elliott Major, "Pupil Premium Toolkit: What Works Best at Raising School Achievement," available at: http://educationendowmentfoundation.org.uk/uploads/pdf/Toolkit_presentation_-_Lee_Elliot_Major.pdf (accessed July 14, 2014).
61. OECD (2011).
62. Ibid.
63. Rivkin, Hanushek, and Kain (2005).
64. Boyd et al. (2008).
65. As discussed later in the chapter, when Roland Fryer (2014) applied models from successful charter schools to public schools in Houston, the result was improvements in achievement for disadvantaged students. One of the five elements in the reform package was replacing existing teachers with more committed ones.
66. Chetty, Friedman, and Rockoff (2013a, 2013b).
67. For example, the Bill and Melinda Gates Foundation has devoted considerable resources to the Measures of Effective Teaching project (http://www

.metproject.org/index.php), which is focused on identifying and developing effective teaching.

68. Sahlberg (2011).
69. Waldfogel (2012b).
70. OECD (2011). See also Barber and Mourshed (2007).
71. OECD (2011), 70.
72. See, for example, Clotfelter, Ladd, and Vidgor (2011).
73. OECD (2011).
74. Cohen et al. (2013).
75. See the review in Jacob and Lefgren (2004).
76. Ibid.; see also Greene and Winters (2007) and Winters and Greene (2012). Retention may also have effects on the students who are not retained—by changing the peer groups with whom they are taught or the allocation of school resources. One study that examined the effects of retention on entire cohorts found benefits of retention (as measured by adult wage gains) across the whole distribution, suggesting that benefits accrued to both the retained and the nonretained; see Babcock and Bedard (2011).
77. In one type of whole school reform, the "turnaround school," an outside leader or organization is brought in to change the culture of a failing school. Turnaround school reforms have been used in the United States as well as in other countries. See, for example, Jensen and Sonnemann (2014).
78. See the overview in Nisbett (2009) and a review of the evidence in Borman et al. (2003).
79. For an overview of KIPP and its approach, see Matthews (2009).
80. Angrist, Pathak, and Walters (2013).
81. Dobbie and Fryer (2011) and Tough (2008).
82. The five policies are discussed in Dobbie and Fryer (2013). The Houston reforms are described in Fryer (2014).
83. Waldfogel (2012b).
84. OECD (2012), table D4.1.
85. The earliest studies were carried out by Richard Murnane (1975) and Barbara Heyns (1978, 1987). These studies were followed by an important examination of Baltimore school children by Doris Entwistle and Karl Alexander (1992). More recently, analyses of children from the ECLS-K have also documented a summer learning loss between kindergarten and first grade (Benson and Borman 2010; Burkam et al. 2004; Downey, von Hippel, and Broh 2004). For a review of this literature, see McCombs et al. (2011); for a meta-analysis, see Cooper et al. (1996) and Cooper et al. (2000).
86. Cooper et al. (1996), Cooper et al. (2000), and McCombs et al. (2011).
87. McCombs et al. (2011).
88. Allington et al. (2010), Kim (2004, 2006), Kim and Guryan (2010), and Kim and White (2008).

89. Travis Andersen and Evan Allen, "Program to Offer Longer School Days Expanding in Massachusetts, Four Other States," *Boston Globe,* December 2, 2012.
90. Desimone and Long (2010).
91. Checkoway et al. (2012).
92. See the review in Bloom (1984).
93. See, for example, Menesses and Gresham (2009).
94. Fryer (2014) and Cook et al. (2014).
95. Ladd (2012); see also Reback (2010) and Carrell and Hoekstra (2010).
96. Ladd (2012) and Rothstein (2004).
97. OECD (2012), table D2.1. Average student-teacher ratios are also higher in the other countries than they are in the United States. For example, in primary schools in 2010, average student-teacher ratios were 14.5 in the United States, 15.7 in Australia, and 19.8 in the United Kingdom. (Primary school data for Canada are not available, but the lower secondary ratio that year was 17.7.). See OECD (2012), table D2.2.
98. *The Guardian* (2012). "Class Size, Teacher's Pay and Spending: Which Countries Spend the Most and Pay the Least in Education?" available at: www.theguardian.com/news/datablog/2012/sep/11/education-compared-oecd-country-pisa (accessed March 6, 2015).
99. Krueger and Whitmore (2001), Ready (2008), and Whitehurst and Chingos (2011).
100. Mosteller (1995) and Krueger (1999). A comprehensive non-experimental study carried out in the United Kingdom found similar results: the benefits of smaller class sizes were concentrated in the early grades and they were particularly pronounced for disadvantaged children (Blatchford 2003).
101. Krueger (1999) and Chetty et al. (2011).
102. Hanushek (1999), Ready (2008), and Whitehurst and Chingos (2011). For both sides of the debate, see Mishel and Rothstein (2002).
103. Putnam (2015).

References

Aaronson, Daniel, Lisa Barrow, and William Sander. 2007. "Teachers and Student Achievement in the Chicago Public High Schools." *Journal of Labor Economics* 25: 95–135.

Allington, Richard, Anne McGill-Franzen, Gregory Camilli, Lunetta Williams, Jennifer Graff, Jacqueline Zeig, Courtney Zmach, and Rhonda Nowak. 2010. "Addressing Summer Reading Setback Among Economically Disadvantaged Elementary Students." *Reading Psychology* 31(5): 411–27.

Almond, Douglas, and Janet Currie. 2011. "Human Capital Development Before Age Five." In *Handbook of Labor Economics*, vol. 4b, edited by Orley Ashenfelter and David Card. Amsterdam: Elsevier.

Angrist, Joshua, Parag A. Pathak, and Christopher R. Walters. 2013. "Explaining Charter School Effectiveness." *American Economic Journal: Applied Economics* 5(4): 1–27.

Aos, Steve, Roxanne Lieb, Jim Mayfield, Marna Miller, and Annie Pennucci. 2004. *Benefits and Costs of Prevention and Early Intervention Programs for Youth*. Olympia: Washington State Institute for Public Policy.

Babcock, Philip, and Kelly Bedard. 2011. "The Wages of Failure: New Evidence on School Retention and Long-Run Outcomes." *Education Finance and Policy* 6(3): 293–322. DOI:10.1162/EDFP_a_00037.

Barber, Michael, and Mona Mourshed. 2007. *How the World's Best-Performing School Systems Come Out on Top*. London: McKinsey and Company.

Barnett, Steven, Dale Epstein, Megan Carolan, Jen Fitzgerald, Debra Ackerman, and Alison Friedman. 2010. *The State of Preschool, 2010*. New Brunswick, N.J.: Rutgers University, National Institute for Early Education Research. Available at: http://nieer.org/publications/state-preschool-2010 (accessed April 30, 2015).

Bartel, Ann, Charles Baum, Maya Rossin-Slater, Christopher Ruhm, and Jane Waldfogel. 2014. "California's Paid Family Leave Law: Lessons from the First Decade." Report prepared for the U.S. Department of Labor, Office of the As-

175

sistant Secretary for Policy, Chief Evaluation Office (June 23). Available at: http://www.dol.gov/asp/evaluation/reports/PaidLeaveDeliverable.pdf (accessed January 5, 2015).

Bartik, Timothy. 2014. "Whitehurst's Latest Comments on Pre-K." Available at investinginkids (blog by Tim Bartik), April 7, http://investinginkids.net/2014/04/07/whitehursts-latest-comments-on-pre-k (accessed June 13, 2014).

Bassok, Daphna, and Sean F. Reardon. 2013. "'Academic Redshirting' in Kindergarten: Prevalence, Patterns, and Implications." *Educational Evaluation and Policy Analysis* 35(3): 283–97. DOI:10.3102/0162373713482764.

Benson, James, and Geoffrey Borman. 2010. "Family, Neighborhood, and School Settings Across Seasons: When Do Socioeconomic Context and Racial Composition Matter for the Reading Achievement Growth of Young Children?" *Teachers College Record* 112(5): 1338–90.

Betts, Julian R., Kim S. Reuben, and Anne Danenberg. 2000. *Equal Resources, Equal Outcomes? The Distribution of School Resources and Student Achievement in California.* San Francisco: Public Policy Institute of California. Available at: http://www.ppic.org/content/pubs/report/R_200JBR.pdf (accessed July 8, 2014).

Blanden, Jo, and Dalia Ben-Galim. 2014. "Why Is Early Years Important?" Guildford, Surrey, and London: University of Surrey and Institute for Public Policy Research (IPPR).

Blatchford, Peter. 2003. *The Class Size Debate: Is Small Better?* Maidenhead, U.K.: Open University Press.

Bloom, Benjamin S. 1984. "The Search for Methods of Group Instruction as Effective as One-to-One Tutoring." *Educational Leadership* (May): 4–17.

Bond, Timothy M., and Kevin Lang. 2013. "The Evolution of the Black-White Test Score Gap in Grades K–3: The Fragility of Results." *Review of Economics and Statistics* 95(5): 1468–79.

Borman, Geoffrey D., Gina M. Hewes, Laura T. Overman, and Shelly Brown. 2003. "Comprehensive School Reform and Achievement: A Meta-analysis." *Review of Educational Research* 73: 125–230.

Boudarbat, Brahim, Thomas Lemieux, and W. Craig Riddell. 2006. "Recent Trends in Wage Inequality and the Wage Structure in Canada." In *Dimensions of Inequality in Canada,* edited by David A. Green and Jonathan R. Kesselman. Vancouver: UBC Press.

Boyd, Donald, Hamilton Lankford, Susanna Loeb, Jonah Rockoff, and James Wyckoff. 2008. "The Narrowing Gap in New York City Teacher Qualifications and Its Implications for Student Achievement in High-Poverty Schools." *Journal of Policy Analysis and Management* 27(4): 793–818. DOI:10.1002/pam.20377.

Bradbury, Bruce, Miles Corak, Jane Waldfogel, and Elizabeth Washbrook. 2012. "Inequality During the Early Years: Child Outcomes and Readiness to Learn in Australia, Canada, United Kingdom, and United States." In *From Parents to*

Children: The Intergenerational Transmission of Advantage, edited by John Ermisch, Markus Jäntti, and Timothy Smeeding. New York: Russell Sage Foundation.

Bradbury, Bruce, and Markus Jäntti. 2001. "Child Poverty Across Twenty-Five Countries." In *The Dynamics of Child Poverty in Industrialized Countries*, edited by Bruce Bradbury, Stephen Jenkins, and John Micklewright. Cambridge: Cambridge University Press.

Brennan, Deborah, and Marianne Fenech. 2014. "Early Education and Care in Australia: Equity in a Mixed Market System?" In *An Equal Start? Providing Quality Early Education and Care for Disadvantaged Children*, edited by Ludovica Gambaro, Kitty Stewart, and Jane Waldfogel. Bristol, U.K.: Policy Press.

Brennan, Lauretta M., Elizabeth C. Shelleby, Daniel S. Shaw, Frances Gardner, Thomas J. Dishion, and Melvin Wilson. 2013. "Indirect Effects of the Family Check-Up on School-Age Academic Achievement Through Improvements in Parenting in Early Childhood." *Journal of Educational Psychology* 105(3). DOI: 10.1037/a0032096.

Brooks-Gunn, Jeanne, and Lisa Markman. 2005. "The Contribution of Parenting to Racial and Ethnic Gaps in School Readiness." *The Future of Children* 15(1): 139–68.

Burkam, David T., Douglas D. Ready, Valerie E. Lee, and Laura F. LoGerfo. 2004. "Social-Class Differences in Summer Learning Between Kindergarten and First Grade: Model Specification and Estimation." *Sociology of Education* 77(1): 1–31.

Card, David, and A. Abigail Payne. 2002. "School Finance Reform, the Distribution of School Spending, and the Distribution of Student Test Scores." *Journal of Public Economics* 83(1): 49–82.

Carneiro, Pedro, and James Heckman. 2003. "Human Capital Policy." In *Inequality in America: What Role for Human Capital Policies?* edited by James Heckman, Alan Krueger, and Benjamin Friedman. Cambridge, Mass.: MIT Press.

Carnoy, Martin, and Richard Rothstein. 2013. "What Do International Tests Really Show About U.S. Student Performance?" Washington, D.C.: Economic Policy Institute (January 28). Available at: http://www.epi.org/publication/us-student-performance-testing/ (accessed July 3, 2014).

Carrell, Scott E., and Mark L. Hoekstra. 2010. "Externalities in the Classroom: How Children Exposed to Domestic Violence Affect Everyone's Kids." *American Economic Journal: Applied Economics* 2(1): 211–28. DOI:10.1257/app.2.1.211.

Champagne, Frances A. 2010. "Epigenetic Influence of Social Experiences Across the Lifespan." *Developmental Psychobiology* 52: 299–311.

Checkoway, Amy, Beth Gamse, Melissa Velez, Meghan Caven, Rodolfo de la Cruz, Nathaniel Donoghue, Kristina Kliorys, Tamara Linkow, Rachel Luck, Sarah Sahni, and Michelle Woodford. 2012. *Evaluation of the Massachusetts Expanded Learning Time (ELT) Initiative Year Five Final Report: 2010–2011*. Report prepared for the Massachusetts Department of Elementary and Secondary Education.

Available at: http://www.abtassociates.com/AbtAssociates/files/fe/fe87ef4f-3978-4e07-9704-2acbb010680c.pdf (accessed January 5, 2015).

Cherlin, Andrew. 2014. *Labor's Love Lost: The Rise and Fall of the Working-Class Family in America*. New York: Russell Sage Foundation.

Chetty, Raj, John N. Friedman, Nathaniel Hilger, Emmanuel Saez, Diane Whitmore Schanzenbach, and Danny Yagan. 2011. "How Does Your Kindergarten Classroom Affect Your Earnings? Evidence from Project STAR." *Quarterly Journal of Economics* 126(4): 1593–1660.

Chetty, Raj, John N. Friedman, and Jonah E. Rockoff. 2013a. "Measuring the Impacts of Teachers I: Evaluation Bias in Teacher Value-Added Estimates." Working Paper 19423. Cambridge, Mass.: National Bureau of Economic Research (NBER).

———. 2013b. "Measuring the Impacts of Teachers II: Teacher Value-Added and Student Outcomes in Adulthood." Working Paper 19424. Cambridge, Mass.: National Bureau of Economic Research (January).

Clinton Foundation and Next Generation. 2014. "Preparing America's Children for Success in the 21st Century: Too Small to Fail." Available at: http://toosmall.org/news/press-releases/body/strategicroadmap.pdf (accessed June 11, 2014).

Clotfelter, Charles T., Helen F. Ladd, and Jacob L. Vigdor. 2006. "Teacher-Student Matching and the Assessment of Teacher Effectiveness." *Journal of Human Resources* 41(4): 778–820.

———. 2011. "Teacher Mobility, School Segregation, and Pay-Based Policies to Level the Playing Field." *Association for Education Finance and Policy* 6(3): 399–438.

Cohen, David K., Donald J. Peurach, Joshua L. Glazer, Karen E. Gates, and Simona Goldin. 2013. *Improvement by Design: The Promise of Better Schools*. Chicago: University of Chicago Press.

Cole, Tim J., Mary C. Bellizzi, Katherine M. Flegal, and William H. Dietz. 2000. "Establishing a Standard Definition for Child Overweight and Obesity Worldwide: International Survey." *British Medical Journal* 320(7244): 1240.

Coleman, James S., et al. 1966. *The Coleman Report: Equality of Educational Opportunity*. Washington: U.S. Department of Health, Education, and Welfare, Office of Education.

Collins, Courtney A., and Li Gan. 2013. "Does Sorting Students Improve Scores? An Analysis of Class Composition." Working Paper 18848. Cambridge, Mass.: National Bureau of Economic Research (February).

Cook, Philip J., Kenneth Dodge, George Farkas, Roland G. Fryer Jr., Jonathan Guryan, Jens Ludwig, Susan Mayer, Harold Pollack, and Laurence Steinberg. 2014. "The (Surprising) Efficacy of Academic and Behavioral Intervention with Disadvantaged Youth: Results from a Randomized Experiment in Chicago." Working Paper 19862. Cambridge, Mass.: National Bureau of Economic Research (January).

Cooper, Harris, Kelly Charlton, Jeff C. Valentine, Laura Muhlenbruck, and Geoffrey D. Borman. 2000. "Making the Most of Summer School: A Meta-Analysis and Narrative Review." *Monographs of the Society for Research in Child Development* 65(1): i–127.

Cooper, Harris, Barbara Nye, Kelly Charlton, James Lindsay, and Scott Greathouse. 1996. "The Effects of Summer Vacation on Achievement Test Scores: A Narrative and Meta-Analytic Review." *Review of Educational Research* 66(3): 227–68.

Cowan, Philip, Carolyn Pape-Cowan, and Virginia Knox. 2010. "Marriage and Fatherhood Programs." *Future of Children* 20(2): 205–30.

Crosnoe, Robert. 2007. "Early Child Care and the School Readiness of Children from Mexican Immigrant Families." *International Migration Review* 41(1): 152–81.

Cunha, Flavio, Irma Elo, and Jennifer Culhane. 2013. "Eliciting Maternal Expectations About the Technology of Cognitive Skill Formation." Working Paper 19144. Cambridge, Mass.: National Bureau of Economic Research (June).

Dahl, Gordon B., and Lance Lochner. 2012. "The Impact of Family Income on Child Achievement: Evidence from the Earned Income Tax Credit." *American Economic Review* 105(5): 1927–56.

Davies, Scott, and Floyd M. Hammack. 2005. "The Channeling of Student Competition in Higher Education: Comparing Canada and the U.S." *Journal of Higher Education* 76(1): 89–106.

Dee, Thomas S., and Brian Jacob. 2011. "The Impact of No Child Left Behind on Student Achievement." *Journal of Policy Analysis and Management* 30(3): 418–46.

Deming, David, and Susan Dynarski. 2008. "The Lengthening of Childhood." Working Paper 14124. Cambridge, Mass.: National Bureau of Economic Research (June).

Department for Children, Schools, and Families (DCSF). 2009. *Deprivation and Education: The Evidence on Pupils in England, Foundation Stage to Key Stage 4.* Available at: http://dera.ioe.ac.uk/9431/1/DCSF-RTP-09-01.pdf (accessed April 30, 2015).

Department for Education. 2013. "Raising the Achievement of Disadvantaged Children: Pupil Premium." April 22; updated November 13, 2014. Available at: https://www.gov.uk/government/policies/raising-the-achievement-of-disadvantaged-children/supporting-pages/pupil-premium (accessed May 23, 2014).

Department of Health. 2013. "Family Nurse Partnership Programme to Be Extended." April 4. Available at: https://www.gov.uk/government/news/family-nurse-partnership-programme-to-be-extended (accessed June 11, 2014).

Desimone, Laura, and Daniel A. Long. 2010. "Teacher Effects and the Achievement Gap: Do Teacher and Teaching Quality Influence the Achievement Gap Between Black and White and High- and Low-SES Students in the Early Grades?" *Teachers College Record* 112(12): 3024–73.

Dobbie, Will, and Roland G. Fryer. 2011. "Are High-Quality Schools Enough to Increase Achievement Among the Poor? Evidence from the Harlem Children's Zone." *American Economic Journal: Applied Economics* 3(3): 158–87.

———. 2013. "Getting Beneath the Veil of Effective Schools: Evidence from New York City." *American Economic Journal: Applied Economics* 5(4): 28–60.

Doherty, Gillian, Martha Friendly, and Jane Beach. 2003, "OECD Thematic Review of Early Childhood Education and Care: Canadian Background Report." Available at: http://www.oecd.org/education/school/33852192.pdf (accessed July 21, 2014).

Downey, Douglas, Paul von Hippel, and Beckett Broh. 2004. "Are Schools the Great Equalizer? Cognitive Inequality During the Summer Months and the School Year." *American Sociological Review* 69: 613–35.

Duckworth, Angela Lee, and Lauren Eskreis-Winkler. 2013. "True Grit." *Observer* 26(4, April). Available at: https://www.psychologicalscience.org/index.php/publications/observer/2013/april-13/true-grit.html (accessed January 10, 2014).

Duckworth, Angela Lee, and Patrick D. Quinn. 2009. "Development and Validation of the Short Grit Scale (Grit-S)." *Journal of Personality Assessment* 91(2): 166–74.

Duckworth, Angela Lee, and Martin E. P. Seligman. 2005. "Self-Discipline Outdoes IQ in Predicting Academic Performance of Adolescents." *Psychological Science* 16(12): 939–44.

Duncan, Greg, and Jeanne Brooks-Gunn, eds. 1997. *Consequences of Growing Up Poor.* New York: Russell Sage Foundation.

Duncan, Greg, Chantelle Dowsett, Amy Claessens, Katherine Magnuson, Aletha Huston, Pamela Klebanov, Linda Pagani, Leon Feinstein, Mimi Engel, Jeanne Brooks-Gunn, Holly Sexton, Kathryn Duckworth, and Crista Japel. 2007. "School Readiness and Later Achievement." *Developmental Psychology* 43(6): 1428–46.

Duncan, Greg, and Katherine Magnuson. 2011. "The Nature and Impact of Early Achievement Skills, Attention Skills, and Behavior Problems." In *Whither Opportunity? Rising Inequality, Schools, and Children's Life Chances,* edited by Greg Duncan and Richard Murnane. New York: Russell Sage Foundation.

———. 2013. "Investing in Preschool Programs." *Journal of Economic Perspectives* 27(2): 109–32.

Duncan, Greg J., and Richard J. Murnane, eds. 2011. *Whither Opportunity? Rising Inequality, Schools, and Children's Life Chances.* New York: Russell Sage Foundation.

———. 2014. *Restoring Opportunity: The Crisis of Inequality and the Challenge for American Education.* New York and Cambridge, Mass.: Russell Sage Foundation and Harvard Education Press.

Eckenrode, John, Mary Campa, Dennis W. Luckey, Charles R. Henderson Jr., Robert Cole, Harriet Kitzman, Elizabeth Anson, Kimberly Sidora-Arcoleo, Jane Powers, and David L. Olds. 2010. "Long-Term Effects of Prenatal and Infancy Nurse Home Visitation on the Life Course of Youths: 19-Year Follow-up of a Randomized Trial." *Archives of Pediatrics and Adolescent Medicine* 164(1): 9–15.

Edin, Kathryn, and Maria Kefalas. 2011. *Promises I Can Keep: Why Poor Women Put Motherhood Before Marriage.* Berkeley: University of California Press.

Eisenberg, Nancy, Angela L. Duckworth, Tracy L. Spinrad, and Carlos Valiente. In press. "Conscientiousness: Origins in Childhood?" *Developmental Psychology.*

Entwistle, Doris, and Karl Alexander. 1992. "Summer Setback: Race, Poverty, School Composition, and Math Achievement in the First Two Years of School." *American Sociological Review* 57: 72–84.

Ermisch, John, and Emilia Del Bono. 2012. "Inequality in Achievement in Adolescence." In *From Parents to Children: The Intergenerational Transmission of Advantage,* edited by John Ermisch, Markus Jäntti, and Timothy Smeeding. New York: Russell Sage Foundation.

Ermisch, John, Markus Jäntti, Timothy Smeeding, and James Wilson. 2012. "What Have We Learned?" In *From Parents to Children: The Intergenerational Transmission of Advantage,* edited by John Ermisch, Markus Jäntti, and Timothy Smeeding. New York: Russell Sage Foundation.

Esping-Andersen, Gøsta. 1990. *The Three Worlds of Welfare Capitalism.* Princeton, N.J.: Princeton University Press.

———. 2004. "Untying the Gordian Knot of Social Inheritance." *Research in Social Stratification and Mobility* 21: 115–38.

Evangelou, Maria, Greg Brooks, Sally Smith, and Denise Jennings. 2005. *The Birth to School Study: A Longitudinal Evaluation of the Peers Early Education Partnership (PEEP) 1998–2005.* Sure Start Unit Report SSU/2005/SF/0717. Available at: www.worldforumfoundation.org/wf/global_leaders/pdf/BirthtoSchoolStudy.pdf (accessed May 20, 2008).

Evangelou, Maria, and Kathy Sylva. 2003. *The Effects of the Peers Early Education Partnership (PEEP) on Children's Developmental Progress.* Research Brief RB489. Manchester, U.K.: Department for Education and Skills.

Evans, William, and Craig Garthwaite. 2010. "Giving Mom a Break: The Impact of Higher EITC Payments on Maternal Health." Working Paper 16296. Cambridge, Mass.: National Bureau of Economic Research (August).

Feinstein, Leon. 2003. "Inequality in the Early Cognitive Development of British Cohort Children in the 1970 Cohort." *Economica* 70(1): 73–77.

———. 2004. "Mobility in Pupils' Cognitive Attainment During School Life." *Oxford Review of Economic Policy* 20(2): 213–29.

Field, Simon, Malgorzata Kuczera, and Beatriz Pont. 2007. *No More Failures: Ten Steps to Equity in Education.* Paris: OECD. Available at: http://www.oecd -ilibrary.org/content/book/9789264032606-en (accessed July 8, 2014).

Fishkin, Joseph. 1983. *Justice, Equal Opportunity, and the Family.* New Haven, CT: Yale University Press.

———. 2014a. *Bottlenecks: A New Theory of Equal Opportunity.* Oxford: Oxford University Press.

———. 2014b. "Bottlenecks: The Real Opportunity Challenge." Brookings (April 28). Available at: http://www.brookings.edu/blogs/social-mobility-memos /posts/2014/04/28-bottlenecks-real-opportunity-challenge (accessed June 24, 2014).

Fryer, Roland G. 2014. "Injecting Charter School Best Practices into Traditional Public Schools: Evidence from Field Experiments." *Quarterly Journal of Economics* 129(3): 1355–1407.

Fryer, Roland, and Steven Levitt. 2004. "Understanding the Black-White Test Score Gap in the First Two Years of School." *Review of Economics and Statistics* 86(2): 447–64.

Furstenberg, Frank F., Jeanne Brooks-Gunn, and Lindsay Chase-Lansdale. 1989. "Teenaged Pregnancy and Childbearing." *American Psychologist* 44(2): 313–20.

Galton, Francis. 1886. "Regression Towards Mediocrity in Hereditary Stature." *Journal of the Anthropological Institute of Great Britain and Ireland,* 246–63.

Gamoran, Adam. 2010. "Tracking and Inequality: New Directions for Research and Practice." In *The Routledge International Handbook of the Sociology of Education,* edited by Michael W. Apple, Stephen J. Ball, and Luís Armando Gandin. London: Routledge.

Gamoran, Adam, and Daniel A. Long. 2007. "Equality of Educational Opportunity: A 40-Year Retrospective." In *International Studies in Educational Inequality, Theory and Policy,* edited by Richard Teese, Stephen Lamb, and Marie Duru-Bellat. Dordrecht, Netherlands: Springer. Available at: http://link.springer .com/chapter/10.1007/978-1-4020-5916-2_2 (accessed April 30, 2015).

Garfinkel, Irwin, Lee Rainwater, and Timothy Smeeding. 2010. *Wealth and Welfare States: Is America a Laggard or Leader?* New York: Oxford University Press.

Goldin, Claudia, and Lawrence Katz. 2008. *The Race Between Technology and Education.* Cambridge, Mass.: Harvard University Press.

Goodman, Alissa, and Paul Gregg. 2010. *Poorer Children's Educational Attainment: How Important Are Attitudes and Behaviour?* York, U.K.: Joseph Rowntree Foundation (March 28). Available at: http://www.jrf.org.uk/publications /educational-attainment-poor-children (accessed July 21, 2014).

Goodman, Alissa, Luke Sibieta, and Elizabeth Washbrook. 2009. *Inequalities in Educational Outcomes Among Children Aged 3 to 16.* London: Institute for Fiscal Studies.

Gormley, William, Ted Gayer, Deborah Phillips, and Brittany Dawson. 2005. "The Effects of Universal Pre-K on Cognitive Development." *Developmental Psychology* 41(6): 872–84.

Gormley, William, Deborah Phillips, and Ted Gayer. 2008. "Preschool Programs Can Boost School Readiness." *Science* 320: 1723–24.

Greene, Jay P., and Marcus A. Winters. 2007. "Revisiting Grade Retention: An Evaluation of Florida's Test-Based Promotion Policy." *Education Finance and Policy* 2(4): 319–40. DOI:10.1162/edfp.2007.2.4.319.

The Guardian. 2012. "Class Size, Teacher's Pay, and Spending: Which Countries Spend the Most and Pay the Least in Education?" Available at: http://www.theguardian.com/news/datablog/2012/sep/11/education-compared-oecd-country-pisa (accessed March 6, 2015).

Hanushek, Eric A. 1999. "Some Findings from an Independent Investigation of the Tennessee STAR Experiment and from Other Investigations of Class Size Effects." *Educational Evaluation and Policy Analysis* 21(2): 143–63.

Hanushek, Eric A., John F. Kain, and Steven G. Rivkin. 2004. "Why Public Schools Lose Teachers." *Journal of Human Resources* 39(2): 326–54.

Hanushek, Eric, and Ludger Woessmann. 2011. "The Economics of International Differences in Educational Achievement." In *Handbook of the Economics of Education*, vol. 3(1), edited by Eric Hanushek, Stephen Machin, and Ludger Woessmann. Amsterdam: Elsevier.

Hart, Betty, and Todd Risley. 1995. *Meaningful Differences in the Everyday Experience of Young American Children*. Baltimore: Paul H. Brookes Publishing Co.

Haskins, Ron, and Greg Margolis. 2014. *Show Me the Money: Obama's Fight for Rigor and Results in Social Policy*. Washington, D.C.: Brookings Institution Press.

Haskins, Ron, and Isabel Sawhill. 2009. *Creating an Opportunity Society*. Washington, D.C.: Brookings Institution Press.

Heckman, James J. 2008. "Schools, Skills, and Synapses." *Economic Inquiry* 46(3): 289–324.

Heckman, James, and Stefano Musso. 2014. "The Economics of Human Development and Social Mobility." Working Paper 19925. Cambridge, Mass.: National Bureau of Economic Research (February).

Hedges, Larry, and Eric C. Hedberg. 2007. "Intraclass Correlation Values for Planning Group-Randomized Trials in Education." *Educational Evaluation and Policy Analysis* 29(1): 60–87.

Herman, Juliana. 2013. "Canada's Approach to School Funding: The Adoption of Provincial Control of Education Funding in Three Provinces." Washington, D.C.: Center for American Progress. Available at: http://cdn.americanprogress.org/wp-content/uploads/2013/05/HermanCanadaReport.pdf (accessed July 8, 2014).

Heyns, Barbara. 1978. *Summer Learning and the Effects of Schooling*. Salt Lake City, Utah: Academic Press.

———. 1987. "Schooling and Cognitive Development: Is There a Season for Learning?" *Child Development* 58: 1151–60.

Hoffman, Saul, and Rebecca Maynard. 2008. *Kids Having Kids: Economic Costs and Social Consequences of Teen Pregnancy*, 2nd ed. Washington, D.C.: Urban Institute Press.

Holmlund, Helena, Sandra McNally, and Martina Viarengo. 2010. "Does Money Matter for Schools?" *Economics of Education Review* 29(6): 1154–64. DOI:10.1016/j.econedurev.2010.06.008.

Jackson, C. Kirabo, Rucker Johnson, and Claudia Persico. 2014. "The Effect of School Finance Reforms on the Distribution of Spending, Academic Achievement, and Adult Outcomes." Working Paper 20118. Cambridge, Mass.: National Bureau of Economic Research (May). Available at: http://www.nber.org/papers/w20118 (accessed May 22, 2014).

———. 2015. "The Effect of School Spending on Educational and Economic Outcomes: Evidence from School Finance Reforms." Working Paper 20847. Cambridge, Mass.: National Bureau of Economic Research (January). Available at: http://www.nber.org/papers/w20847 (accessed January 19, 2015).

Jacob, Brian A., and Lars Lefgren. 2004. "Remedial Education and Student Achievement: A Regression-Discontinuity Analysis." *Review of Economics and Statistics* 86(1): 226–44.

Jacob, Brian, and Jens Ludwig. 2009. "Improving Educational Outcomes for Poor Children." In *Changing Poverty, Changing Policies*, edited by Maria Cancian and Sheldon Danziger. New York: Russell Sage Foundation.

Jencks, Christopher, et al. 1972. *Inequality: A Reassessment of the Effect of Family and Schooling in America*. New York: Basic Books.

Jencks, Christopher, and Meredith Phillips, eds. 1998. *The Black-White Test Score Gap*. Washington, D.C.: Brookings Institution.

Jensen, Ben, and Julie Sonnemann. 2014. "Turning Around Troubled Schools: It Can Be Done." Melbourne, Australia: Grattan Institute (February). Available at: http://grattan.edu.au/wp-content/uploads/2014/04/805-turning-around-schools.pdf (accessed April 30, 2015).

Jerrim, John, and Anna Vignoles. 2013. "Social Mobility, Regression to the Mean, and the Cognitive Development of High Ability Children from Disadvantaged Homes." *Journal of the Royal Statistical Society: Series A (Statistics in Society)* 176(4): 887–906.

Jones, Ken, David Daley, Judy Hutchings, Tracey Bywater, and Catrin Eames. 2007. "Efficacy of the Incredible Years Basic Parenting Training Programme as an Early Intervention for Children with Conduct Problems and ADHD." *Child: Care, Health, and Development* 33: 749–56.

Kalil, Ariel, and Tom DeLeire, eds. 2004. *Family Investments in Children's Potential:*

Resources and Parenting Behaviors That Predict Children's Success. Mahwah, N.J.: Lawrence Erlbaum.

Kalogrides, Demetra, Susanna Loeb, and Tara Béteille. 2013. "Systematic Sorting Teacher Characteristics and Class Assignments." *Sociology of Education* 86(2): 103–23. DOI:10.1177/0038040712456555.

Kane, Thomas J., Jonah E. Rockoff, and Douglas O. Staiger. 2008. "What Does Certification Tell Us About Teacher Effectiveness? Evidence from New York City." *Economics of Education Review* 27(6): 615–31.

Karoly, Lynn, Peter Greenwood, Susan Everingham, Jill Hoube, Rebecca Kilburn, Peter Rydell, Matthew Sanders, and James Chiesa. 1998. *Investing in Our Children: What We Know and Don't Know About the Costs and Benefits of Early Childhood Interventions.* Santa Monica, Calif.: RAND.

Karoly, Lynn, Rebecca Kilburn, and Jill Cannon. 2005. *Early Childhood Interventions: Proven Results, Future Promise.* Santa Monica, Calif.: RAND.

Kaushal, Neeraj, Katherine Magnuson, and Jane Waldfogel. 2011. "How Is Family Income Related to Investments in Children's Learning?" In *Whither Opportunity? Rising Inequality, Schools, and Children's Life Chances,* edited by Greg Duncan and Richard Murnane. New York: Russell Sage Foundation.

Kearney, Melissa S., and Phillip B. Levine. 2014. "Media Influences on Social Outcomes: The Impact of MTV's *16 and Pregnant* on Teen Childbearing." Working Paper 19795. Cambridge, Mass.: National Bureau of Economic Research (January).

Keating, Daniel P., and Clyde Hertzman, eds. 1999. *Developmental Health and the Wealth of Nations: Social, Biological, and Educational Dynamics.* New York: Guilford Press.

Kelly, Dana, Holly Xie, Christine Winquist Nord, Frank Jenkins, Jessica Ying Chan, and David Kastberg. 2013. "Performance of U.S. 15-Year-Old Students in Mathematics, Science, and Reading Literacy in an International Context: First Look at PISA 2012." Washington: U.S. Department of Education, National Center for Education Statistics. Available at: https://nces.ed.gov/pubs2014/2014024rev.pdf (accessed July 3, 2014).

Kerr, Sari Pekkala, Tuomas Pekkarinen, and Roope Uusitalo. 2013. "School Tracking and Development of Cognitive Skills." *Journal of Labor Economics* 31(3): 577–602.

Kim, James. 2004. "Summer Reading and the Ethnic Achievement Gap." *Journal of Education for Students Placed at Risk* 9(2): 169–88.

———. 2006. "Effects of a Voluntary Summer Reading Intervention on Reading Achievement: Results from a Randomized Field Trial." *Educational Evaluation and Policy Analysis* 28(4): 335–55.

Kim, James, and Jonathan Guryan. 2010. "The Efficacy of a Voluntary Summer Book Reading Intervention for Low-Income Latino Children from Language-Minority Families." *Journal of Educational Psychology* 102(1): 20–31.

Kim, James, and Thomas White. 2008. "Scaffolding Voluntary Summer Reading for Children Grades 3 to 5: An Experimental Study." *Scientific Studies of Reading* 12(1): 1–23.

Kitzman, Harriet J., David L. Olds, Robert E. Cole, Carole A. Hanks, Elizabeth A. Anson, Kimberly J. Arcoleo, Dennis W. Luckey, Michael D. Knudtson, Charles R. Henderson Jr., and John R. Holmberg. 2010. "Enduring Effects of Prenatal and Infancy Home Visiting by Nurses on Children: Follow-up of a Randomized Trial Among Children at Age 12 Years." *Archives of Pediatric and Adolescent Medicine* 164(5): 412–18.

Knudsen, Eric I., James J. Heckman, Judy L. Cameron, and Jack P. Shonkoff. 2006. "Economic, Neurobiological, and Behavioral Perspectives on Building America's Future Workforce." *Proceedings of the National Academy of Sciences of the United States of America* 103(27): 10155–62.

Kornrich, Sabino, and Frank Furstenberg. 2013. "Investing in Children: Changes in Parental Spending on Children: 1972 to 2007." *Demography* 50(1): 1–23.

Kornrich, Sabino, Anne Gauthier, and Frank Furstenberg. 2011. "Comparing Private Investments in Children Across Three Liberal Welfare States: Australia, Canada, and the United States." Paper presented to the annual meeting of the Population Association of America. Washington, D.C. (March 31–April 2).

Krueger, Alan B. 1999. "Experimental Estimates of Education Production Functions." *Quarterly Journal of Economics* 119: 497–532.

Krueger, Alan B., and Diane Whitmore. 2001. "The Effect of Attending a Small Class in the Early Grades on College-Test Taking and Middle School Test Results: Evidence from Project Star." *Economic Journal* 111: 1–28.

Ladd, Helen F. 2012. "Education and Poverty: Confronting the Evidence." *Journal of Policy Analysis and Management* 31(2): 203–27. DOI:10.1002/pam.21615.

Ladd, Helen F., and Edward B. Fiske. 2011. "Weighted Student Funding in the Netherlands: A Model for the U.S.?" *Journal of Policy Analysis and Management* 30(3): 470–98. DOI:10.1002/pam.20589.

Landry, Susan H. 2008. "The Role of Parents in Early Childhood Learning." In *Encyclopedia on Early Childhood Development (online)*, edited by Richard E. Tremblay, Ronald G. Barr, Ray D. Peters, and Michel Boivin. Montreal: Centre of Excellence for Early Childhood Development. Available at: http://www.child-encyclopedia.com/sites/default/files/textes-experts/en/654/the-role-of-parents-in-early-childhood-learning.pdf (April 30, 2015).

Landry, Susan H., Karen E. Smith, and Paul R. Swank. 2006. "Responsive Parenting: Establishing Early Foundations for Social, Communication, and Independent Problem-Solving Skills." *Developmental Psychology* 42: 627–42.

Landry, Susan H., Karen E. Smith, Paul R. Swank, and Cathy Guttentag. 2008. "A Responsive Parenting Intervention: The Optimal Timing Across Early Childhood for Impacting Maternal Behaviors and Child Outcomes." *Developmental Psychology* 44(5): 1335–53.

Lankford, Hamilton, Susanna Loeb, and James Wyckoff. 2002. "Teacher Sorting and the Plight of Urban Schools: A Descriptive Analysis." *Educational Evaluation and Policy Analysis* 24(1): 37–62.

Lareau, Annette. 2003. *Unequal Childhoods: Class, Race, and Family Life.* Berkeley: University of California Press.

Lareau, Annette, and Kimberly Goyette. 2014. *Choosing Homes, Choosing Schools: Residential Segregation and the Search for a Good School.* New York: Russell Sage Foundation.

Lee, Valerie, and David Burkam. 2002. *Inequality at the Starting Gate: Social Background Differences in Achievement as Children Begin School.* Washington, D.C.: Economic Policy Institute.

Lemann, Nicholas. 1999. *The Big Test: The Secret History of the American Meritocracy.* New York: Farrar, Straus and Giroux.

Levey, Hilary Leigh. 2009. "Playing to Win: Raising Children in a Competitive Culture." PhD diss., Princeton University.

Lipsey, Mark, Kerry Hofer, Nianbo Dong, Dale Farran, and Carol Bilbrey. 2013. "Evaluation of the Tennessee Voluntary Prekindergarten Program: Kindergarten and First Grade Follow-up Results from the Randomized Control Design." Research Report. Nashville: Vanderbilt University, Peabody Research Institute.

Lleras, Christy, and Claudia Rangel. 2009. "Ability Grouping Practices in Elementary School and African American/Hispanic Achievement." *American Journal of Education* 115(2): 279–304.

Love, John M., Rachel Chazan-Cohen, Helen Raikes, and Jeanne Brooks-Gunn. 2013. "What Makes a Difference: Early Head Start Evaluation Findings in a Developmental Context." *Monographs of the Society for Research in Child Development* 78: vii–173.

Loveless, Tom. 2012. *The 2012 Brown Center Report on American Education.* Washington, D.C.: Brown Center for Education Policy at Brookings (February 16). Available at: http://www.brookings.edu/research/reports/2012/02/16-brown-education (accessed July 3, 2014).

———. 2013. "The Resurgence of Ability Grouping and Persistence of Tracking." Part II of *2013 Brown Center Report on American Education: How Well Are American Students Learning?* Washington, D.C.: Brown Center on Education Policy at Brookings (March 18). Available at: http://www.brookings.edu/research/reports/2013/03/18-tracking-ability-grouping-loveless (accessed July 8, 2014).

Lunkenheimer, Erika S., Thomas J. Dishion, Daniel S. Shaw, Arin M. Connell, Frances Gardner, Melvin N. Wilson, and Emily M. Skuban. 2008. "Collateral Benefits of the Family Check Up on Early Childhood School Readiness: Indirect Effects of Parents' Positive Behavior Support." *Developmental Psychology* 44(6): 1737–52.

Luthar, Suniya, and Bronwyn Becker. 2002. "Privileged but Pressured? A Study of Affluent Youth." *Child Development* 73(5): 1593–1610.

MacKenzie, Michael, Eric Nicklas, Jane Waldfogel, and Jeanne Brooks-Gunn. 2013. "Spanking and Child Development Across the First Decade of Life." *Pediatrics* 132(5): e1118–25.

Magnuson, Katherine, Claudia Lahaie, and Jane Waldfogel. 2006. "Preschool and School Readiness of Children of Immigrants." *Social Science Quarterly* 87(1): 1241–62.

Magnuson, Katherine, and Jane Waldfogel, eds. 2008. *Steady Gains and Stalled Progress: Inequality and the Black-White Test Score Gap.* New York: Russell Sage Foundation.

———. 2012. "The Role of Early Childhood Education in Changing SES Gaps in Achievement." Working paper. New York: Columbia University School of Social Work.

———. 2014. "Delivering High-Quality Early Childhood Education and Care to Low-Income Children: How Well Is the U.S. Doing?" In *An Equal Start? Providing Quality Early Education and Care for Disadvantaged Children,* edited by Ludovica Gambaro, Kitty Stewart, and Jane Waldfogel. Bristol, U.K.: Policy Press.

Magnuson, Katherine, Jane Waldfogel, and Elizabeth Washbrook. 2012. "The Development of SES Gradients in Skills During the School Years: Evidence from the United States and England." In *From Parents to Children: The Intergenerational Transmission of Advantage,* edited by John Ermisch, Markus Jäntti, and Timothy Smeeding. New York: Russell Sage Foundation.

Matthews, Jay. 2009. *Work Hard, Be Nice: How Two Inspired Teachers Created the Most Promising Schools in America.* Chapel Hill, N.C.: Algonquin Books.

Mayer, Susan E. 1998. *What Money Can't Buy: Family Income and Children's Life Chances.* Cambridge, Mass.: Harvard University Press.

McCombs, Jennifer Sloan, Catherine H. Augustine, Heather L. Schwartz, Susan J. Bodilly, Brian McInnis, Dahlia S. Lichter, and Amanda Brown Cross. 2011. *Making Summer Count: How Summer Programs Can Boost Student Learning.* Santa Monica, Calif.: RAND.

McLanahan, Sara. 2004. "Diverging Destinies: How Children Are Faring Under the Second Demographic Transition." *Demography* 41(4): 606–27.

———. 2011. "Family Instability and Complexity After a Nonmarital Birth: Outcomes for Children in Fragile Families." In *Social Class and Changing Families in an Unequal America,* edited by Marcia Carlson and Paula England. Stanford, Calif.: Stanford University Press.

McLanahan, Sara, and Gary Sandefur. 1997. *Growing Up with a Single Parent: What Hurts, What Helps.* Cambridge, Mass.: Harvard University Press.

McLanahan, Sara, Laura Tach, and Daniel Schneider. 2013. "The Causal Effects of Father Absence." *Annual Review of Sociology* 39: 399–427.

Menesses, Keri F., and Frank M. Gresham. 2009. "Relative Efficacy of Reciprocal and Nonreciprocal Peer Tutoring for Students At-Risk for Academic Failure." *School Psychology Quarterly* 24(4): 266–75. DOI:10.1037/a0018174.

Milligan, Kevin, and Mark Stabile. 2008. "Do Child Tax Benefits Affect the Wellbeing of Children? Evidence from Canadian Child Benefit Expansions." Working Paper 14624. Cambridge, Mass.: National Bureau for Economic Research (December).

Mishel, Laurence, and Richard Rothstein, eds. 2002. *The Class Size Debate.* Washington, D.C.: Economic Policy Institute.

Mosteller, Charles Frederick. 1995. "The Tennessee Study of Class Size in the Early School Grades." *The Future of Children* 5: 113–27.

Mosteller, Frederick, and Daniel Patrick Moynihan, eds. 1972. *On Equality of Educational Opportunity: Papers Deriving from the Harvard University Faculty Seminar on the Coleman Report.* New York: Random House.

Mullainathan, Sendhil, and Eldar Shafir. 2013. *Scarcity: Why Having Too Little Means So Much.* New York: Macmillan.

Mullis, Ina V. S., Michael O. Martin, Pierre Foy, and Kathleen T. Drucker. 2012. *PIRLS 2011 International Results in Reading.* Chestnut Hill, Mass.: Boston College, Lynch School of Education, TIMSS & PIRLS International Study Center. Available at: http://timssandpirls.bc.edu/pirls2011/downloads/P11_IR_Full Book.pdf (accessed July 8, 2014).

Murnane, Richard. 1975. *The Impact of School Resources on the Learning of Inner City Children.* Cambridge, Mass.: Ballinger.

Murnane, Richard J., and Jennifer L. Steele. 2007. "What Is the Problem? The Challenge of Providing Effective Teachers for All Children." *The Future of Children* 17(1): 15–43.

Murnane, Richard, John B. Willett, Kristen L. Bub, and Kathleen McCartney. 2006. "Understanding Trends in the Black-White Achievement Gaps During the First Years of School." *Brookings-Wharton Papers on Urban Affairs,* 97–135.

Nisbett, Richard. 2009. *Intelligence and How to Get It: Why Schools and Cultures Count.* New York: W. W. Norton.

Nisbett, Richard, Joshua Aronson, Clancy Blair, William Dickens, James Flynn, Diane Halpern, and Eric Turkheimer. 2012. "Intelligence: New Findings and Theoretical Developments." *American Psychologist* 67(2): 130–59.

Nomi, Takako. 2010. "The Effects of Within-Class Ability Grouping on Academic Achievement in Early Elementary Years." *Journal of Research on Educational Effectiveness* 3(1): 56–92.

Nurse Family Partnership. 2014. Nurse Family Partnership Snapshot. Available at: http://www.nursefamilypartnership.org/assets/PDF/Fact-sheets/NFP_April_2015_Snapshot.aspx (accessed May 11, 2015).

Olds, David L., John Eckenrode, Charles Henderson, Harriet Kitzman, Robert Cole, Dennis W. Luckey, John R. Holmberg, Pilar Baca, and Peggy Hill. 2007.

"Preventing Child Abuse and Neglect with Home Visiting by Nurses." In *Community Prevention of Maltreatment*, edited by Kenneth Dodge and Doriane Lambelet Coleman. New York: Guilford Press.

Olds, David L., John R. Holmberg, Nancy Donelan-McCall, Dennis W. Luckey, Michael D. Knudtson, and JoAnn Robinson. 2014. "Effects of Home Visits by Paraprofessionals and by Nurses on Children: Follow-up of a Randomized Trial at Ages 6 and 9 Years." *JAMA Pediatrics* 168(2): 114–21.

Organization for Economic Cooperation and Development (OECD). 2011. *Strong Performers and Successful Reformers in Education: Lessons from PISA for the United States*. Paris: OECD Publishing. Available at: http://dx.doi.org/10.1787/9789264096660-en (accessed July 3, 2014).

———. 2012. *Education at a Glance 2012*. Paris: OECD Publishing.

———. 2013a. *PISA 2012 Results: Excellence Through Equity: Giving Every Student the Chance to Succeed*, vol. 2. Paris: OECD Publishing. Available at: http://www.oecd.org/pisa/keyfindings/pisa-2012-results-volume-II.pdf (accessed July 3, 2014).

———. 2013b. *OECD Skills Outlook 2013—First Results from the Survey of Adult Skills*. Paris: OECD Publishing. Available at: http://skills.oecd.org/OECD_Skills_Outlook_2013.pdf (accessed July 3, 2014).

———. 2013c. *Education at a Glance 2013*. Paris: OECD Publishing.

Paine, Steven Louis, and Andreas Schleicher. 2011. "What the U.S. Can Learn from the World's Most Successful Education Reform Efforts." New York: McGraw-Hill Research Foundation. Available at: http://www.mcgraw-hillresearchfoundation.org/wp-content/uploads/pisa-intl-competitiveness.pdf (accessed April 30, 2015).

Pew Charitable Trust (2011). "Poll Results: Economic Mobility and the American Dream." Available at: http://www.pewtrusts.org/en/research-and-analysis/analysis/2009/03/12/opinion-poll-on-economic-mobility-and-the-american-dream (accessed May 4, 2015).

Phillips, Meredith. 2011. "Parenting, Time Use, and Disparities in Academic Outcomes." In *Whither Opportunity? Rising Inequality, Schools, and Children's Life Chances*, edited by Greg Duncan and Richard Murnane. New York: Russell Sage Foundation.

Phillips, Meredith, Jeanne Brooks-Gunn, Greg J. Duncan, Pamela Klebanov, and Jonathan Crane. 1998. "Family Background, Parenting Practices, and the Black-White Test Score Gap." In *The Black-White Test Score Gap*, edited by Christopher Jencks and Meredith Phillips. Washington, D.C.: Brookings Institution.

Putnam, Robert. 2015. *Our Kids: The American Dream in Crisis*. New York: Simon & Schuster.

Ramey, Garey, and Valerie A. Ramey. 2010. "The Rug Rat Race." *Brookings Papers on Economic Activity* (Spring): 129–201.

Rathbun, Amy, Jerry West, and Elvira Germino Hausken. 2004. *From Kindergarten Through Third Grade: Children's Beginning School Experiences.* Washington: U.S. Department of Education, National Center for Education Statistics.

Ravitch, Diane. 2010. *The Death and Life of the Great American School System.* New York: Basic Books.

Ready, Douglas D. 2008. "Class-Size Reduction: Policy, Politics, and Implications for Equity." Research Review 2. New York: Columbia University, Teachers College, Campaign for Educational Equity. Available at: http://www .schoolfunding.info/policy/Poverty/Ready-ClassSizeResearchReview.pdf (accessed September 13, 2013).

Reardon, Sean. 2008. "Thirteen Ways of Looking at the Black-White Test Score Gap." Working Paper 2008-08. Stanford, Calif.: Stanford University, Institute for Research on Education Policy and Practice (IREPP).

———. 2011. "The Widening Academic Achievement Gap Between the Rich and the Poor: New Evidence and Possible Explanations." In *Whither Opportunity? Rising Inequality, Schools, and Children's Life Chances,* edited by Greg J. Duncan and Richard J. Murnane. New York: Russell Sage Foundation.

Reardon, Sean F., Rachel A. Valentino, and Kenneth A. Shores. 2012. "Patterns of Literacy Among U.S. Students." *The Future of Children* 22(2): 17–38.

Reback, Randall. 2010. "Schools' Mental Health Services and Young Children's Emotions, Behavior, and Learning." *Journal of Policy Analysis and Management* 29(4): 698–725.

Reback, Randall, Jonah Rockoff, and Heather Schwartz. 2014. "Under Pressure: Job Security, Resource Allocation, and Productivity in Schools Under NCLB." *American Economic Journal: Economic Policy* 6(3): 207–41.

Ridley, Matt. 2003. *Nature Via Nurture: Genes, Experience, and What Makes Us Human.* New York: HarperCollins.

Ripley, Amanda. 2013. *The Smartest Kids in the World: And How They Got That Way.* New York: Simon & Schuster.

Rivkin, Steven G., Eric A. Hanushek, and John F. Kain. 2005. "Teachers, Schools, and Academic Achievement." *Econometrica* 73(2): 417–58.

Rockoff, Jonah E. 2004. "The Impact of Individual Teachers on Student Achievement: Evidence from Panel Data." *American Economic Review* 94(2): 247–52.

Roemer, John E., and Alain Trannoy. 2013. "Equality of Opportunity," unpublished draft dated November 18. Available at https://milescorak.files.wordpress .com/2014/06/roemer-trannoy-equality-of-opportunity-journal-of-economic -literature.pdf (accessed April 27, 2015).

Ronfeldt, Matthew, Susanna Loeb, and James Wyckoff. 2013. "How Teacher Turnover Harms Student Achievement." *American Educational Research Journal* 50(1): 4–36.

Rothstein, Richard. 2004. *Class and Schools: Using Social, Economic, and Educational*

Reform to Close the Black-White Achievement Gap. Washington, D.C.: Economic Policy Institute.

Rowe, Meredith. 2008. "Child-Directed Speech: Relation to Socioeconomic Status, Knowledge of Child Development, and Child Vocabulary Skill." *Child Language* 35: 185–205.

Ruhm, Christopher, and Jane Waldfogel. 2012. "Long-Term Effects of Early Childhood Care and Education." *Nordic Economic Policy Review* 1: 23–51.

Sahlberg, Pasi. 2011. *Finnish Lessons: What Can the World Learn from Educational Change in Finland?* New York: Teachers College Press.

Sanders, Matthew R. 1999. "Triple P-Positive Parenting Program: Towards an Empirically Validated Multilevel Parenting and Family Support Strategy for the Prevention of Behavior and Emotional Problems in Children." *Clinical Child and Family Psychology Review* 2: 71–90.

Sanders, William L., and June Rivers. 1996. "Cumulative and Residual Effects of Teachers on Future Academic Achievement." Research Progress Report. Knoxville: University of Tennessee, Value-Added Research and Assessment Center (November). Available at: http://www.cgp.upenn.edu/pdf/Sanders_Rivers-TVASS_teacher%20effects.pdf (accessed July 8, 2014).

Sawhill, Isabel. 2014. *Generation Unbound: Drifting into Sex and Parenthood Without Marriage.* Washington, D.C.: Brookings Institution Press.

Sawhill, Isabel, Adam Thomas, and Emily Monea. 2010. "An Ounce of Prevention: Policy Prescriptions to Reduce the Prevalence of Fragile Families." *Future of Children* 20(2): 133–56.

Schleicher, Andreas. 2009. "Securing Quality and Equity in Education: Lessons from PISA." *PROSPECTS* 39(3): 251–63. DOI:10.1007/s11125-009-9126-x.

Schütz, Gabriela, Heinrich W. Ursprung, and Ludger Woessmann. 2008. "Education Policy and Equality of Opportunity." *Kyklos* 61(2): 279–308.

Seawright, Jason, and John Gerring. 2008. "Case Selection Techniques in Case Study Research: A Menu of Qualitative and Quantitative Options." *Political Research Quarterly* 61(2): 294–308.

Shonkoff, Jack, and Deborah Phillips, eds. 2000. *From Neurons to Neighborhoods: The Science of Early Childhood Development.* Washington, D.C.: National Academies Press.

Smolensky, Eugene, and Jennifer Appleton Gootman, eds. 2003. *Working Families and Growing Kids: Caring for Children and Adolescents.* Washington, D.C.: National Academies Press.

Sonuga-Barke, Edmund J. S., David Daley, Margaret Thompson, Cathy Laver-Bradbury, and Anne Weeks. 2001. "Parent-Based Therapies for Attention-Deficit/Hyperactivity Disorder: A Randomized Controlled Trial with a Community Sample." *Journal of the American Academy of Child and Adolescent Psychiatry* 40: 402–8.

Steinberg, Lawrence. 2011. *You and Your Adolescent: The Essential Guide for Ages 10–25.* New York: Simon & Schuster.

Stipek, Deborah, and Rosaleen Ryan. 1997. "Economically Disadvantaged Preschoolers: Ready to Learn but Further to Go." *Developmental Psychology* 33(4): 711–23.

Strully, Kate, David Rehkopf, and Ziming Xuan. 2010. "Effects of Prenatal Poverty on Infant Health: State Earned Income Tax Credits and Birth Weight." *American Sociological Review* 75(4): 534–62.

Tough, Paul. 2008. *Whatever It Takes: Geoffrey Canada's Quest to Change Harlem and America.* New York: Houghton Mifflin.

———. 2012. *How Children Succeed: Grit, Curiosity, and the Hidden Power of Character.* New York: Houghton Mifflin.

University of London, Institute of Education, Centre for Longitudinal Studies. 2012a. *Millennium Cohort Study: First Survey, 2001–2003.* 11th ed. Colchester: UK Data Archive, December 2012. SN: 4683.

___. 2012b. *Millennium Cohort Study: Second Survey, 2003–2005.* 8th ed. Colchester: UK Data Archive, December 2012. SN: 5350.

___. 2012c. *Millennium Cohort Study: Third Survey, 2006.* 6th ed. Colchester: UK Data Archive, December 2012. SN: 5795.

___. 2012d. *Millennium Cohort Study: Fourth Survey, 2008.* 4th ed. Colchester: UK Data Archive, December 2012. SN: 6411.

___. 2014. *Millennium Cohort Study: Fifth Survey, 2012.* Colchester: UK Data Archive, February 2014. SN: 7464.

Van der Klaauw, Wilbert. 2008. "Breaking the Link Between Poverty and Low Student Achievement: An Evaluation of Title I." *Journal of Econometrics* 142(2): 731–56. DOI:10.1016/j.jeconom.2007.05.007.

Van de Werfhorst, Herman G., and Jonathan J. B. Mijs. 2010. "Achievement Inequality and the Institutional Structure of Educational Systems: A Comparative Perspective." *Annual Review of Sociology* 36(1): 407–28.

Waldfogel, Jane. 2006. *What Children Need.* Cambridge, Mass.: Harvard University Press.

———. 2010. *Britain's War on Poverty.* New York: Russell Sage Foundation.

———. 2012a. "Out-of-School Influences on the Literacy Problem." *Future of Children* 22(2): 39–54.

———. 2012b. "Review of *Finnish Lessons: What Can the World Learn from Educational Change in Finland?* by Pasi Sahlberg." *Journal of Policy Analysis and Management* 31(4): 970–74.

Waldfogel, Jane, Terry-Ann Craigie, and Jeanne Brooks-Gunn. 2010. "Fragile Families and Child Wellbeing." *Future of Children* 20(2): 87–112.

Waldfogel, Jane, and Elizabeth Washbrook. 2011a. "Early Years Policy." *Child Development Research* 2011: 1–12. Available at: http://academiccommons.columbia.edu/item/ac:152348 (accessed April 30, 2015).

————. 2011b. "Income-Related Gaps in School Readiness in the United States and United Kingdom." In *Persistence, Privilege, and Parenting: The Comparative Study of Intergenerational Mobility*, edited by Timothy Smeeding, Robert Erikson, and Markus Jäntti. New York: Russell Sage Foundation.

Webster-Stratton, Carolyn. 1994. "Advancing Videotape Parent Training: A Comparison Study." *Journal of Consulting and Clinical Psychology* 62: 583–93.

Weiland, Christina, and Hiro Yoshikawa. 2013 "Impacts of a Prekindergarten Program on Children's Mathematics, Language, Literacy, Executive Function, and Emotional Skills." *Child Development* 84: 2112–30.

Whitehurst, Grover J. "Russ." 2013. "New Evidence Raises Doubts on Obama's Preschool for All." Washington, D.C.: Brookings Institution (November 20). Available at: http://www.brookings.edu/research/papers/2013/11/20-evidence -raises-doubts-about-obamas-preschool-for-all-whitehurst (accessed April 30, 2015).

Whitehurst, Grover J., David S. Arnold, Jeffery N. Epstein, Andrea L. Angell, Meagan Smith, and Janet E. Fischel. 1994. "A Picture Book Reading Intervention in Day Care and Home for Children from Low-Income Families." *Developmental Psychology* 30(5): 679–89.

Whitehurst, Grover J. "Russ," and Matthew M. Chingos. 2011. "Class Size: What Research Says and What It Means for State Policy." Washington, D.C.: Brown Center on Education Policy at Brookings Institution (May 11). Available at: http://www.brookings.edu/research/papers/2011/05/11-class-size-white hurst-chingos (accessed September 13, 2013).

Whitehurst, Grover J., and Christopher J. Lonigan. 1998. "Child Development and Emergent Literacy." *Child Development* 69(3): 848–72.

Wilson, Kathryn, Kristina Lambright, and Timothy M. Smeeding. 2006. "School Finance, Equivalent Educational Expenditure, and the Income Distribution: Equal Dollars or Equal Chances for Success?" *Education Finance and Policy* 1(4): 396–424.

Winters, Marcus A., and Jay P. Greene. 2012. "The Medium-Run Effects of Florida's Test-Based Promotion Policy." *Education Finance and Policy* 7(3): 305–30. DOI:10.1162/EDFP_a_00069.

Wong, Vivian, Thomas Cook, Steven Barnett, and Kwanghee Jung. 2008. "An Effectiveness-Based Evaluation of Five State Pre-Kindergarten Programs." *Journal of Policy Analysis and Management* 27(1): 122–54.

Wooldridge, Jeffrey M. 2002. *Econometric Analysis of Cross Section and Panel Data*. Cambridge, Mass.: MIT Press.

Yoshikawa, Hirokazu, Christina Weiland, Jeanne Brooks-Gunn, Margaret R. Burchinal, Linda M. Espinoza, William T. Gormley, Jens Ludwig, Katherine A. Magnuson, Deborah Phillips, and Martha J. Zaslow. 2013. "Investing in Our

Future: The Evidence Base on Preschool Education." Society for Research in Child Development and Foundation for Child Development policy brief (October). Available at: http://www.srcd.org/sites/default/files/documents/washington/mb_2013_10_16_investing_in_children.pdf (accessed January 10, 2014).

Index